Inside Sales and Leases

What Matters and Why

ASPEN PUBLISHERS

Inside Sales and Leases

What Matters and Why

Bryan D. Hull
Professor of Law
Loyola Law School

Wolters Kluwer
Law & Business

AUSTIN   BOSTON   CHICAGO   NEW YORK   THE NETHERLANDS

To contact Customer Care, e-mail customer.care@aspenpublishers.com,
call 1-800-234-1660, fax 1-800-901-9075, or mail correspondence to:

Aspen Publishers
Attn: Order Department
PO Box 990
Frederick, MD 21705

Printed in the United States of America.

1 2 3 4 5 6 7 8 9 0

ISBN 978-0-7355-6996-6

Library of Congress Cataloging-in-Publication Data

Hull, Bryan, 1957-
  Inside sales and leases : what matters and why / Bryan D. Hull.
    p. cm.
  Includes index.
    ISBN 978-0-7355-6996-6 (pbk. : alk. paper) 1. Sales—United States. 2. Leases—United
States. I. Title.

KF915.Z9H85 2008
346.7307′2—dc22

                                                        2008022167

About Wolters Kluwer Law & Business

Wolters Kluwer Law & Business is a leading provider of research information and workflow solutions in key specialty areas. The strengths of the individual brands of Aspen Publishers, CCH, Kluwer Law International and Loislaw are aligned within Wolters Kluwer Law & Business to provide comprehensive, in-depth solutions and expert-authored content for the legal, professional and education markets.

CCH was founded in 1913 and has served more than four generations of business professionals and their clients. The CCH products in the Wolters Kluwer Law & Business group are highly regarded electronic and print resources for legal, securities, antitrust and trade regulation, government contracting, banking, pension, payroll, employment and labor, and healthcare reimbursement and compliance professionals.

Aspen Publishers is a leading information provider for attorneys, business professionals and law students. Written by preeminent authorities, Aspen products offer analytical and practical information in a range of specialty practice areas from securities law and intellectual property to mergers and acquisitions and pension/benefits. Aspen's trusted legal education resources provide professors and students with high-quality, up-to-date and effective resources for successful instruction and study in all areas of the law.

Kluwer Law International supplies the global business community with comprehensive English-language international legal information. Legal practitioners, corporate counsel and business executives around the world rely on the Kluwer Law International journals, loose-leafs, books and electronic products for authoritative information in many areas of international legal practice.

Loislaw is a premier provider of digitized legal content to small law firm practitioners of various specializations. Loislaw provides attorneys with the ability to quickly and efficiently find the necessary legal information they need, when and where they need it, by facilitating access to primary law as well as state-specific law, records, forms and treatises.

Wolters Kluwer Law & Business, a unit of Wolters Kluwer, is headquartered in New York and Riverwoods, Illinois. Wolters Kluwer is a leading multinational publisher and information services company.

To my brother-in-law Tom Kellerman—the quintessential "reasonable man"

Summary of Contents

Contents

Chapter 9. Third Parties Involved in the Sales Transaction 177

Preface

Inside Sales and Leases: What Matters and Why offers a succinct overview of the law governing sales and leases of goods. It is for the reader who wants to gain a firm grasp of the topic without reading a 500-page treatise. Students taking a course specifically covering sales and leases will find it very helpful, but it would also be useful for anyone taking a first-year Contracts class that spends significant time on the Uniform Commercial Code (UCC) or the Convention on Contracts for the International Sale of Goods (CISG). In addition, it certainly can be used to advantage by general practitioners as a way to become more familiar with the law governing sales and leases of goods.

This book is different from most other study guides in the following ways:

- **Visual aids** such as charts and diagrams are frequently used to illustrate concepts. For some students and lawyers, this makes it easier to understand and remember the subject matter.
- *Overviews* at the beginning of each chapter offer a brief summary of the topics covered therein. This is a convenient reference tool when looking for a specific topic or trying to see how all of the pieces fit together.
- *Chapter Summaries* in each chapter highlight key points.
- *Connections* at the end of each chapter explain how the salient topics just covered are important in the overall scheme of sales and leases, and how they connect with other topics in the book.
- *FAQs* (Frequently Asked Questions) and *Sidebars* within the chapters clear up common misconceptions, offer additional examples and anecdotal information from the real world, and provide study tips.
- **Key terms** in this book are boldfaced, to help you become familiar with the jargon of sales and leasing law. Like so many areas of law, learning the terminology will help you understand the concepts.

In writing this book, I have drawn on my many years of teaching; in so doing, I have chosen to hone in on the particular areas that have been troublesome for my students. Some of the charts in this book have been developed to help students overcome specific hurdles on their way to understanding challenging topics. Writing this book has forced me to think very clearly about how to explain difficult concepts to students. I hope that you, the reader, will benefit from the insights that I have gained from this experience.

I would remind students that I do not intend for this book to be a substitute for assigned readings or class attendance. In my opinion, a law student can best learn the law by trying to figure things out—first, by carefully reading the assigned course materials; second, by attending class; and third, by participating in classroom discussion. I believe that students should try to prepare their own course outlines. This book, however, can ensure that students do understand the basic concepts of a topic so that they can get the most out of their assigned readings and be more prepared to participate in class discussion.

Inside Sales and Leases has been reviewed not only by faculty members, but also by law students. Students were asked to review the book to make sure that it would be understandable and useful to them and, by extension, to you—the ultimate test of its success.

Thanks for buying my book. I do think that it will help you better understand sales and leases, and I hope that it makes a real contribution to your success in class.

Bryan D. Hull

June 2008

Acknowledgments

Thanks to my employer, Loyola Law School, Los Angeles, for its financial support. Thanks also to Ben Stevens of the International Warehouse Logistics Association for giving me permission to reproduce a couple of their forms. Thanks to my research assistants, Brian Harlan and Soheyl Tahsildoost, for reviewing an earlier draft of the book and assisting me with the Table of Statutes, respectively. Thanks to all of the reviewers and Aspen editors for all of their hard work and helpful comments in making this a better product. Finally, thanks to my colleague, Professor John McDermott, for motivating me to become more interested in international sales law through his work with me as co-coach of the Loyola Law School international commercial arbitration team that has competed in the Willem C. Vis International Arbitration Moot competition.

Inside Sales and Leases

What Matters and Why

Introduction

1

In this chapter we discuss the types of transactions covered by this book, that is, sales and leases of goods. We discuss the law governing

O V E R V I E W

these transactions, both domestic and international. Finally, we discuss the overall structure of the book.

A. SALES AND LEASES OF GOODS

B. THE LAW APPLICABLE TO DOMESTIC SALES AND LEASE TRANSACTIONS

C. THE LAW APPLICABLE TO INTERNATIONAL SALES

D. THE STRUCTURE OF THIS BOOK

A. Sales and Leases of Goods

We all frequently enter into sales of goods contracts. Whenever we purchase a head of lettuce from the grocery store, we have entered into a sales contract with the grocer. Sometimes the contracts are more substantial, such as when we purchase an automobile. We generally do not give much thought to the law governing these contracts, and often the contracts themselves are very informal, not in any way evidenced by a writing. Thankfully, most of the time there are no problems with the goods we purchase or sell, and there is no need to be concerned with the law. But what if a good that we purchased breaks right after we purchase it and the seller refuses to fix it or refund our money? At that point, we need to focus on the law that determines our rights.

S i d e b a r

THE AMERICAN LAW INSTITUTE AND THE NATIONAL CONFERENCE OF COMMISSIONERS ON UNIFORM STATE LAWS

The American Law Institute (ALI), founded in 1923, is a private organization consisting of lawyers, judges, and law professors that is dedicated to studying and proposing changes to the law to promote its clarification and simplification and to improve the administration of justice. Among other things, the ALI is responsible for the Restatements of the law, including the *Restatement (Second) of Contracts* that you probably studied in your Contracts class. One of the ALI's projects is the Uniform Commercial Code (UCC).

The National Conference of Commissioners on Uniform State Laws (NCCUSL) is a nonprofit organization that was organized in 1892. The Commissioners are all members of the bar that are appointed by each state government. As its title would suggest, NCCUSL is dedicated to formulating uniform laws in various areas. The UCC is one of its projects, but it has also sponsored other uniform laws in the probate and family law areas, among other things. Both the ALI and NCCUSL sponsor the UCC. For more information on both organizations, see their Web sites at http://www.ali.org and http://www.nccusl.org.

Of course, sales of goods transactions are not limited to purchases by consumers. If a large retailer like Wal-Mart orders goods from overseas for its many retail establishments, the contract may be worth millions of dollars. As commerce becomes increasingly global, international sales become increasingly common. Again, most of the time it does not matter what law governs the transaction as goods will be delivered and paid for as the parties intended. But what happens if the seller fails to deliver the goods on time and the buyer then loses the opportunity to resell the goods? In that situation, it will again be important to focus on the law that determines the rights of the parties.

A transaction that can be similar to the sales transaction is a lease of goods. For people who plan to use goods for only a short time, it might make sense to lease them for the time needed and then return the goods to the owner, the lessor. People who like to drive late-model cars will sometimes find it better to lease a car for a few years, then return it to the dealer and lease a newer model. When things go wrong with leased goods, questions will arise as to whether the lessee can stop paying for use of the goods and/or can sue the lessor for damages. The law governing the lease transaction is similar, but not identical, to the law governing the sales transaction.

This book is designed to take you "inside" the law governing both consumer and commercial sales and leases of goods in a way that will make that law more accessible to you and easy to understand. The book seeks to do this through charts and simple explanations designed to demystify some of the difficultly worded statutes that govern sales and leases of goods transactions. The book will not necessarily go into all of the legal nuances in this area, but will help you get a good understanding of the basic law, the law that is most likely to matter in the course that you are taking.

B. The Law Applicable to Domestic Sales and Lease Transactions

The primary law governing sales and leases of goods in the United States is the Uniform Commercial Code (UCC). The relevant article of the UCC covering sales is Article 2, and the relevant article covering leases is Article 2A. The UCC is a set of rules drafted and sponsored by the National Conference of Commissioners on Uniform State Laws (NCCUSL) and the American Law Institute (ALI). The UCC covers various commercial law topics, ranging from sales and leases of goods (the subject of this book) to secured transactions in personal property (UCC Article 9). It covers ten topics in Articles 2 through 9 (including Articles 2A and 4A) and has one article, Article 1, which contains general provisions applicable to all of the Articles under the UCC.

The UCC is not "law" until it has been adopted by state legislatures — NCCUSL and ALI sponsor the UCC for adoption by legislatures. Articles 2 and 2A of the UCC have been adopted in some form by all of the United States except for Louisiana. States do not necessarily enact all sections of the UCC without change — there are a number of non-uniform provisions, the number of which varies from state to state. When you are in practice, you will need to be alert to whether the state in which you are practicing has made any non-uniform changes to the UCC — it will be malpractice if you don't check!

HOW THE UCC AND UNIFORM AMENDMENTS TO UCC BECOME "LAW"

Drafted by drafting committees selected by NCCUSL & ALI

↓
↓

Draft ultimately approved by NCCUSL & ALI

↓
↓

Approved draft introduced in state legislatures

↓
↓

Legislature adopts approved draft with or without non-uniform amendments

---

NCCUSL and ALI are constantly studying the UCC to make sure that its rules keep up with current commercial practices. In 2001, Article 1 of the UCC was revised and the majority of the states have now adopted the revision, at least in part. In 2003, ALI and NCCUSL approved proposed amendments to Articles 2 and 2A. At the time of this writing, no state has adopted these proposed amendments and there is some question as to how many states will ultimately adopt them. In this book, references to Article 1 will be to the version as revised in 2001, unless otherwise indicated. References to Article 2 and 2A will be to the versions of Article 2 and 2A without the proposed amendments, unless otherwise indicated.

It is important to note that the UCC is not the exclusive source of law governing domestic sales or leasing law. To the extent that the U.S. Congress has enacted laws that impact sales and leases of goods in interstate commerce, those laws take precedence over the UCC by virtue of the Supremacy Clause of the U.S. Constitution.[1]

---

[1] U.S. Const., Art. VI, cl. 2.

One example of a federal law that "trumps" the UCC to some extent is the federal Magnuson-Moss Warranty Act, which provides greater rights to consumers than does the UCC. We will talk in some detail about this law later in the book.[2]

Sometimes, other state laws will trump the UCC. The UCC itself notes that consumer protection law may sometimes override its provisions.[3] So-called state lemon laws that require sellers of goods to repair goods within certain time periods or give buyers their money back are examples of state laws that to some extent override the UCC. We will talk a little about these laws later in the book.[4]

The UCC also recognizes the continued role of the common law—the UCC does not seek to displace all common law rules that might impact on a sales case. UCC §1-103(b) states:

> Unless displaced by the particular provisions of the Uniform Commercial Code, the principles of law and equity, including the law merchant and the law relative to capacity to contract, principal and agent, estoppel, fraud, misrepresentation, duress, coercion, mistake, bankruptcy, and other validating or invalidating cause supplement its provisions.

For example, if an issue came up in a sales contract as to whether an employee of a company was authorized to enter into a contract to sell goods to somebody else, Article 2 would not supply the rule and the law of agency would have to be consulted. Case law must also be consulted to view courts' interpretations of the UCC provisions. Because the UCC is a uniform law, case authority from all states should be persuasive to a court facing a UCC issue.

C. The Law Applicable to International Sales

In 1980, the United Nations Commission on International Trade Law (UNCITRAL) promulgated the United Nations Convention on Contracts for the International Sale of Goods (CISG), which is also referred to as the "Vienna Sales Convention" because it was promulgated in Vienna, Austria. It is a "convention" because it is

---

Sidebar

THE UCC OFFICIAL COMMENTS

The official comments to the UCC are helpful in understanding the various statutory provisions. They are not "law" unless the state legislature adopts them, but they are useful persuasive authority for courts in that they explain the intent of the people drafting the Code. They are typically prepared by the Reporter to the drafting committee with input from the members of the committee. Often, because they contain examples and are written in a more "user-friendly" way than the statutes, courts rely more on them than the statutes themselves! But, you should be careful in relying too heavily on them since it is the statute that is the "law."

Sidebar

THE UNITED NATIONS COMMISSION ON INTERNATIONAL TRADE LAW

The United Nations Commission on International Trade Law (UNCITRAL) was established by the United Nations in 1966. The purpose of UNCITRAL is to try to improve the flow of trade by bringing about uniform laws covering international commerce. UNCITRAL has 60 member nations, each of which is elected to a six-year term. The United Nations Convention on Contracts for the International Sale of Goods (CISG) is one of its projects. Among its other projects are laws and rules governing international arbitration and a model law governing electronic fund transfers. For more information regarding UNCITRAL, see its Web site at http://www.uncitral.org.

---

[2]See pp. 67-70, *infra.*
[3]UCC §2-102.
[4]See pp. 70-71, *infra.*

an agreement among the nations adopting it that its rules will govern sales of goods between parties that reside in the adopting nations. At the time of this writing, there are 70 nations that are a party to the CISG, including the United States, China, France, and Germany. Noteworthy of nations that have <u>not</u> adopted the CISG are Japan and the United Kingdom, which prefer their own domestic sales law.

Unless the parties have agreed otherwise, the CISG will apply to a commercial (not consumer) sale of goods transaction in which the seller is located in one nation that has adopted the CISG and the buyer is located in another nation that has adopted the CISG.[5] Parties in their contract are allowed to opt out of all or part of the CISG if they so choose.[6] The CISG may also apply to transactions in which one of the parties is in a nation that has not adopted the CISG if choice of law rules lead to application of the nation's laws that has adopted the CISG.[7]

THE CISG WILL APPLY IF:

(1) The transaction is predominantly for the sale of goods;
(2) The buyer has not supplied a substantial part of the materials used in manufacturing the goods;
(3) Each party is in a different nation that has adopted the CISG;
(4) The sale is not a consumer transaction;
(5) The contract does not exclude application of the CISG;
(6) The dispute does not involve injury to person or property; and
(7) The transaction is not excluded under CISG Article 6.

Even if the CISG does apply to the transaction, it will not necessarily provide all of the rules that will govern the transaction. Unlike the UCC, the CISG does not cover situations involving personal injury and does not provide any rules regarding title to goods (other than providing that a warranty of good title is given by the seller).[8] The CISG also does not provide rules covering validity of the contract, such as unconscionability, mistake, or duress.[9] In some cases, it may thus be necessary to apply domestic law to fill in the gaps of the CISG. The domestic law that will apply is determined by choice of law rules.[10]

D. The Structure of This Book

The primary focus of this book is on the law governing sales of goods. Chapters 2 through 9 deal with sales. In Chapter 10, we will discuss the law governing leases. The focus of that chapter will be on areas in which leasing law differs from sales law.

---

[5]CISG Arts. 1 & 2.
[6]CISG Art. 6.
[7]CISG Art. 1(1)(b).
[8]CISG Arts. 2 & 4.
[9]CISG Art. 4.
[10]CISG Art. 7.

SUMMARY

- This book covers the law governing sales and leases of goods.

- The primary law governing domestic sales of goods is Article 2 of the Uniform Commercial Code (UCC).

- The primary law governing domestic leases of goods is Article 2A of the UCC.

- UCC Article 1 provides general rules of law that apply to all transactions within the UCC, so it will work together with Article 2 in sales transactions and with Article 2A in lease transactions.

- The common law supplements the UCC to the extent there are gaps.

- Sometimes other state and federal law, such as consumer protection law, will take precedence over the UCC.

- The Convention on Contracts for the International Sale of Goods (CISG) governs commercial international sales of goods if each party is in a country that has adopted it. Parties are permitted, however, to opt out of all or part of the CISG if they wish.

- The CISG does not cover all issues that might arise in an international sale, so sometimes other law will need to be consulted.

CONNECTIONS

The Law Governing Sales and Leases

This chapter introduced you to the law that governs domestic sales and leases of goods, namely Articles 2 and 2A of the Uniform Commercial Code (UCC), respectively. It also gave an introduction to the law governing international sales of goods, the United Nations Convention on Contracts for the International Sale of Goods (CISG). The following chapters of the book explore in more detail how to apply these laws.

Choice of Law

In the next chapter, we explore in more detail whether we have a sale of goods covered by the UCC or the CISG or if instead we have some other type of contract covered by other law, for example a service contract. The focus of this book is on contracts for the sale and lease of goods. Other types of contracts are beyond the scope of this book. The choice of law is important because different bodies of law use different standards for determining whether a party has acted in accordance with the contract at issue. For example, we will see that the standard for imposing liability in a sale of goods case is strict liability while the standard of liability in a service contract is negligence.

Contract Formation

Once we have determined the governing law, we must determine under that law whether an enforceable contract has been formed. As we will see, the law governing contract formation in a sale of goods contract under both the CISG and the UCC is more liberal than under common law, permitting an enforceable contract to exist even if the parties have not agreed on all terms. Parties often form contracts in sales cases by exchanging pre-printed forms, and both the UCC and CISG have rules for determining in those cases whether a contract has been formed at all and for determining the terms of such a contract.

Contract Terms

If a contract exists, we must determine the terms of the contract. This will involve interpreting the contract and filling in gaps. As we will see, both the UCC and CISG provide gap filler terms in the event that the parties have not agreed on everything.

Performance

Once we have determined the terms of the contract, we can then determine if the parties have performed. If there is a failure to perform exactly in accordance with contract requirements, we must determine the consequences. For example, if the seller does not ship goods that are exactly as promised, can the buyer terminate the contract? Is the seller allowed to cure any problems? These issues will be discussed in Chapter 6.

Remedies

If there is a failure to perform, what can the injured party obtain in terms of a remedy? Can the injured party sue for specific performance, or is the injured party limited to recovering damages? These issues are discussed in Chapters 7 and 8.

Is the Transaction a Sale of Goods Transaction?

2

The first question that a lawyer must consider when faced with a client with a problem is which law applies to the situation. Was the transaction

O V E R V I E W

a sale of goods? Was it a lease? Was it a service contract? Different laws govern different transactions, and the ultimate result in a case may hinge on the choice of law. In this chapter we discuss when the law considers a transaction to be a "sale" covered by Article 2 of the Uniform Commercial Code (UCC) or the international law governing sales of goods, the United Nations Convention on Contracts for the International Sale of Goods (CISG).

A. "GOODS" AND "SALE" DEFINED

B. SALES INVOLVING MERCHANTS AND NON-MERCHANTS

C. MIXED GOODS/SERVICES CONTRACTS AND SALES OF BUSINESSES

    1. The "Predominant Purpose" Approach
    2. The "Gravamen" Approach

D. MIXED GOODS/REAL ESTATE TRANSACTIONS

E. SOFTWARE TRANSACTIONS AND THE USE OF ARTICLE 2 BY ANALOGY

F. INTERNATIONAL SALES

A. "Goods" and "Sale" Defined

Article 2 of the UCC applies to contracts for the sale of goods.[1] *"Goods"* are defined basically as tangible, personal property—"things" that "move."[2] Article 2 of the UCC thus does not cover a sale of real estate, such as an apartment house, or the transfer of intangible property rights ("things in action"), such as an assignment of a right to be paid money for services rendered (e.g., an account receivable). Article 2 also does not cover a service contract, such as when someone hires a lawyer to provide legal services. A *"sale"* of goods is defined as the transfer of title to the goods for a price.[3] A sale should thus be contrasted with a lease, in which the person leasing goods retains title and agrees to let the lessee use the goods for a fixed period of time in exchange for rent. Leases of goods are also not covered by Article 2 of the UCC but are covered by Article 2A, and are considered in more detail in Chapter 10 of this book. The following diagram links up different types of transactions with the laws that govern them.

DIFFERENT TRANSACTIONS AND THE LAWS GOVERNING THEM

Sale of goods	Real estate contract	Service contract	Lease of goods
↓	↓	↓	↓
↓	↓	↓	↓
UCC Article 2 or CISG	Real estate law, general contract law	General contract law, any law governing specific service	UCC Article 2A

Intellectual property license

↓

↓

Law governing particular intellectual property, general contract law (courts will sometimes use Article 2)

Many times it will be very clear whether or not a transaction is one for the sale of goods. For example, if you go to the local hardware store and buy a wrench, it is clearly a sale of goods. If you go to the doctor and ask her to look at your sore throat in exchange for the cost of an office visit, that is not a sale of goods transaction (assuming she didn't give you anything other than a diagnosis and a prescription). Other times, however, there may be a question as to whether a transaction is a sale of goods transaction or some other kind of transaction. For example, if you hire a contractor to build you a backyard pool, is that a sale of goods or a contract for a service? The contractor will be providing a service in digging a hole, pouring concrete and installing tile. But the contractor will also be providing goods as part of the price—the concrete, tile, filter, heater, and diving board are all goods.

---

[1] UCC §2-102.
[2] UCC §2-105.
[3] UCC §2-106.

You might be asking, what difference does it make? Why do we care if the contract is for goods, services, or something else? The reason is because if something goes wrong with a transaction, we need to know which rules will determine responsibility. If we say that the transaction is a sale of goods, Article 2 of the UCC will govern if the transaction is in a state that has adopted it. If Article 2 governs, the seller of the goods will be deemed to have given an *implied warranty of merchantability* if the seller is in the business of selling the goods of the kind involved. The implied warranty of merchantability can be disclaimed in the contract; if it isn't, the warranty of merchantability means that the goods will be fit for their ordinary purpose.[4] This means that if the goods don't work, the seller is strictly liable. On the other hand, in a service contract, we don't hold the provider of the service strictly liable; instead, we apply a standard of reasonable care. If the doctor doesn't cure your sore throat, you can't sue her for breach of the warranty of merchantability; you can only sue her if her services did not reach the standard of reasonable care (i.e., she committed malpractice). By comparison, if you buy a defectively manufactured product and it injures you, the seller of the goods is strictly liable and we do not care if the seller exercised reasonable care.

F   A   Q

Q: Why should strict liability apply to a sale of goods while a negligence standard is applied to service contracts?

A: Public policy dictates that defective goods should not be put into the stream of commerce. Strict liability is imposed to prevent that from happening. Presumably, the fear of strict liability will cause sellers of goods to take care to make sure that defective products do not wind up in the marketplace. On the other hand, there is a public policy against imposing strict liability on service providers, such as doctors. We do not want to deter people from providing vital public services. Also, people contracting with service providers do not reasonably expect that the services will be perfect. All that can be reasonably expected is that the person providing the service will make a reasonable effort to perform the service well. People do reasonably expect, however, that goods will not harm them. For a good discussion of the policies underlying the distinction between contracts for goods and contracts for services, see *Milau Associates, Inc. v. North Avenue Development Corp.*, 42 N.Y.2d 482, 368 N.E.2d 1247, 398 N.Y.S.2d 882 (1977).

Besides the question of whether we apply a standard of strict liability or one of reasonable care, there are other differences between the law governing sales of goods (i.e., UCC Article 2) and the laws governing service contracts. For example, the UCC has a *statute of frauds* requiring contracts for the sale of goods where the price is $500 or more to be evidenced by a writing.[5] There is no statute of frauds for service contracts over $500, although you may remember from your Contracts class that contracts that are not to be performed within one year of their making must be

---

[4]UCC §2-314. This topic is discussed more fully at pp. 57-60, *infra*.
[5]UCC §2-201. This topic is discussed more fully at pp. 23-25, *infra*.

evidenced by a writing. Another difference may involve the statute of limitations. The UCC provides a four-year *statute of limitations* that most of the time begins to run when the goods are delivered.[6] In non-sales cases, the statute of limitations may be shorter or longer, depending on the state, and may not begin to run until the injured party discovers or should have discovered the problem. So, deciding whether a transaction is a sales transaction covered by UCC Article 2 or some other kind of transaction may be determinative as to whether a plaintiff wins or loses the case.

B. Sales Involving Merchants and Non-Merchants

Students sometimes think that Article 2 of the UCC only applies to sales between merchants. Wrong! Although Article 2 distinguishes between merchants and non-merchants in some cases, it applies to sale of goods transactions regardless of whether the sale is from merchant to merchant, merchant to non-merchant, or non-merchant to non-merchant. In other words, if you were to buy a used laptop computer from your friend, the transaction would be subject to Article 2 even though you are both non-merchants.

     As noted previously, the UCC does sometimes apply different rules to *merchants*, so it is important to know the definition of merchant and to be able to distinguish between merchants and non-merchants. A "merchant" is defined in the UCC as "a person who deals in goods of the kind or otherwise by his occupation holds himself out as having knowledge or skill peculiar to the practices or goods involved in the transaction."[7] If a hardware store buys paint for its inventory from a supplier, the transaction will be considered between merchants. Someone may also be considered a merchant if the person hires an agent or broker who is experienced in selling the type of goods involved.[8] So, for example, if you own a boat and hire a professional boat broker to sell it to you, you could be considered a "merchant" under the UCC definition even though you don't typically sell boats.

C. Mixed Goods/Services Contracts and Sales of Businesses

Perhaps the most difficult area for determining whether a contract is for a sale of goods involves contracts that call for goods and also for services. The swimming pool example discussed previously is an example of such a contract, as are many contracts for construction. The doctor example provided earlier may also involve both goods and services if the doctor provides you with and charges you for a drug (a good) in addition to providing services.

(1) The "Predominant Purpose" Approach

The mixed goods/services cases are difficult because the UCC does not provide a rule for the courts to use. It is thus left for the courts to decide how to handle these cases as

---

[6]UCC §2-725. This topic is discussed more fully at pp. 153-155, *infra*.
[7]UCC §2-104(1).
[8]*Id.*

a matter of common law. The approach that most courts take in these cases is to ask whether the ***predominant purpose*** of the contract was for the provision of goods or for the provision of services.[9] If the court determines that the parties were predominantly contracting for goods, then Article 2 applies to the transaction. If the court determines that the parties were predominantly contracting for services, then Article 2 does not apply and the common law relating to the particular service contract applies instead.

To show how the predominant purpose test works, assume that you go to the hospital and as part of the hospital stay you are charged for drugs that are administered to you. The drugs are goods, but when you agreed to pay the hospital's daily rates and other charges in exchange for your stay there, were you primarily interested in purchasing the drugs or were you primarily interested in the services provided by the hospital? It is probably fair to say in most cases that such a contract was predominantly for services, so Article 2 would **not** apply to the transaction.[10] Likewise, courts will generally find that construction contracts are predominantly for services, even though the contractor will be providing goods as part of the construction process.[11]

The predominant purpose test is not necessarily that easy to apply in all cases, however. Courts have disagreed whether some types of contracts are predominantly for goods or services, for example with regard to contracts for the sale of electricity and for the sale of water by public utilities.[12] How does one tell whether the predominant purpose of a contract is for the provision of goods or services? Perhaps one could look at the consideration that is being paid for the services as compared to the goods, but that is not necessarily determinative. For example, in a construction contract the cost of the services in doing the construction probably exceeds the cost of the materials in many cases, and courts are generally inclined to find that construction contracts are primarily for services.

Some courts approach this issue by looking at policy and the consequences of saying that Article 2 applies to the transaction. Remember that one aspect of saying that Article 2 applies to the transaction is that the implied warranty of merchantability might apply, meaning strict liability will be imposed if the product does not work properly or harms someone. In a case involving the sale of tainted water by a municipality, the court considered that imposing strict liability on the municipality was too harsh a consequence and ultimately held that the contract was therefore a service contract rather than a sale of goods.[13] Legislatures have also stepped into the fray in some situations. For example, an issue might exist as to whether the provision of blood in a transfusion at a hospital is a sale of goods or is a service. Imposing strict liability on hospitals in such a situation has been considered to be too harsh a consequence in that it would potentially chill the willingness of hospitals to provide transfusions for fear of liability. Thus, some states have enacted statutes apart

---

[9]See, e.g., *Milau Associates, Inc. v. North Avenue Development Corp.*, 42 N.Y.2d 482, 368 N.E.2d 1247, 398 N.Y.S.2d 882 (1977).
[10]See *Batiste v. American Home Products Corp.*, 32 N.C. App. 1, 231 S.E.2d 269 (1977).
[11]See, e.g., *Milau Associates, Inc. v. North Avenue Development Corp.*, 42 N.Y.2d 482, 368 N.E.2d 1247, 398 N.Y.S.2d 882 (1977).
[12]*Compare Cincinnati Gas & Electric Co. v. Goebel*, 28 Ohio Misc. 2d 4, 502 N.E.2d 713, 2 UCC Rep. Serv. 2d 1187 (1986) (not a sale of goods covered by Article 2), *with New Balance Athletic Shoe, Inc. v. Boston Edison Co.*, 29 UCC Rep. Serv. 2d 397 (Mass. Super. Ct. 1996) (is a sale of goods covered by Article 2).
[13]*Mattoon v. City of Pittsfield*, 56 Mass. App. Ct. 124, 775 N.E.2d 770, 49 UCC Rep. Serv. 2d 52 (2002).

from the UCC that state that the provision of blood is not a sale and that strict liability should not apply to entities that provide it.[14]

The UCC expressly states that "goods" include "***specially manufactured goods***," namely, goods that are specially made by the seller for the buyer.[15] But what if a famous painter is commissioned to paint a portrait of someone? Arguably, the creation of the painting is a "specially manufactured good." But, is the canvas with the paint what is being contracted for, or is the contract really for the services of the artist? In one case, a court held that a contract for a painting to be provided by the famous artist Salvador Dali was a contract for his services and not a sale of goods.[16] In cases involving specially manufactured goods, courts might thus look to whether the purchaser is looking for a special design (i.e., a service) or is instead looking for manufacture of goods pursuant to an already existing design (i.e., a sale of goods).

(2) The "Gravamen" Approach

Another approach that courts take is to ask whether the issue in the case involves problems with the goods or problems with something else. If the problem involves the goods, then Article 2 of the UCC applies. If the problem involves the service or something else other than the goods, then Article 2 does not apply and some other law applies instead. This approach has been referred to as the "***gravamen test***" because it focuses on the substantial part (or gravamen) of the claim. Chancellor William Hawkland is given the credit for coming up with this approach.[17]

In an example of the application of the gravamen test, a court found that Article 2 applied to a case involving an allegedly defective diving board that was installed in conjunction with the construction of a swimming pool.[18] Even though the predominant purpose of such a contract was for the services of the contractor in building the pool, the court believed that because the problem was with a good, the diving board, Article 2 should apply to the lawsuit against the contractor. Public policy supported this approach, the court believed, because the swimming pool owner could have sued under Article 2 if he had purchased the diving board separately and had it installed.[19] Why should it not apply just because the board was installed as part of the overall construction of the pool?

A gravamen approach is also used in cases involving the sale of entire businesses that include the business' inventory of goods. In a sale of a business, a number of assets are sold, which might include real estate, intangible goodwill of the business, accounts receivable owed to the business, and inventory. Article 2 might not apply to the majority of the assets being sold—it would not apply to a transfer of accounts receivable, goodwill, or real estate. But, if goods that are sold turn out to be defective, courts have used Article 2 to resolve that liability issue.[20]

---

[14]See, e.g., Cal. Health & Safety Code §1606.
[15]UCC §2-105.
[16]*National Historic Shrines Foundation v. Dali*, 4 UCC Rep. Serv. 71 (N.Y. Super. Ct. 1967).
[17]See *Anthony Pools v. Sheehan*, 295 Md. 285, 455 A.2d 434, 35 UCC Rep. Serv. 408 (1983).
[18]*Id.*
[19]*Id.*
[20]See *Miller v. Belk*, 23 N.C. App. 1, 207 S.E.2d 792, 15 UCC Rep. Serv. 627 (1974).

DIFFERENT APPROACHES TO MIXED GOODS/SERVICES PROBLEM	
Predominant Purpose Approach Contract predominantly for goods?	Gravamen Approach Problem involving the goods?
↓ ↓	↓ ↓
Yes ↓ No ↓	Yes ↓ No ↓
↓ ↓	↓ ↓
Article 2 applies Article 2 does not apply	Article 2 applies Article 2 does not apply

D. Mixed Goods/Real Estate Transactions

It is clear that Article 2 does not apply to the sale of land. But what about the sale of things that are attached to land but can be severed, such as crops, timber, or a house that sits on the land? Are such sales considered "sales of goods" that are covered by Article 2?

Article 2 is clearer on how these cases should be handled than it is with respect to mixed goods/services contracts. Section 2-107 of the UCC indicates that sales of crops, timber to be cut, or other things that are attached to realty that can be removed without material harm to the realty are sales of goods within the scope of Article 2. It does not matter if such goods are to be severed by the buyer or the seller. For goods like minerals, oil or gas, or a structure or its materials to be removed from realty, a contract for sale of such goods is within the scope of Article 2 only if such goods are to be removed by the seller. If these goods are to be severed by the buyer, the transaction is considered to be a real property transaction covered by real property law. For example, if a buyer is removing minerals from land, it is likely pursuant to a long-term mining lease giving the buyer the right to enter and mine the land.

E. Software Transactions and the Use of Article 2 by Analogy

One area in which there has been some litigation involves contracts for the provision of software. Is the person obtaining the software contracting for a tangible good, for intellectual property, or for the services of the programmer? The software cases are complicated by the fact that most software is provided via license. When you "buy" software, you are not really receiving title to it; instead, you are being given permission (i.e., a license) to use it pursuant to the terms of the license. Because there is technically not a "sale" of anything, Article 2 arguably should not apply to the transaction. General contract law should apply or laws (if any) that are specifically tailored to the licensing of intellectual property.

Many courts apply Article 2 to software licenses, at least if the software is generally available to "buyers" (licensees) and is not custom designed.[21] Courts view the licensing of prepackaged software as analogous to sale of goods contracts in that the

---

[21]Many of these cases are discussed and criticized in Lorin Brennan, *Why Article 2 Cannot Apply to Software Transactions*, 38 Duq. L. Rev. 459 (2000).

"buyer" is primarily interested in purchasing a product, the software package. It may also be tempting for courts to apply Article 2 in these cases because there is no other widely enacted uniform law that covers these transactions. In cases involving custom-designed software, courts might find that the contract is primarily for the services of the software programmer.[22]

Courts will sometimes use UCC Article 2 by analogy even in cases that are clearly not within its scope. Courts will do this if they believe a rule in Article 2 is suitable for the case before it as the case is analogous to a sale of goods. Cases applying Article 2 to software licenses are arguably analogous applications, although courts do not always acknowledge that they are doing that. They are using Article 2 by analogy because there is no "sale" of a good. Sometimes courts will apply parts of Article 2 to real estate contracts or sales of investment securities (e.g., stocks and bonds).[23]

Software providers have not been happy with the application of Article 2 to their licensing transactions. They do not like strict liability rules of Article 2 and also do not like the contract formation rules, which may render unenforceable some provisions of their "shrinkwrap" or "click through" licenses (more on this later).[24] The proposed 2003 amendments to Article 2 would exclude pure software licensing transactions from the scope of Article 2 (called "information" under the proposed amendments).[25] If the proposed amendments become law, courts will have to look to law other than the UCC to resolve disputes involving software licenses. NCCUSL has sponsored the Uniform Computer Information Transactions Act (UCITA), which would cover software licenses, but thus far UCITA has only been adopted by two states, Virginia and Maryland.

F. International Sales

As noted in the previous chapter, the CISG applies to contracts for the sale of goods where each party is in a different nation that has adopted the CISG, unless the parties have contractually agreed that the CISG will not apply.[26] The CISG does not define "goods." This is consistent with the general approach of the CISG, which is not to define terms as precisely as the UCC, leaving more room for courts and arbitral tribunals to interpret its provisions. It is likely, however, that courts and arbitral tribunals will define goods in a manner similar to the UCC—tangible personal property.

Unlike the UCC, the CISG does provide a rule for the treatment of mixed goods/services contracts. It expressly provides that if the predominant part of the contract is the provision of services, the CISG does **not** apply.[27] Similarly, the CISG does not apply to transactions involving manufactured goods if the buyer provides a substantial part of the materials, because what the buyer is contracting for in such a situation is really the seller's service in manufacturing the goods.[28] The CISG also has some express exclusions. It does not apply to any of the following: (1) consumer goods transactions (unless the seller did not know

---

[22]See, e.g., *Data Processing Services v. L.H. Smith Oil Corp.*, 492 N.E.2d 314 (Ind. App. 1986).
[23]See, e.g., *Romig v. De Vallance*, 637 P.2d 1147 (Haw. App. 1981)(applying part of Article 2 to the sale of real estate).
[24]*Id.* For further discussion on this issue, see pp. 39-41, *infra*.
[25]See Amended UCC §2-103(k) and its official comment.
[26]CISG Arts. 1 & 6.
[27]CISG Art. 3(2).
[28]*Id.*

nor should have known that the goods were for the personal, family, or household use of the buyer and thus thought that the CISG would apply); (2) auction sales; (3) execution sales and other sales under authority of law; (4) sales of investment securities, negotiable instruments, and money; (5) sales of ships, hovercraft, or aircraft; and (6) sales of electricity.[29] The CISG also does not apply to cases involving the liability of the seller for death or personal injury (the UCC may apply to such cases, as we will see).[30] The reasons for these exclusions are that the transactions involved are not necessarily commercially significant and also raise questions best left to domestic law. For example, the amount of protection given to consumers varies from country to country. Sales of ships, aircraft, and electricity also raise regulatory issues that are best left to domestic law.[31]

The CISG may also apply to cases in which one of the parties resides in a nation that has adopted the CISG and the other party resides in a nation that has not adopted the CISG if applicable choice of law rules call for application of the law of a country that has adopted it.[32] Countries are given the option of not permitting application of the CISG in such cases — the United States is one of those nations.[33] So, if one of the parties to the sale of goods transaction is located in the United States, the CISG will only apply if the other party resides in another nation that has adopted the CISG. If one party resides in the United States and the other party resides in a nation that has not adopted the CISG, for example, the United Kingdom, then the domestic sales law of one of the nations will apply (e.g., the UCC or the domestic sales law of the United Kingdom).

Sidebar

THE LESS PRECISE DRAFTING STYLE OF THE CISG

The CISG needed to be drafted in a way that would make it acceptable to a large number of nations. Not all nations follow the same legal systems. For example, the United States and the United Kingdom are common law countries. Many other countries, such as those in continental Europe, are civil law countries. The Codes in civil law countries tend to be written in a broader way because the rules in those Codes are what the courts use to decide the case before it — case law precedent is not as important. In common law countries, statutes tend to be drafted more precisely. Courts can rely on case law to decide cases that are not within the narrow scope of the statute. Also, different legal systems follow different rules, and to make the CISG acceptable, it had to be written ambiguously to reflect compromises.

F A Q

Q: Why did the United States (and a few other nations) make a declaration under CISG Article 95?

A: As noted previously, when the United States adopted the CISG, it made a declaration under CISG Article 95 to the effect that the CISG would only apply

---

[29]CISG Art. 2.
[30]CISG Art. 5.
[31]See Secretariat Commentary to 1978 Draft Counterpart to Article 2, http://www.cisg.law.pace.edu/cisg/text/secomm/secomm-02.html.
[32]CISG Article 1(1)(b).
[33]A country opts out of Art. 1(1)(b) by making a declaration under CISG Art. 95.

to contracts involving U.S. parties if the other party to the contract resided in a nation that had also adopted the CISG. The reason given was that choice of law analysis is difficult, and the rule applying the CISG only if each party is in a different nation that has adopted it is easy to apply. If one party is in the United States and the other party is in a nation that has not adopted the CISG, it might be difficult to tell which nation's law should apply, and if the court has to do the analysis, it might just as well apply whichever nation's domestic law winds up being chosen. See Michael Douglas, *The Lex Mercatoria and the Culture of Transnational Industry*, 13 U. Miami Int'l & Comp. L. Rev. 367, 377 n.33 (2006).

One other circumstance in which the CISG would apply would be if the parties to the contract actually state that the CISG should govern the transaction. If the transaction is international, it seems likely that courts would uphold such a choice of law even if the CISG would not apply but for the parties having chosen it. It seems, however, that parties infrequently choose the CISG as the governing law and in fact normally opt out of its application. The reason for opting out is probably that parties are more familiar with their own domestic sales law than they are with the CISG.

SUMMARY

- Goods are tangible personal property — things that move. Real estate is not included.

- A "sale" of goods involves the transfer of title to goods for a price.

- UCC Article 2 covers "sales" of goods, not leases of goods (covered by Article 2A) and not service contracts or sales of real estate.

- The determination of applicable law is important because the liability of the parties differs depending on which law applies. For example, sellers are often held strictly liable if goods do not work properly whereas providers of services are liable only if they act negligently.

- In mixed goods/services contracts, most courts will apply Article 2 if the predominant purpose of the contract is the sale of goods.

- Some courts will apply Article 2 if the "gravamen" of the claim involves the goods. In other words, is the problem with the goods or with the services?

- Article 2 applies to sales of timber, crops, and other items that can be easily severable from the land.

- Article 2 applies to sales of minerals, oil, gas, and structures only if the seller is to sever those items from the land.

- Many courts will apply Article 2 to licenses of software, finding these transactions to be analogous to sales of goods. The 2003 amendments to Article 2, if adopted by the states, would exclude pure software licenses from the scope of Article 2.

- The CISG applies to contracts for the sale of goods if each party is in a different nation that has adopted the CISG. Parties may, however, opt out of the CISG either in whole or in part, in which case other law will apply.

- The CISG may also apply if one party is in a nation that has adopted the CISG and the other party is in another nation that has not adopted it if choice of law rules point to the law of the nation that has adopted the CISG. The United States has opted out of this provision, however, so the CISG will apply to a U.S. party only if the nation in which the other party resides has also adopted it.

- In mixed goods/services contracts, the CISG applies if the predominant purpose of the contract is the sale of goods.

- The CISG does **not** apply in the following transactions: (1) consumer goods transactions (unless the seller did not know nor should have known that the goods were for the personal, family, or household use of the buyer and thus thought that the CISG would apply); (2) auction sales; (3) execution sales and other sales under authority of law; (4) sales of investment securities, negotiable instruments, and money; (5) sales of ships, hovercraft, or aircraft; and (6) sales of electricity.

- The CISG does not apply to personal injury cases.

CONNECTIONS

Choice of Law

This chapter deals with the first question that any lawyer must consider when faced with a problem — which law applies? As we saw, if the contract is for a sale of goods, Article 2 applies in a domestic sale within the United States and the CISG may apply in an international sale. If the contract is for something else, like a sale of real estate or a service contract, other contract law applies. The analysis can get tricky especially when the contract is partially for goods and partially for services, and we saw that most courts (and the CISG) focus on the predominant purpose of the contract — was it for goods or for services? If for goods, then the UCC or the CISG apply and if for services, the law governing service contracts applies. The consequences of the determination can be significant — if Article 2 applies the provider of defective goods is strictly liable, whereas under the law governing service contracts the service provider is liable only if negligent.

Contract Formation

Once we determine that we have a sale of goods, we then analyze whether a contract has been formed under the UCC or the CISG. We will see that the law governing contract formation under both laws is more liberal than under common law, permitting contract formation even if the parties have not agreed on all terms, and permitting contract formation through exchanges of forms in which the forms differ from one another.

Contract Terms

If we determine that the transaction is a sale of goods, contract terms will be determined based on what the parties agree to and gap filler provisions provided by either the UCC or the CISG. As we will see, the two laws imply some warranties of quality to which the goods must conform unless the warranties are validly disclaimed.

Contract Performance

The choice of law will determine the law governing contract performance. If we have a domestic sale of goods in the United States, Article 2 of the UCC requires the seller to make a perfect tender of goods before the buyer is required to accept them in non-installment sale situations. This rule should be contrasted to the common law, which generally does not permit a party to terminate a contract unless there is an uncured material breach. The CISG is more like the common law in requiring a fundamental breach before a party is allowed to avoid a contract.

Remedies

The remedies available to the injured party also depend on the choice of law. Under the CISG, parties are generally allowed to obtain specific performance, although the CISG defers to domestic law if a court would not order specific performance under its own law. By contrast, both the UCC and the common law prefer that the injured party obtain damages as a remedy rather than specific performance.

Contract Formation

3

Once it is determined that a transaction is a sale of goods transaction, we must then explore whether a contract has been validly formed.

The Uniform Commercial Code (UCC) and the United Nations Convention on Contracts for the International Sale of Goods (CISG) both have fairly liberal contract formational rules, not requiring that the parties necessarily agree on all terms. It is even possible for parties to form an enforceable contract without agreeing on a definite price. In this chapter we will first focus on the UCC rules dealing with contract formation and will then focus on the different approaches to formational issues taken by the CISG.

OVERVIEW

A. BASIC FORMATIONAL RULES

1. Formal Requirements — Must the Contract Be Evidenced by a Writing?
2. "Offer" and the "Firm Offer Rule"
3. The Acceptance

B. THE "BATTLE OF THE FORMS"

1. The Writings Form a Contract
2. The Parties Informally Contract and Follow with Confirmations
3. The Writings of the Parties Do Not Form a Contract, But a Contract Is Formed by Performance

C. THE "ROLLING CONTRACT" APPROACH, OR "MONEY NOW, TERMS LATER"

D. MODIFICATIONS

1. No Consideration Required
2. Formal Requirements for Modification

E. DIFFERENCES IN CISG APPROACH TO CONTRACT FORMATION

1. Definition and Revocation of Offers
2. Acceptances Are Generally Effective on Receipt
3. CISG Approach to the "Battle of the Forms"
4. Generally, No Writings Are Required Under the CISG

A. Basic Formational Rules

The UCC indicates that a contract for sale "may be made in any manner sufficient to show agreement."[1] The parties may form a contract through conduct, such as by the seller shipping goods to a buyer after the buyer has ordered them or by a buyer accepting the goods and paying for them after they have been shipped.[2] In addition, it is not necessary to show the exact moment that the contract was formed.

The UCC reflects the understanding that parties to a sale of goods contract often deal informally. Lawyers are generally not present when parties contract to buy and sell goods. The agreement may occur during a casual conversation at which the parties agree only on the most fundamental of terms, such as the quantity of goods sold and the price. The parties may then follow up the conversation by exchanging "confirmations," which memorialize the agreement of the parties and which might flesh out the terms of the agreement. UCC §2-204 indicates that it is not necessary for the parties to agree on all details for an enforceable contract to exist; the question is whether the parties intend to be bound and have agreed on enough terms so that there is reasonably certain basis for enforcing the contract.

To assist courts in enforcing agreements in which the parties have not agreed on all details, the UCC provides a number of "*gap filler*" terms. We will talk in more detail about these gap filler terms later in the book, but for now you should understand that such terms as delivery date and location of delivery are provided by the Code if the parties have indicated an intent to be bound to a contract but have not agreed on delivery date and location. For example, assume that a buyer and seller have a signed, written agreement for the sale of a specific automobile for $20,000 but have not indicated in the contract when delivery will occur or when the buyer will pay the price. The UCC will fill these gaps by saying that delivery must occur within a reasonable time at the seller's place of business, and that payment is due at the time that delivery is tendered.[3]

Courts may also look at industry practice (*usage of trade*), *courses of dealing* between the parties in prior transactions, and how the parties have been performing in the current transaction (*course of performance*) to flesh out the parties'

---

[1]UCC §2-204.
[2]UCC §2-206(1).
[3]UCC §§2-308-2-310.

agreement.[4] For example, if in past dealings the seller has always delivered goods 30 days after the parties contracted and the contract is silent as to delivery date, it is probably fair to assume that the parties intend delivery in 30 days in the current transaction.

(1) Formal Requirements — Must the Contract Be Evidenced by a Writing?

As noted previously, the UCC permits contracts to be formed informally, but UCC §2-201 provides a **statute of frauds** requiring that any contract for the sale of goods for the price of $500 or more be evidenced by a writing sufficient to indicate that a contract was made signed by the party to be charged (i.e., the person being sued). Under the proposed amendments to Article 2, the threshold price for requiring written evidence is raised to $5,000 or more. Notice that the contract itself need not be in writing — what is needed is written evidence of the contract. The evidence could take the form of a confirmatory letter sent by one of the parties or even scribbled notes on a cocktail napkin, at least as long as it is signed. Also noted previously, parties will often follow an informal contract formed during a conversation with a written "confirmation" laying out the terms of the deal.

The statute is very liberal about the requirements of the writing. All that is necessary is that it evidences a contract. A purchase order or an advertisement containing the name of the party making the order or the advertisement may not be enough as such writings at most are evidence of an offer. Nevertheless, some courts have held that purchase orders and advertisements satisfy §2-201.[5]

The terms in the writing do not need to be correct. The writing is not really used to demonstrate the terms of the contract, but rather to show that a contract actually exists. The one requirement is that the contract will not be enforced beyond the quantity that is stated in the writing. So, for example, if a signed contract indicates that 500 bushels of wheat will be sold, neither party can assert that the contract is really for 700 bushels.

Q: Why don't all contracts have to be in writing?

A: Life would be easier if all contracts were in writing. Unfortunately, that's not the way that people act. People orally contract all of the time, and expect that the contract will be honored. Transaction costs would increase if every time that somebody contracted, the contract needed to be put in writing. Of course, for major transactions, parties will go to the expense of putting the terms of the contract in writing. But the law does not make people do it — the law generally seeks to reflect the way people do business rather than change the way they do business. See Gilmore, *The Ages of American Law* 85 (1977).

---

[4]See UCC §1-303.
[5]See *Donovan v. RRL Corp.*, 26 Cal. 4th 261, 27 P.2d 702, 109 Cal. Rptr. 2d 807 (2001).

The **signature** requirement is also very liberal. All that is required is an intent of a party to authenticate the document.[6] This could be done with a printed name, a name stamp, a typed name or an "X."

In this day and age of electronic contracting, a question might come up as to whether an e-mail or other form of electronic communication satisfies the requirement of written evidence signed by the party to be charged. The Uniform Electronic Transactions Act (UETA), a uniform state law, and the federal Electronic Signatures in Global and National Commerce Act[7] (sometimes referred to as the "E-Sign Act") both indicate that contracts are not to be considered unenforceable simply because they are in electronic form and contain electronic signatures. Courts might in any event find that an e-mail satisfies the statute of frauds because it can be printed out and the sender's name might constitute a sufficient "signature."[8] Revised Article 1 and the approved amendments to Article 2 generally refer to "record," which includes electronic records, rather than writing.[9]

In some cases, a party does not even have to sign the document to be precluded from asserting the statute of frauds as a defense. If both parties are merchants and one party sends a signed writing to the other party that satisfies the statute of frauds, the recipient must object in writing to the existence of the contract within ten days after receipt of the document or be barred from asserting the statute of frauds as a defense.[10]

For example, assume that both the buyer and seller are merchants, and the seller sends a signed "Order Acknowledgment" to the buyer that spells out the quantity, price, and delivery date for the goods. The buyer receives the document, but does not object. The buyer will not be allowed to assert the statute of frauds as a defense, even though the buyer did not sign the document. You should note, however, that even if a party is precluded from asserting the statute of frauds, the party may still claim that no contract was actually formed. The buyer could assert that the Order Acknowledgment was really an offer to sell sent by the seller to which the buyer never agreed.

STATUTE OF FRAUDS EXCEPTIONS

1) Specially manufactured goods
2) Party admits contract during course of proceeding under oath
3) Goods paid for or accepted
4) Promissory estoppel (general principles of law & equity)
5) Promissory fraud (general principles of law & equity)

---

[6]UCC §1-201(b)(37).
[7]15 U.S.C. §§7001, *et seq.*
[8]*Cloud Corp. v. Hasbro, Inc.*, 314 F.2d 289, 49 UCC Rep. Serv. 2d 413 (7th Cir. 2002).
[9]UCC §1-201(b)(31); Amended UCC §2-201.
[10]UCC §2-201(2). For a discussion of "merchants," see p. 12, *supra.*

Even if there is no writing at all, a contract may nevertheless be enforceable if one of the exceptions to the statute of frauds applies. Under the ***specially manufactured goods exception***, no writing is required if (i) the goods are specially manufactured for the buyer; (ii) the goods are not for sale to others in the ordinary course of the seller's business; (iii) circumstances reasonably indicate that the goods are for the buyer; and (iv) before the seller receives notice that the buyer has repudiated, the seller has made either a substantial beginning of the goods' manufacture or commitments for the goods' procurement.[11]

Another situation in which no writing is required is if the party being sued admits during the litigation that a contract exists. This is called the ***admissions exception*** to the statute of frauds. The admission must be in a pleading, in testimony, or otherwise in court.[12] The admission probably doesn't have to be as direct as saying "I admit there is a contract," but rather can probably be of facts that show the existence of a contract ("plaintiff and I agreed that I would sell him 400 bushels of wheat at $4 a bushel"). There is judicial authority for the proposition that the defendant must deny under oath that there is a contract before that party may assert the statute of frauds as a defense.[13]

A third exception to the §2-201 statute of frauds is for ***goods that have been paid for or accepted***. This exception is good only to the extent that goods have been paid for or accepted, meaning that the party trying to assert the contract cannot use this exception to assert obligations to deliver or pay for more than what has been paid for or accepted. For example, if parties have an oral agreement for the purchase and sale of 500 bushels of wheat and 200 bushels have been accepted by the buyer, the seller may sue for the price of those 200 bushels. The seller may not, however, sue for damages with respect to the bushels that have not been delivered, namely, the 300 additional bushels.

Another exception to the statute of frauds that is applied by the majority of jurisdictions is ***promissory estoppel***, or reliance. Section 2-201 does not provide for an exception based on reliance. Nevertheless, courts applying general principles of law and equity will sometimes bar a party from asserting the statute of frauds as a defense in a sale of goods case if a party has reasonably relied on an oral contract. For example, in one case a seller was allowed to sue on an oral contract for the sale of grapes when the seller relied on the contract by canceling another contract and where it was too late to resell the grapes when the buyer repudiated.[14]

Finally, another exception to the statute of frauds that is not mentioned in §2-201 but that might apply as a general principle of law and equity is ***promissory fraud***. Promissory fraud is a tort in which somebody makes a promise with no intention of keeping it. Some courts have held that the statute of frauds does not bar an action for promissory fraud in cases in which the promise is oral.[15]

---

[11]UCC §2-201(3)(a).
[12]UCC §2-201(3)(b).
[13]*DF Activities Corp. v. Brown*, 851 F.2d 920 (7th Cir. 1988).
[14]*Allied Grape Growers v. Bronco Wine Co.*, 203 Cal. App. 3d 432, 249 Cal. Rptr. 872 (1988).
[15]See, e.g., *Tenzer v. Superscope, Inc.*, 39 Cal. 3d 18, 702 P.2d 212 (1985) (although not a sale of goods case).

(2) "Offer" and the "Firm Offer Rule"

One way that a contract can be formed is through the traditional offer and acceptance. The UCC does not define *"offer,"* leaving the question of whether an offer has been made to general principles of law and equity.[16] One should then ask whether a proposal made by a seller or buyer is sufficiently definite that the recipient would reasonably believe that all that the recipient needs to do is accept the proposal for a contract to be formed?[17] In determining whether an offer has been made (as compared to a mere ***invitation to bargain***), one should look at whether the proposal indicates a price or method of determining the price, the quantity, and a time for acceptance. It is particularly important that a quantity be provided, as the UCC does not provide any gap-filler provision to help a court determine the quantity, except in cases involving so-called output or requirements contracts.[18] In addition, the proposal should be limited in terms of the number of persons to whom it is directed; catalogs and other advertisements to the general public are generally considered invitations to bargain and are not offers, unless the catalog or advertisement is so specific in describing the terms of the deal that someone hearing it reasonably believes that all they have to do is accept for a contract to be formed.[19]

IMPORTANT ISSUES REGARDING "OFFERS"

(1) Is communication an "offer" or an "invitation to bargain"?
   ■ Does recipient reasonably believe it is an offer to contract?
   ■ Could court enforce a contract upon acceptance?
(2) If an offer, is it irrevocable?
   ■ Is it a "firm offer" under §2-205?
   ■ Is it a binding option supported by consideration?
   ■ Is it irrevocable because the offeree reasonably relied on it?

As noted previously, one of the important issues regarding any offer is whether it can be revoked before acceptance. As under the common law, an offer can generally be revoked at any time before it is accepted, unless it is a binding option contract supported by consideration or is a *"firm offer"* under UCC §2-205. A firm offer is one made by a merchant in a signed writing that indicates that it is "irrevocable" or "firm."[20] An example of a firm offer would be the statement, "I will sell you 2,000 bushels of wheat at $5 per bushel. This offer is firm until June 25, 2008." This should be contrasted with the statement, "I will sell you 2,000 bushels of wheat at $5 per

---

[16]See p. 26, *supra*.
[17]See *Restatement (Second) of Contracts* §24. The *Restatement* provides some general rules of contract law that courts might use in filling gaps left by the UCC.
[18]Output and requirements contracts are discussed more fully at pp. 145-146, *infra*.
[19]*Restatement (Second) of Contracts* §26, comment b. The classic example of an advertisement that was found sufficiently definite as to be an offer is *Lefkowitz v. Great Minneapolis Surplus Store, Inc.*, 281 Minn. 188, 86 N.W.2d 689 (1957), in which the court held that an advertisement of one fur stole "worth $139.50" for $1, "first come, first served," was an enforceable offer.
[20]For the definition of "merchant," see p. 12, *supra*.

bushel. The offer expires June 25, 2008." The latter proposal does not indicate that it is irrevocable until June 25, 2008; it simply indicates a deadline for acceptance without any assurance that it will be held open until that time. It could thus be revoked before June 25, 2008.

The requirements for an offer to be "firm" and thus irrevocable are the following:

1. it is made by a merchant;
2. it is in a signed writing; and
3. it gives assurance that it will be held open.

If the offer meets these requirements it will be irrevocable during any time stated for irrevocability, as long as the time stated is not beyond three months. If no time is stated, it will be irrevocable for a reasonable time, again not exceeding three months. An example of such an offer would be if a merchant stated in a signed writing, "I will sell you 2,000 bushels of wheat for $5 per bushel; this offer is irrevocable." The firm-offer rule provides an additional requirement if the firm offer is contained on a form document that is provided by the offeree. In such a case, it must be separately signed by the offeror. For example, a buyer might have a form proposal that it requires the seller to sign, indicating the seller's willingness to supply goods for a specific project at a designated price. If that form states that the proposal is "firm" or "irrevocable," the seller must separately sign the language providing for irrevocability.

Offers that do not qualify as firm offers under UCC §2-205 may nevertheless be irrevocable if the promise to keep the offer open is supported by consideration. For example, somebody could say, "In exchange for $500, I give you the option to purchase my car for $20,000 with the option expiring in seven months." Although this offer would not be irrevocable under §2-205, it would be irrevocable as an option contract supported by consideration.

Another basis for holding an offer open is **promissory estoppel**. Let us assume, for example, that a supplier of concrete writes a letter to a general contractor offering to sell all the concrete the contractor requires for a set price for one year. The general contractor relies on this offer in submitting its bid to build a building. Six months later, the seller of concrete attempts to revoke its offer. The offer would not be irrevocable under the firm offer rule of UCC §2-205 because the period of irrevocability stated in the offer is over three months, but the general contractor might try to argue that it reasonably and detrimentally relied on the concrete supplier's promise to sell concrete at a set price for one year.

Under general principles of law and equity, some courts might hold the concrete supplier liable under the principle of promissory estoppel. The *Restatement*

Sidebar

THE POLICY FAVORING REVOCABILITY OF OFFERS

Not all offers are irrevocable because the law generally does not like to expose parties to speculation and also does not like to give people something for nothing. If all offers were irrevocable until the time stated for expiration, the offeree could decide whether or not to accept (i.e., speculate) without giving up anything in return. Meanwhile, the offeror would be bound and might have to pass up other opportunities. See E. Allan Farnsworth, *Mutuality of Obligation in Contract Law*, 3 U. Dayton L. Rev. 271 (1978). The drafters of the UCC decided that in some cases it made sense to allow for irrevocable offers so that the offeree could rely on it, for example, by obtaining financing to go through with a purchase. Note, however, that only experienced business people (i.e., merchants) can make firm offers and they must be in writing.

(Second) of Contracts formulation of the rule reads, "An offer which the offeror should reasonably expect to induce action or forbearance of a substantial character on the part of the offeree before acceptance and which does induce such action or forbearance is binding as an option contract to the extent necessary to prevent injustice."[21]

(3) The Acceptance

ISSUES INVOLVING THE ACCEPTANCE

(1) Is it definite—i.e., is the offeree agreeing with the terms of the offer?
(2) Is it timely, within the time indicated in the offer?
(3) Is it in the manner reasonably permitted by the offer?

The offeror is the "master" of the offer and can dictate the mode of *acceptance*. An exception to this rule would be that the offeror cannot compel the offeree to speak—that is, the offeror cannot say that by remaining silent, the offeree will be deemed to have accepted the offer.[22] The UCC does not provide this rule, but this is a situation in which the common law rule supplements the UCC.[23] The issues involved in determining whether an offer has been accepted are noted previously.

Unless the offeror unambiguously indicates an exclusive mode of acceptance, however, the offeree may accept in any manner that is reasonable. Article 2 provides that unless unambiguously stated otherwise, an offer for prompt or current shipment is construed as inviting either a prompt promise to ship or the prompt or current shipment of conforming or nonconforming goods. If nonconforming goods are shipped, this means that the seller has accepted the offer and breached the contract at the same time, unless the seller seasonably notifies the buyer that the goods are merely being shipped as an accommodation.[24]

To demonstrate how this works, assume that a buyer sends a purchase order to a seller that says "ship at once." The official commentary to UCC §2-206 indicates that such an offer would still invite a promissory acceptance, meaning that the seller could send an acknowledgment of the order, which would form a contract before the goods were actually shipped. Likewise, a purchase order that says "please respond with an acknowledgment of order" might permit acceptance by the seller promptly shipping the goods. If the offeror really wants to limit the mode of acceptance, it must be very clear about it, such as by saying "the only permissible mode of acceptance is by responding with an acknowledgment of this order within 24 hours."

---

[21]See Janke Constr. Co. v. Vulcan Materials Co., 386 F. Supp. 697, 16 UCC Rep. Serv. 937 (W.D. Wis. 1974), *aff'd*, 527 F.2d 772 (7th Cir. 1976); *Restatement (2d) of Contracts* §87(2).
[22]*Restatement (Second) of Contracts* §69.
[23]UCC §1-103(b).
[24]UCC §2-206.

One thing that the Code requires in cases in which acceptance by performance is permissible is that the offeree notify the offeror of acceptance within a reasonable time.[25] If the offeree does not do this, the offer is deemed to have lapsed before acceptance.

As noted previously, if the offeree chooses to accept by sending nonconforming goods, the offer is accepted and the contract is breached at the same time. For example, let us assume that the buyer sends a purchase order for 1,000 bushels of wheat but the seller responds by shipping only 800 bushels. The seller in such a case would be accepting the buyer's offer but would be deemed to have breached the contract at the same time. If the seller wishes to avoid liability in such a case and has only those 800 bushels to ship, the seller could send a notification at the same time as shipment that the 800 bushels are being sent as an accommodation, which means that essentially the seller is making a counteroffer of 800 bushels. The buyer could then choose to accept the counteroffer or reject it, but the seller would not be responsible in either case for delivering an additional 200 bushels.

B. The "Battle of the Forms"

As noted previously, parties to a sales contract often contract informally and do not expressly agree on all terms of the deal. Parties might have an informal conversation in which they agree on the price of the goods and the quantity to be purchased. One or both parties will then follow up with "*confirmation*" or "*acknowledgment*" forms that confirm the basic points of the deal but then add other details, such as how the goods will be shipped or how disputes will be resolved (e.g., through arbitration). The written confirmation may be sent for the purpose of satisfying the statute of frauds. Another way of contracting is for the parties to exchange form offers and acceptances, for example, by the buyer sending a "*purchase order*" (offer) and the seller sending an "*order acknowledgment*" (acceptance). The forms will be in agreement regarding the basic terms of the contract, but the buyer's form may have terms that vary from the terms in the seller's form. Yet another way that parties may form a contract is through performance. Perhaps they will exchange a purchase order and order acknowledgment that do not form a contract, but goods will subsequently be shipped and the buyer will accept them and pay for them. In all of these situations, courts will have to try to figure out what to do with the terms that are in the parties' forms — are they part of the contract or are they not? Courts may also have to use gap fillers, as discussed previously, to flesh out the terms of the deal.

Sidebar

SHIPMENT OF NONCONFORMING GOODS AS AN ACCEPTANCE

Shipment of nonconforming goods is an acceptance rather than a rejection and counteroffer because otherwise the buyer could not hold the seller responsible for shipping goods that are defective in some way. As noted previously, if the seller wants to make a counteroffer by sending nonconforming goods, the seller can indicate to the buyer that the goods shipped are an "accommodation," which puts the buyer on notice to check the goods and see if they are suitable for the buyer. See UCC §2-206(1)(b).

---

[25]UCC §2-206(2).

The drafters of the UCC attempted to come up with a rule that would deal with these situations, namely, §2-207. This statute is one of the most difficult to study in the law of sales because the statute is not clearly worded. Because the question considered is which party's form contract should control, this topic is referred to as the "***battle of the forms***."

Section 2-207 should be viewed against the backdrop of the common law. Under the common law approach, an acceptance could not have different or additional terms from the offer. If it did, it was not truly an acceptance but was instead a rejection and counteroffer. The power of acceptance under the original offer was also terminated. This was the so-called ***mirror image rule***, and to some extent is still the rule under the *Restatement (Second) of Contracts*.[26] If the parties went ahead and performed after the rejection and counteroffer, it was deemed to be an acceptance of the counteroffer and the terms in the counteroffer controlled. This is referred to as the *"**last shot doctrine**."*[27]

The drafters of the UCC thought that the mirror image rule and last shot doctrine were arbitrary rules that could result in injustice. The drafters recognized the reality that parties do not read all of the terms in the forms that are used in contracting. Each party uses its own form over and over again, with the only terms that change being the quantity of the goods, the price, and the delivery date. When one party receives the other party's form, that party probably only checks to make sure that the fundamental terms are correct. Under a "mirror image" rule, parties could seize on technical differences between forms to get out of agreements that had become unfavorable.[28] For example, assume that parties exchange forms that are in agreement regarding price and quantity of goods and think they have a deal. Delivery is to be in two months. One month later, the market price of the goods drops, and so now the buyer does not want to go through with the transaction. Under a strict application of the mirror image rule, if the buyer could show even a slight difference between the forms, the buyer could assert that there never had been an acceptance and thus there was no deal.

The last shot doctrine is also arbitrary if parties are not paying much attention to the forms that are being used. In the days when parties more carefully negotiated the terms of their contracts and read the documents that were exchanged, it might have made sense to say that performance indicated tacit acceptance of terms contained in a counteroffer. Why would a party perform unless the party agreed to all of the terms in the counteroffer? It is a fiction, however, to say that parties are necessarily agreeing to terms in a form document that the parties do not read (and that we do not necessarily expect them to read).

UCC §2-207 was thus drafted to permit contract formation even in situations in which there are discrepancies between the forms exchanged by the parties. Rather than always providing that the terms in the last form "win" the battle of the forms, §2-207 also attempts to come up with a more fair consideration of which terms in the forms should become part of the contract. We will now consider application of §2-207 in three different situations: (1) where the parties form a contract by offer and acceptance but the acceptance contains different or additional terms from those

---

[26]*Restatement (Second) of Contracts* §39.
[27]See *Richardson v. Union Carbide Industrial Gases*, 347 N.J. Super. 524, 790 A.2d 962 (App. Div. 2002).
[28]See, e.g., *Poel v. Brunswick-Balke-Collender Co.*, 216 N.Y. 310, 110 N.E. 619 (1915).

in the offer; (2) where the parties informally contract, perhaps by an oral conversation, and then one or both parties sends a confirmation that contains terms in addition to those on which they have verbally agreed; and (3) where the parties' exchange of forms does not cause a contract to be formed, perhaps because the purported acceptance was conditional on assent to all of its terms and there was no express assent, but the parties' performance indicates the existence of a contract.[29]

(1) The Writings Form a Contract

To demonstrate how §2-207 works in the context of the writings forming a contract let us consider the following hypothetical fact pattern:

(1) Buyer, a merchant, sends a "purchase order" to Seller seeking to purchase a specified quantity of carpeting at a specified price. The purchase order says nothing about dispute resolution and does not state that it is limited to its terms.

(2) Seller, also a merchant, responds with an "order acknowledgment" that is in agreement with the purchase order on price and quantity. Seller's form states that acceptance of Buyer's order is "subject to" terms and conditions on the reverse of the order acknowledgment. Included among those terms is a provision requiring arbitration of all disputes.

(a) Identify the Offer

The first step in doing the analysis of whether the writings form a contract under UCC §2-207 is to identify the offer. This is important because §2-207 really favors the party who sends the offer — it is more likely that its terms will be included in the contract (as compared to the last shot doctrine at common law). In this case it appears that Buyer's purchase order is the offer, as it called for specific goods at a specific price. Remember that an offer to purchase goods need not spell out all terms of the contract. In doing this analysis, one should also remember that advertisements and price quotes are generally not considered offers, they are invitations to bargain. So, a purchase order sent after a price quote is given may very well constitute the "offer."

(b) Identify the Acceptance

UCC §2-207(1) provides that a definite and seasonable expression of acceptance is operative as an acceptance even if it contains different or additional terms from the offer as long as it is not expressly conditional on assent to the different or additional terms. The UCC thus obviously rejects the common law mirror image rule. The question that remains is how different an acceptance can be from the offer and still be an acceptance.

Commentators suggest that if the offer and acceptance are in agreement on the fundamental terms of the contract, such as the price, quality, quantity, and delivery date, a contract may be found to exist even if non-negotiated "boilerplate" terms on the buyer's and seller's forms are different or additional.[30] The fundamental terms of the contract are sometimes called "*dicker terms*" as they are terms over which parties

---

[29]See UCC §2-207, official comment 1.
[30]See White & Summers, *Uniform Commercial Code* §1.3 (5th ed.).

will dicker, or negotiate. In our hypothetical, it appears that the purchase order and the order acknowledgment are in agreement on the dicker terms.

There is a question then as to whether the order acknowledgment was expressly conditional on assent to its additional terms. A provision in a purported acceptance indicating that it is expressly conditional on asset to additional or different terms in the acceptance is sometimes referred to as a "***proviso clause***," because it indicates that there is a contract only on the condition that the other side agrees to all terms in the form. If a purported acceptance has a proviso clause, it is not an acceptance but is instead a rejection and counteroffer.

In our hypothetical, does the statement that the order acknowledgment is "subject to" all of the terms and conditions on the back of the form mean that it is expressly conditional on Buyer's assent to all of its terms? Courts have indicated, "the conditional nature of the acceptance must be clearly expressed in a manner sufficient to notify the offeror that the offeree is unwilling to proceed with the trans-action unless the additional or different terms are included in the contract."[31] When one thinks about it, this makes sense because the party receiving the form (the offeror) is looking primarily at the dicker terms and if they are in agreement with the offer, the offeror reasonably believes that there is a contract. The offeror will be surprised later to find out that what appeared to be an acceptance was really a rejection and a counteroffer. In our hypothetical, the language "subject to" has been held by at least one court to be **not** sufficiently clear to make the acceptance expressly conditional on the offeror's assent to the additional terms.[32] To make an acceptance expressly conditional (and therefore not really an acceptance, but a rejec-tion and counteroffer), the acceptance should probably say something like, "this acceptance is conditional on assent to all of its terms and there will be no contract unless the recipient so assents." It is probably better if the language is in bold print and in all capital letters.

Thus, the bottom line in our hypothetical is that the order acknowledgment was an operative acceptance, even though it had the arbitration clause in it. The next question is what happens to the arbitration clause—does it become part of the contract?

(c) What Happens to the Additional or Different Terms in the Acceptance?

According to subsection 2 to §2-207, additional terms in the acceptance are to be considered as proposals for addition to the contract. If the two parties are merchants, the terms automatically become part of the contract unless (1) the offer is expressly limited to its terms, (2) the terms *materially alter* the contract, or (3) the offeror has objected to the terms or objects within a reasonable time after notice of the terms is received.

Note that if the contract is between a merchant and a non-merchant or between two non-merchants, additional or different terms in an acceptance will not automat-ically become part of the contract. Such terms are merely proposals, and it is necessary for the offeror to agree to them for the terms to become part of the contract.

The facts of our hypothetical indicate that both Buyer and Seller are merchants. The facts also state that the purchase order was not limited to its terms. That means

---

[31]*Brown Machine v. Hercules, Inc.*, 770 S.W.2d 416 (Mo. App. 1989).
[32]*Dorton v. Collins & Aikman Corp.*, 453 F.2d 1163, 10 UCC Rep. Serv. 585 (1972).

that the arbitration provision in the order acknowledgment will become part of the contract unless it materially alters the contract or the offeror objects within a reasonable time. There is no evidence of objection to the term by Buyer. We must then examine whether the arbitration provision "materially alters" the contract. Official comment 4 to §2-207 gives guidance about what is meant by the language "materially alter." The test, according to the comment, is one of "surprise or hardship" to the offeror. The comment gives some examples of such provisions, including disclaiming of standard warranties and clauses imposing responsibilities on a party that are greater than prevailing industry practices. Comment 5 gives examples of clauses that do **not** materially alter the contract, such as clauses that fix a reasonable time for customer complaints and allow for interest on unpaid invoices. The comments say nothing about whether arbitration provisions are material.

Arbitration is an alternative means of resolving disputes. It is favored by some because of the belief that it is more expeditious than litigation and because arbitrators have more expertise than jurors (and also some judges). It is disfavored because the procedural safeguards present in litigation, such as a right to discovery, are largely absent. There might also be concern regarding the bias of some arbitrators.[33]

Some courts hold that arbitration is always material—parties must expressly agree to it before they will be required to arbitrate.[34] Other courts hold that the materiality of arbitration is a question of fact to be determined on a case-by-case basis.[35] For example, if both parties frequently arbitrate disputes and there is nothing unusual about the arbitration clause, it is not a "surprise or hardship" for either party to arbitrate disputes between them.

Returning to our hypothetical, if the court takes the position that arbitration clauses are *per se* material, the clause will not be included in the contract unless the offeror expressly assents to it. If the court takes the position that materiality of an arbitration provision is a question of fact, it might be useful to examine whether arbitration is common in sales transactions comparable to the one between Seller and Buyer. The terms of arbitration may also be important—would Buyer be required to pay more to arbitrate than to litigate and travel a long distance to the place of arbitration? If the terms of arbitration are normal in this industry, it would be hard for Buyer to argue that arbitration is either a "surprise" or a "hardship," and the arbitration provision would thus be included in the contract.

One issue under §2-207 that is not clearly answered is what to do if terms in an acceptance differ from terms in the offer? Subsection 2 to §2-207 says that additional terms are to be considered, but does not say anything about different terms. It may sometimes be difficult to determine if a term is "additional" or "different." Obviously, if the offer says that disputes will be resolved in court while the acceptance states that disputes will be resolved by arbitration, the term in the acceptance would be a different term. In our hypothetical, the purchase order said nothing about dispute resolution, so the arbitration provision would probably be considered to be "additional." But, one could argue that because the default term is that disputes will be litigated rather than arbitrated, implied in the purchase order is that any disputes will be litigated. That would make the arbitration provision in the order acknowledgment a "different" term.

---

[33]For a discussion of some of the problems posed by arbitration, see *Armendariz v. Foundation Health Psychcare Services, Inc.*, 24 Cal. 4th 83, 6 P.3d 669, 99 Cal. Rptr. 2d 745 (2000).
[34]See *Application of Doughboy Industries, Inc.*, 17 A.D.2d 216, 233 N.Y.S.2d 488 (1962).
[35]See *Dorton v. Collins & Aikman Corp.*, 453 F.2d 1161, 10 UCC Rep. Serv. 585 (1972) (6th Cir. 1972).

Courts and commentators split on what is to be done with different terms in an acceptance. Official comment 3 to §2-207 suggests that additional or different terms should both be considered under subsection 2. This suggests that the drafters were not as careful as they should have been in drafting subsection 2 as they left out the word "different." An advantage to this approach is that we do not have to deal with the determination of whether a term is "different" or "additional." Another approach, however, is to say that any term in an acceptance that contradicts a term in the offer is not included in the contract unless the offeror assents. One can take the position that if the term contradicts the offer, the offeror has already objected to it. A third approach, which is suggested in official comment 6 to §2-207, is to say that conflicting terms in forms exchanged by the parties cancel each other out. This approach is referred to as the "*knock out doctrine.*" Under this third approach, the terms of the contract are then those on which the forms of the parties agree, terms on which the parties otherwise agree, and terms provided by the UCC, including course of dealing and usage of trade.

THREE APPROACHES TO TREATMENT OF DIFFERENT TERMS IN AN ACCEPTANCE

(1) Different terms in the acceptance are not included in the contract unless the offeror assents to them.
(2) Different terms in the acceptance are treated the same as additional terms under §2-207(2).
(3) Different terms in the offer and acceptance cancel each other out, and the term is supplied by the UCC.

The knock out doctrine has a certain appeal, at least if the offer and the acceptance clearly contradict each other. For example, if the offer says that delivery of goods is to be on May 3 while the acceptance says that delivery is to be on May 10, it is clear that the parties are in disagreement on this point. If the date of delivery is significant in the transaction, it probably makes the most sense to say that there is no contract at all until there is further agreement between the parties on the date of delivery. If the date of delivery is not that significant (i.e., it wasn't the topic of negotiation or dickering), it seems arbitrary to pick one date or the other. It might make the most sense to just "knock out" the conflicting terms and use the UCC gap filler on delivery date, which is that delivery will be at a reasonable time.[36]

Under the 2003 approved amendments to Article 2, a contract can still be formed with different or additional terms in an acceptance.[37] To the extent that terms in the offer and acceptance vary, neither the terms in the offer nor the terms in the acceptance control. The terms of the contract consist of those on which the forms agree, terms on which both parties otherwise agree, and terms supplied by the UCC, which would include "gap filler" terms and terms supplied by course of performance,

---

[36]UCC §2-309.
[37]Amended UCC §2-206(3).

course of dealing, and usage of trade.[38] The proposed amendments thus adopt the knock out approach discussed previously, giving neither party the victory in the "battle of the forms."

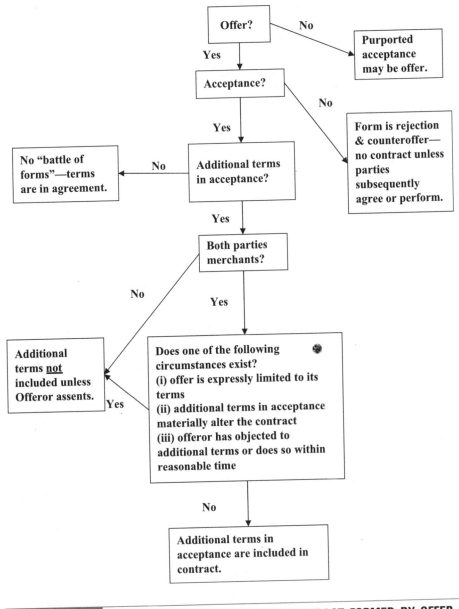

---

[38]Amended UCC §2-207.

The above flowchart demonstrates the logical flow of analysis to be done in situations in which a contract is formed through the exchange of forms. We must first identify the offer. Once we have done that, we must ask whether there has been an acceptance. Remember that the acceptance must be definite — there needs to be a fundamental agreement on basic terms such as price and quantity. Also, a purported acceptance containing additional or different terms must not be expressly conditional on the offeror's assent to those terms — if it is expressly conditional, it is a rejection and counteroffer. If a purported acceptance is a rejection and counteroffer, there is no contract between the parties unless they subsequently reach agreement or perform.

THE STATUTORY MESS THAT IS UCC §2-207

If you have a hard time figuring out how to analyze cases under UCC §2-207, you can take comfort in the fact that you are not alone. Professor Grant Gilmore, one of the people responsible for the UCC, referred to §2-207 as "arguably the greatest statutory mess of all time." Mark Roszkowski, *Revised Article 2 of the Uniform Commercial Code — Section-by-Section Analysis*, 54 SMU L. Rev. 927, 932 (2001) (quoting from Gilmore). Professors White & Summers have described it as being "like the amphibious tank that was originally designed to fight in the swamps but was sent to fight in the desert." White & Summers, *Uniform Commercial Code* §1.3 (5th ed.). In other words, it doesn't work very well! In doing UCC §2-207 analysis, you must be aware that arguments can be made on several sides of the issues of which form constitutes the offer, which constitutes the acceptance, and whether terms in the acceptance are material. In terms of analyzing materiality and whether a term is a "surprise or hardship," it is useful to look at the facts of the case and determine if the additional term in the acceptance is consistent with trade usage (industry practice) or prior dealings between the parties. If so, it is probably no surprise or hardship, and is not material.

Assuming we have an acceptance, we must then ask if the acceptance has additional terms in it. If it has different terms, remember that there are three approaches as to how to deal with them because §2-207 is not clear — treat them the same as additional terms, consider them as mere proposals that must be assented to by the offeror for them to become part of the contract, or "knock out" the conflicting terms and use gap fillers. If the acceptance does not contain additional or different terms from the offer, there is no "battle of the forms" as the parties are in agreement.

If the acceptance has additional terms to those in the offer, we must ask whether both parties are merchants. If not, the additional terms are merely proposals and must be assented to by the offeror to become part of the contract. If the parties are merchants, we must ask if the offer was limited to its terms, if the term materially alters the contract, or if the offeror objected to the terms in a timely fashion. If any of those circumstances exists, then the additional terms are merely proposals that must be assented to by the offeror for the terms to become part of the contract. If none of those circumstances exists, the additional terms in the acceptance are included in the contract.

(2) The Parties Informally Contract and Follow with Confirmations

The second situation we will consider is the situation in which the parties informally contract, either orally or through correspondence, and then one or both parties follow up with a "confirmation" that fleshes out the terms of the agreement. This situation was considered in *Ohio Grain Co. v. Swisshelm*,[39] a case in which the parties orally agreed to a sale of 1,500 bushels of

---

[39]40 Ohio App. 2d 203, 318 N.E.2d 428 (1973).

soybeans at $5 per bushel. On the same day as the conversation, the buyer sent a confirmation form that provided certain specifications for the soybeans, such as the amount of foreign material allowed, the amount of damage, and the percentage of moisture. Subsequently, the seller claimed that there was no contract as the confirmation changed the terms of the deal and the seller never agreed to it.

The first question that has to be considered in a case like this is whether the parties agreed on enough terms during the conversation or through correspondence for a contract to be formed. Remember that the UCC does not require that the parties agree on all details—all that is necessary is that the parties intended to contract and that there is a reasonably certain basis for giving an appropriate remedy.[40] The UCC provides a number of gap filler provisions to help the court in fleshing out the agreement between the parties.[41] The court held in *Ohio Grain* that agreeing to the quantity and the price of the beans was enough for an enforceable contract to be formed.

Once we determine that there is an enforceable contract, we must then consider the enforceability of the terms in any confirmation that is sent. Section 2-207(1) requires any written confirmation to be sent within a reasonable time. Any confirmation that is sent more than a reasonable time after the parties have contracted would have to be considered as a proposal for a modification since there is already an enforceable contract based on the conversation between the parties. In *Ohio Grain*, the confirmation was sent on the same day as the oral agreement, so it was within a reasonable time. It is arguable whether terms that are included in invoices sent at the same time or after goods have been shipped should be considered for inclusion under UCC §2-207(2) or should instead be considered proposals for modification.

Assuming that the confirmation is sent within a reasonable time, additional terms are considered as proposals for the contract under subsection 2 of §2-207. Remember that the parties have already entered into an enforceable contract, so a confirmation cannot be expressly conditional upon assent to its terms. Once an agreement has been made, a party cannot insist on additional terms and threaten not to perform. Also, a party cannot unilaterally change the terms that have been agreed on by sending a confirmation. For example, if you and I agree that you will buy my car for $10,000 with delivery to be on June 1, you cannot send me a "confirmation" changing the date to May 15 and expressly condition your obligation on my assent to that term. I am entitled to enforce the agreement that we initially made.

As is the case with the situation in which the writings of the parties form a contract, if the contract is between merchants, the additional terms in the confirmations will become part of the contract unless (a) the offer expressly limits acceptance to the terms of the offer, (b) the terms materially alter the contract, or (c) notification of objection to the terms has already been given or is given within a reasonable time after notice of them is received.

In *Ohio Grain*, the seller tried to argue that it was not a merchant, and therefore should not have been bound to the buyer's form. There is some authority for the proposition that farmers are not sophisticated in business and thus should not be considered merchants.[42] The court in *Ohio Grain*, however, held that farmers who are experienced in the farming industry should be considered merchants just like other business persons.

---

[40]UCC §2-204.
[41]See pp. 85-89, *supra*.
[42]*Cook Grains, Inc. v. Fallis*, 239 Ark. 962, 395 S.W.2d 555 (1965).

As for the terms in the confirmation in *Ohio Grain*, the court found them to be normal terms in the industry and thus not a "surprise or hardship." Because there had been no objection to the terms either before they had been given or within a reasonable time after notice of them had been received, they were part of the contract.

What happens if both parties send forms that have conflicting terms? For example, let us assume that in *Ohio Grain* the buyer sent a form allowing for 15 percent moisture while the seller sent a form allowing for 13 percent moisture. According to official comment 6 to §2-207, where terms conflict, neither term is part of the contract, the "knock out" doctrine applies. In such a situation, the court would have to resort to industry practice or any prior usage between the parties to determine the appropriate moisture content.

The 2003 approved amendments to Article 2 do not include in the contract terms in a confirmation unless they are also in a confirmation sent by the other party or both parties otherwise agree to them.[43] Gaps in the contract are filled by gap filler terms supplied by the UCC and by course of performance, course of dealing, and usage of trade.

(3) The Writings of the Parties Do Not Form a Contract, But a Contract Is Formed by Performance

The third case covered by §2-207 is when the writings of the parties do not form a contract but the parties go ahead and perform anyway: Goods are shipped, accepted, and paid for. There is thus some kind of a contract, but we must determine the terms. Let us return to the original hypothetical fact pattern that we used in analyzing contracts formed by an exchange of form offers and acceptances, except now the "order acknowledgment" is expressly conditional on assent to its additional terms:

(1) Buyer, a merchant, sends a "purchase order" to Seller seeking to purchase a specified quantity of carpeting at a specified price. The purchase order says nothing about dispute resolution and does not state that it is limited to its terms.

(2) Seller, also a merchant, responds with an "order acknowledgment" that is in agreement with the purchase order on price, quantity, and delivery date. Seller's form states that acceptance of Buyer's order is "**conditional on Buyer's assent**" to terms and conditions on the reverse of the order acknowledgment. Included among those terms is a provision requiring arbitration of all disputes.

(3) Shortly after the exchange of forms, Seller ships the carpeting ordered by Buyer. Buyer accepts the carpeting and pays the price. Subsequently, Buyer sues Seller, complaining that the carpeting does not conform to warranties and Seller insists that the dispute must be arbitrated.

In this situation, the writings of the parties do not form a contract because Seller's order acknowledgment is expressly conditional on assent. That means that it is not an acceptance, but is instead a rejection and counteroffer. Buyer did not expressly assent to its terms but arguably accepted it by accepting and paying for the goods.

Under the common law last shot doctrine, the acceptance of and payment for the goods would mean that Buyer was assenting to the terms in the order acknowledgment. The drafters of §2-207 rejected the "last shot" doctrine in §2-207(3). That

---

[43]Amended UCC §2-207.

section provides that where a contract is formed by conduct, the terms of the contract are those on which the writings of the parties agree together with supplementary provisions of the UCC. Official comment 6 to §2-207 indicates that terms provided by the UCC include those terms determined under §2-207(2). They would also include terms provided by the gap fillers of Article 2 and any course of dealing or trade usage that is applicable.

Applying this rule to the preceding hypothetical, the writings of the parties are in agreement regarding the price, quantity, and delivery date of the goods. There was nothing in Buyer's purchase order, however, indicating any assent to arbitration.

The arbitration provision in the order acknowledgment should be treated the same way as additional terms in the acceptance, as discussed previously.[44] This means that the arbitration provision is a proposal by Seller for addition to the contract. Between merchants, it becomes part of the contract unless the offer was expressly limited to its terms, the term materially alters the contract, or objection to the term is given within a reasonable time. As previously noted, some courts might consider an arbitration clause *per se* material, meaning that it will not be included in the contract. Other courts look on arbitration clauses on a case-by-case basis — if in this case arbitration is not a "surprise or hardship" to Buyer, the court would allow the arbitration clause to stand.

As previously noted, the 2003 approved amendments to Article 2 do not include terms provided in the parties' forms unless the forms are in agreement or the parties otherwise agree to the terms.[45] Gaps in the contract are filled by gap filler terms from the UCC or by course of performance, course of dealing, or usage of trade.

C. The "Rolling Contract" Approach, or "Money Now, Terms Later"

Another approach that is followed by some courts, which is arguably contrary to the approach required under UCC §2-207, is one that views the contract as not being fully formed until the buyer has the opportunity to view terms of sale disclosed after the goods are paid for. This approach, which is used most notably by Judge Easterbrook in *ProCD, Inc. v. Zeidenberg*[46] and *Hill v. Gateway 2000, Inc,*[47] has been referred to as the *"rolling contract"* theory or *"money now, terms later."*[48]

The classic example of how this approach works is when a buyer orders goods over the phone. The buyer calls the seller and orders goods. The seller agrees to ship the goods and the buyer pays for them using a credit card. Nothing is really discussed over the phone other than the type and quantity of goods being purchased and the price. When the goods show up, the box containing the goods also contains some documents, such as a description of the warranty and other terms and conditions of sale. In *Hill v. Gateway 2000*, one of the terms of sale was a clause requiring binding arbitration of any disputes. The terms of sale indicated that if the buyers disagreed with them, they had 30 days to return the computer before being bound by the terms.

---

[44]See pp. 32-36, *supra.*
[45]Amended UCC §2-207.
[46]86 F.3d 1447 (7th Cir. 1996).
[47]105 F.2d 1147, 33 UCC Rep. Serv. 2d 303 (7th Cir. 1997).
[48]See Christopher L. Petit, *The Problem with "Money Now, Terms Later": ProCD, Inc. v. Zeidenberg and the Enforceability of "Shrinkwrap" Software Licenses,* 31 Loy. L.A. L. Rev. 325 (1997).

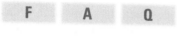

Q: Why is the situation where terms are disclosed after the goods are purchased called a "rolling contract"?

A: The reason is because the contract is not formed at one time, but kind of "rolls" from when the buyer first contacts the seller and agrees on the price until the offer is fully disclosed at the time the goods are received and the buyer has a chance to look at the terms in the box. Acceptance then occurs some time after that when the buyer retains the goods.

The buyers retained the computer for more than 30 days, and when they had problems with the computer they sued the seller. The seller then attempted to enforce the arbitration clause.

Under the rolling contract approach, UCC §2-207 does not apply to the transaction because it involves only one form; it is not a "battle of the forms." The contract is not fully formed when the buyer orders the goods over the phone and pays for them because the buyer reasonably understands that additional terms will be forthcoming. Buyers understand that there will be some documents in the box containing the goods that fully flesh out the obligations of the buyer and the seller in the sale. So, the "offer" is really not fully made until the goods reach the buyer and the buyer has a reasonable opportunity to review the terms. After that happens, if the buyer decides to keep the goods, the buyer has effectively accepted the terms and they are binding on the buyer unless they are unenforceable for some reason, for example, if they are unconscionable.[49]

The rolling contract approach is much more protective of the seller's ability to control the terms of the sale than is §2-207. If §2-207 were to be applied to the fact situation discussed previously, the arbitration provision would not be included in the contract. The contract could be viewed as being formed during the telephone conversation, because the parties agree at that time on the fundamental terms of the subject matter of the sale and the price. The terms contained in the box would be viewed as proposals for addition to the contract. Assuming the buyers were ordering the computer for their own personal use, they would not be considered "merchants" and the terms would not become part of the contract unless they expressly agreed to them. It would be a stretch to say that by retaining the goods and using them, the buyers

---

[49]Unconscionability is discussed in more detail on pp. 97-100, *infra.*

were indicating express assent to the arbitration clause. Because they paid for the goods, they have a right to use them and the use does not necessarily indicate assent to terms that were in the box containing the goods.

Not all courts agree with the rolling contract approach. Some courts in the *Hill v. Gateway 2000* scenario take the position that UCC §2-207 was intended to deal with the situation in which an informal contract was formed during the telephone conversation and the terms in the box are additional terms proposed by the seller that are to be considered under §2-207(2).[50] Section 2-207 does not expressly require two forms in order for its application; in fact, official comment 1 to §2-207 indicates that sometimes only one party will send a confirmation form. The drafters of the 2003 amendments to Article 2 refused to take a position on when, if ever, the rolling contract approach should be used, leaving it to the courts.[51]

It seems that the rolling contract approach is inconsistent with the intent of §2-207 to deal with situations in which contracts are formed informally, followed by one or both parties sending a form or forms that flesh out the transaction. When a buyer calls a seller and orders goods from a seller over the phone and pays for those goods, the buyer reasonably believes that the buyer has a contract with the seller. In this context, it is really the buyer who is making the offer, and the seller accepts it by agreeing to ship the goods and by taking the buyer's money. It is inappropriate to consider the seller as the one making the offer. Unless the buyer is informed to the contrary, the buyer probably doesn't think that the contract is contingent upon the buyer's further approval of terms of the sale. Terms in the box that are adverse to the buyer should probably be considered offers for modification that must be expressly assented to before they become part of the contract.

You should understand, then, that if you see a factual situation in which goods are ordered over the phone or paid for in a store and there are terms in the box that a court might, or might not, apply the rolling contract approach as compared to UCC §2-207. If the approach is applied, it is much more likely that the seller's terms will wind up governing the contract. If §2-207 is applied instead, it is less likely that the seller's terms will apply, especially if the buyer is not a merchant.

D. Modifications

REQUIREMENTS FOR MODIFICATIONS	
Common Law	**UCC Article 2**
1) Offer	1) Offer
2) Acceptance	2) Acceptance
3) Consideration	3) Good faith — "legitimate commercial reason"

---

[50]See *Klocek v. Gateway, Inc.*, 104 F. Supp. 2d 1332 (D. Kan. 2000).
[51]Amended UCC §2-207, official comment 5.

(1) No Consideration Required

A *modification* is a contract to change an existing contract. At common law, the general requirements for contract formation also existed for modifications — there needed to be an offer and acceptance, and the modification needed to be supported by consideration (as noted in the previous boxed text). Although the UCC still requires an agreement to modify (meaning that both parties must agree), no consideration is required.[52]

UCC §2-209 expressly states that an agreement modifying a sale of goods contract within Article 2 needs no consideration in order to be binding. The official commentary to §2-209 makes it clear, however, that any modifications must be in *good faith*. A party is not allowed to extort the other party into agreeing to change the terms of the contract by failing to perform — a legitimate commercial reason is required.

What is meant by "good faith" under the UCC? Under Revised Article 1, "good faith" is defined as "honesty in fact and the observance of reasonable commercial standards of fair dealing." The test is thus partly subjective and partly objective — looking at the subjective honesty of the parties and also focusing on how their conduct compares to other similarly situated parties. The focus could be on what sort of conduct a party should reasonably expect under the circumstances. The commentary to §2-209 suggests that if a market shift occurs that would cause a party to suffer a loss unless a contract is modified, a legitimate commercial reason may exist for a modification and the party requesting it would be in good faith to do so. On the other hand, if a seller knows that a buyer is desperately in need of goods, it would be bad faith for the seller to refuse to deliver unless the buyer paid a handsome premium on top of the agreed price.

Sidebar

A CHANGE IN THE DEFINITION OF "GOOD FAITH"

Before Article 1 was revised, the standard definition of "good faith" was "honesty in fact in the conduct or transaction concerned." Old UCC §1-201(19). This is a completely subjective determination, sometimes called "the pure heart and empty head test." Article 2, however, has always had an objective test of good faith for merchants, "honesty in fact and the observance of reasonable commercial standards of fair dealing in the trade." UCC §2-103(1)(b) (deleted in states that have adopted Revised Article 1). Not all states that have adopted Revised Article 1 have adopted the new definition of "good faith" out of concern that the objective standard may lead to more litigation over the question of whether a party acted in good faith. But, the Article 2 definition of good faith for merchants remains in those states.

(2) Formal Requirements for Modification

A question exists under Article 2 as to when a modification must be evidenced by a signed writing. Does every modification of a contract that is over $500 or more need to be evidenced by a writing? Also, if parties have indicated in their contract that all modifications must be evidenced by a writing, does that mean that all oral modifications are unenforceable?

UCC §2-209(3) states that the requirements of the statute of frauds must be met if the contract as modified is for a sale of goods for a price of $500 or more. There are a several possible interpretations of this section because the statute isn't written that clearly. One possible interpretation is that every modification of a contract with a price of $500 or more must be evidenced by a writing,

---

[52]UCC §2-209.

unless the modification reduces the price below $500.[53] Assume, for example, that in a contract for the sale of goods where the price is over $500, the parties agree to change the delivery date from May 1 to June 1. Under this interpretation of §2-209(3), there must be written evidence of this modification for it to be enforceable (or an applicable exception to the writing requirement, as mentioned in the earlier discussion of the statute of frauds).[54]

Another possible interpretation would be that only modifications that increase the quantity must be evidenced by a writing, at least if there was a sufficient writing to uphold the original contract.[55] Remember that the statute of frauds does not require that all terms in a writing be accurate — it just says that the contract will not be enforced beyond the quantity stated in the writing. So, if the parties modify the contract to change the delivery date, the original writing still satisfies the statute of frauds and no additional writing is required. Parties could prove the change of delivery date by oral testimony. If, on the other hand, the parties agreed to increase the quantity, the original writing would not be sufficient and there would be a need for a writing to show the change.

Section 2-209(2) provides that parties may stipulate in their contract that any modification or rescission of the contract must be evidenced by a writing. This is a so-called **no oral modification** or **NOM clause**. The statute requires that if a merchant uses a form contract in a transaction with a non-merchant, any no oral modification clause in that contract must be separately signed by the non-merchant. There is obviously a concern that non-merchants may unwittingly sign a contract containing such a clause and not understand that all modifications must be evidenced by a writing.

This section is a change from the common law, which did not enforce "no oral modification" clauses.[56] The reason such clauses are viewed with suspicion is because it is recognized that parties frequently orally modify contracts and do not pay much attention to "no oral modification" clauses. Modifications sometimes need to occur quickly and there isn't time to put it in writing.

Section 2-209(4) states, however, that any modification that fails to comply with the statute of frauds or a no oral modification clause may nevertheless operate as a **waiver**. A waiver is frequently defined as an intentional relinquishment of a known right.[57] To demonstrate how this might work, let us assume that the parties orally agree to modify a contract so that delivery will be on June 1 rather than on May 1. Assume that this oral modification is not enforceable because of the statute of frauds or else because the original contract had a no oral modification clause. When the seller delivers on June 1, seller could argue that buyer had effectively waived its right to receive delivery on May 1 and that there was thus no breach.

Section 2-209(5) provides that a party may retract a waiver affecting a part of the contract that has not yet been performed. Reasonable notification of the retraction must be given to the other party, and the other party must not have materially relied on the waiver so that it would be unjust to permit retraction. For example,

---

[53]*Wixon Jewelers v. Di-Star, Ltd.*, 218 F.3d 913 (2000).
[54]See pp. 24-25, *supra*.
[55]*Costco Wholesale Corp. v. World Wide Licensing Corp.*, 898 P.2d 347 (Wash. App. 1995).
[56]*Wagner v. Graziano Construction Co.*, 390 Pa. 445, 136 A.2d 82 (1957).
[57]*Clark v. West*, 86 N.E.1 (N.Y. 1908).

assume in March that the parties orally agreed to change a May 1 delivery date to June 1. In April, the buyer might notify the seller that it is retracting the waiver and is requiring that strict performance will be required under the original contract. An issue will then exist as to whether the notification is reasonable and also whether the seller has relied on the initial agreement so that it would be unfair now for the buyer to insist on the original contract terms. If there is not enough time for the seller to be able to make delivery by May 1, the court might find that the retraction is not allowed.

ISSUES IF MODIFICATION MUST BE EVIDENCED BY A WRITING UNDER EITHER THE STATUTE OF FRAUDS OR A "NO ORAL MODIFICATION" CLAUSE

(1) Is there a sufficient writing to evidence the modification?
(2) If not, is there an applicable statute of frauds exception?
(3) If no writing and no exception, can the oral modification serve as a waiver of a term in the original contract?
(4) Has there been reliance on the oral modification so that allowing retraction of the waiver would be unjust?

E. Differences in CISG Approach to Contract Formation

For the most part, the CISG and the UCC have similar rules with regard to contract formation and modifications. Some of the more significant differences are discussed in the following sections.

(1) Definition and Revocation of Offers

Unlike the UCC, the CISG defines what is meant by "offer." A proposal must be sufficiently definite and indicate the intention of the offeror to be bound in case of acceptance. Article 14 of the CISG goes on to suggest that a proposal would be an offer if "it indicates the goods and expressly or implicitly fixes or makes provision for determining the quantity and the price." Article 14 also expressly provides that proposals directed to the general public like advertisements are generally not offers. There is probably not much difference between the CISG definition of offer and the analysis that courts would go through in determining whether an offer exists in a sale of goods case governed by UCC Article 2.

With regard to revocation of offers, however, the CISG states that an offer is irrevocable if it indicates, whether by stating a fixed time for acceptance or otherwise, that it is irrevocable.[58] Identical to the UCC, the CISG does not require consideration to be given before an offer will be irrevocable. Unlike the UCC, there is no specific requirement that a "firm" offer be in writing and necessarily state that it

---

[58]CISG Art. 16(2)(a).

is "firm" or "irrevocable." There is no limitation of irrevocability of firm offers to three months. In determining whether an offer is irrevocable, courts will probably focus on whether the offeree reasonably understood under the circumstances that the offer was intended to be irrevocable during the time stated in the offer.[59] Parties from civil law countries where offers generally are irrevocable are more likely to think that offers stating a fixed time for acceptance are irrevocable during that time.

(2) Acceptances Are Generally Effective on Receipt

The CISG provides that an acceptance is effective when it reaches the offeror.[60] This is contrary to the "mailbox rule" of the common law that indicates that an acceptance is effective on dispatch if the offeree reasonably believed that acceptance could be via correspondence.[61] There is an exception for situations in which the offeror receives a late acceptance and can tell from the circumstances that there were irregularities that delayed its receipt until after the time for acceptance. In such a case, the offeror must without delay notify the offeree that the offer lapsed before the acceptance was received.[62] If the offeror does not so notify the offeree, the late acceptance is effective and a contract is formed.

(3) CISG Approach to the "Battle of the Forms"

The CISG approach to the "battle of the forms" differs from the UCC. The CISG permits a purported acceptance to contain additional or different terms that do not materially alter the terms of the offer, unless the offeror, without undue delay, objects to the discrepancy. If the offeror objects, there is no contract. In addition, if additional or different terms in a purported acceptance are material, the purported acceptance containing those terms is really a rejection and a counteroffer.[63]

The CISG defines material terms to include the price, payment, quality and quantity of the goods, place and time of delivery, extent of one party's liability to the other, and settlement of disputes.[64] One area in which the CISG would thus differ from the UCC would be if a purported acceptance contained a clause requiring all disputes to be submitted to arbitration. Under the UCC, an acceptance could contain an arbitration clause, but under the CISG the purported acceptance would effectively be a rejection and a counteroffer.

Let us assume that a purported acceptance under the CISG contains an arbitration clause, but the parties pay no attention to the form and go ahead with the transaction. Is the arbitration provision then part of the contract? One could argue under the CISG that performance indicates assent to the form containing the arbitration provision — the CISG follows the last shot doctrine because the CISG provides that conduct indicating assent is an acceptance.[65] Some commentators have argued, however, that the drafters of the CISG did not intend to adopt the last shot doctrine

---

[59]CISG Art. 8. See Honnold, *Uniform Law for International Sales Under the 1980 United Nations Convention* §143.1 (3d ed. 1999).
[60]CISG Art. 18(2).
[61]*Restatement (Second) of Contracts* §63.
[62]CISG Art. 21.
[63]CISG Art. 19.
[64]CISG Art. 19(3).
[65]CISG Art. 18(1).

and that the contract should consist of only those terms on which the parties' forms agree, together with default terms provided by the CISG, industry practice, and any customs between the parties.[66]

Another area of difference between the CISG and the UCC is that the CISG does not expressly contemplate the situation in which parties informally agree to a contract and then follow with confirmations. There is no suggestion that terms in such confirmations should in some cases automatically become part of the contract. One case considering invoices that were sent after the parties had orally contracted suggested that the term in the invoice sent by the seller calling for resolution of all disputes in France was really a proposal for modification to the contract, and the buyer's acceptance of goods after receipt of the invoice did not indicate that the buyer was agreeing to modify the contract. Express assent was required.[67]

(4) Generally, No Writings Are Required Under the CISG

The CISG does not have a statute of frauds; contracts can be oral.[68] The CISG does, however, give nations adopting it the option of opting out of the rule that states that contracts can be oral (Article 11).[69] When a nation does this, it is making a declaration under CISG Article 96. What this means is that if one of the parties has its place of business in a nation that has opted out of Article 11, the CISG says nothing about whether a writing is required or not. The question of whether a writing is required is left to domestic sales law determined under choice of law principles. Let us say, for example, that the seller is located in a nation that has opted out of Article 11. The seller and the buyer have entered into an oral contract for sale. Whether such a contract will be enforceable will depend on whether applicable choice of law principles say that the governing domestic law is from the nation where the seller is located. Choice of law principles most often do lead to application of the law where the seller is located.[70] If the law of the seller's nation applies, whether the oral contract is enforceable or not will depend on that nation's statute of frauds.

Similar to the UCC, the CISG provides that parties to the contract may insert a no oral modification clause in the contract, in which case a writing is required to enforce any modification. Also similar to the UCC, the CISG provides that oral modifications may nevertheless be enforceable if a party has relied on it to its detriment.[71]

The following table briefly summarizes some of the differences between the rules of the CISG and the UCC regarding contract formation.

---

[66]See Vergne, *The "Battle of the Forms" Under the 1980 United Nations Convention on the International Sale of Goods*, 33 Am. J. Comp. L. 233 (1985).
[67]*Chateau Des Charmes v. Sabate USA, Inc.*, 328 F.3d 528 (9th Cir. 2003).
[68]CISG Art. 11.
[69]CISG Art. 12.
[70]See Reich & Halfmeier, *Consumer Protection in the Global Village: Recent Developments in German and European Union Law*, 106 Dick. L. Rev. 111 (2001).
[71]CISG Art. 29.

TABLE 3.1	A Listing of Differences Between UCC and CISG Contract Formation Rules	
Topic	**UCC**	**CISG**
Offer	Not defined; use common law definition (UCC §1-103).	Defined in Art. 14; definition similar to U.S. common law.
"Firm Offer"	Must be from merchant, signed writing, must give assurance of irrevocability, limited to three months in duration.	No writing required, offer simply stating fixed time for acceptance may be irrevocable, no limit in duration.
Acceptance	Effective on dispatch (via common law "mailbox rule").	Effective on receipt by offeror.
"Battle of the Forms"	Acceptance can contain materially different or additional terms, but those terms will not be included in the contract unless offeror assents. "Last shot" rule does not apply.	Purported acceptance containing material terms is rejection and counteroffer. Article 19 defines "material" terms, including terms relating to dispute resolution. "Last shot" rule may apply.
Statute of Frauds	Contract for the sale of goods for $500 or more must be evidenced by a writing, unless there is an applicable exception.	No writing is required, unless a party resides in a nation that has opted out of the CISG on this issue.

SUMMARY

■ The UCC permits parties to contract informally without necessarily agreeing on all terms.

■ The UCC requires a contract for sale of $500 or more to be evidenced by a writing signed by the party to be charged, unless there is an applicable exception.

■ A merchant may make a "firm offer" in a signed writing, meaning that the offer is not revocable even though there is no consideration to support an option. The outside period for irrevocability without consideration is three months.

■ A seller may generally accept an offer for prompt or current shipment by either promising to ship or shipping the goods.

■ The UCC permits parties to contract even though the acceptance of the offer has different or additional terms, as long as there is a definite and seasonable expression of acceptance that is not expressly conditional on assent to the additional or different terms.

■ Additional (and perhaps different) terms in an acceptance or confirmation may become part of the contract if the contract is between merchants, the terms are not material, and the offeror does not object to the terms.

- Under the "rolling contract theory," a seller may delay disclosure of terms to the buyer until receipt of the goods. If the buyer retains the goods after having had a chance to review the terms, the buyer is deemed to have agreed to those terms. Not all courts follow the "rolling contract theory."

- Parties may modify a contract under the UCC without consideration, as long as the parties act in good faith.

- Modifications of contracts within the statute of frauds may need to be evidenced by a writing, unless there is reliance on the modification. Likewise, if the contract contains a "no oral modification" clause, written evidence is required, unless there is reliance.

- Unlike common law contracts, the CISG rejects the "mailbox rule" and states that acceptances are effective on receipt by the offeror.

- The CISG approach to the "battle of the forms" is not to enforce an agreement if there is a material difference between the offer and the acceptance, unless the parties subsequently perform.

- The CISG generally does not require written evidence of contracts or modifications.

CONNECTIONS

Choice of Law

The choice of law is important in determining whether a contract has been formed. If we determine that the contract is a sale of goods and that UCC Article 2 or the CISG applies, then courts may find a contract even though parties have not agreed on all terms or have contracted using forms that do not mirror each other. Under the common law, courts might require agreement on more terms and might not find a contract if there are differences between the offer and acceptance. Also, sales of goods of $500 or more require written evidence under the Article 2 statute of frauds. The CISG does not have a statute of frauds.

Contract Terms

The terms of the contract will depend on how the contract was formed. Under the "battle of the forms," we must determine whether the terms in the offer are included or the terms in the acceptance. If the contract was formed by performance, it may be that neither party's terms will apply and the court will use gap filler terms.

Contract Performance

Whether the parties have properly performed under the contract depends on what the contract requires; in other words, it depends on the terms. The terms of the contract depend on how the contract was formed. For example, if a warranty disclaimer is in a form sent by the seller, there will be an issue as to whether the terms in the seller's form govern the transaction. That might depend on whether the seller's form is viewed as the offer or the acceptance.

Remedies

The remedies available may also depend on how the contract was formed. The seller may have included in its form a provision limiting the buyer's right to recover consequential damages in the event of breach. Whether that limitation is effective may depend on whether the term is deemed "material" so that is excluded under the "battle of the forms," assuming the seller's form was the "acceptance."

Terms of the Contract — Warranties

4

We now turn our attention to the terms of the contract of sale. Among the most important terms in the contract are any warranties that

O V E R V I E W

the seller gives the buyer regarding the goods. The warranties can include whether the seller has good title to the goods being sold and also can promise that the goods will perform in a certain way. The text box on the following page briefly summarizes the warranties discussed in this chapter. Warranties can be either express or implied. We start by looking at the warranty of title.

A. THE WARRANTY OF TITLE

1. UCC Treatment
2. CISG Treatment

B. WARRANTIES OF QUALITY

1. Express Warranties
2. The Implied Warranty of Merchantability
3. The Implied Warranty of Fitness for a Particular Purpose
4. Warranty Disclaimers
5. Privity Issues
6. The Magnuson-Moss Warranty Act and State Consumer Protection Law

> ### WARRANTIES OF TITLE
>
> — seller is conveying good title
> — no security interest encumbers title (unless buyer is aware of it)
> — no infringement on intellectual property rights
>
> ### WARRANTIES OF QUALITY
>
> — express promises regarding goods quality or performance
> — implied warranty of merchantability (good will work as reasonably expected)
> — implied warranty of fitness for particular purpose (if buyer relied on seller to select goods for buyer's purpose and seller had reason to know of reliance, goods will work for buyer's purpose)

A. The Warranty of Title

(1) UCC Treatment

Uniform Commercial Code (UCC) §2-312 provides that unless disclaimed or unless special circumstances exist, the seller gives a warranty to the buyer that the seller rightfully conveyed good title to the goods and that the goods were transferred free of any lien or encumbrance of which the buyer at the time of contracting had no knowledge. Basically, the warranty is to the effect that the buyer receives the goods free of any superior interest unless the buyer knows otherwise.

One question that has been litigated is whether the **warranty of title** protects the buyer against false claims to title brought by a third party. For example, a third party might sue the buyer and attempt to obtain possession of the goods, erroneously claiming that the third party has a **security interest** (i.e., a lien) in the goods. Even if the buyer wins the lawsuit, the buyer will have gone through the time and expense of litigation. The majority of courts hold that the warranty of title protects the buyer from colorable claims to the goods, meaning that the seller would be required to compensate the buyer for any damages suffered in defending the title, even if the buyer ultimately wins.[1] This is the position taken by the 2003 approved amendments to UCC §2-312.

If the seller wishes to disclaim the warranty of title, the seller must use specific language, such as "the goods are sold without any warranty of title." According to the official comments to §2-312, the seller may not use broad language such as "as is" or

---

[1] See, e.g., *Frank Arnold Contractors v. Vilsmeier Auction Co.*, 806 F.2d 462 (3d Cir. 1986).

"with all faults," which can be used to disclaim implied warranties of quality (discussed later in this chapter).

A seller does not give a warranty of title if circumstances exist that would give the buyer reason to know that the seller is not warranting that it is conveying good title. Sheriffs' sales and sales by executors of estates are singled out in the official commentary as being the type of sales at which a buyer reasonably understands that the seller is not claiming to convey any greater title than the seller has. The commentary does state, however, that somebody who is selling goods under a UCC Article 9 foreclosure sale does give a warranty of title, unless it is expressly disclaimed. UCC Article 9 covers consensual liens that somebody might give to a lender to secure a loan, which is called a security interest. For example, if you bought a car on credit and allowed the car dealer or bank financing the loan to retain the pink slip until you paid off the price or loan, you granted an Article 9 security interest in the car. If you defaulted and the bank or dealer foreclosed on the car and sold it, they would be giving a warranty of title to the buyer of the car at the foreclosure sale unless they disclaimed it.[2]

> ### Sidebar
>
> **WARRANTIES COVERING "COLORABLE" CLAIMS TO TITLE**
>
> There is an old saying that a buyer of goods should not have to buy a lawsuit. This is the reason for holding the seller responsible for colorable claims to title, even if the claims ultimately have no merit. The seller is required to defend the buyer against such claims. The seller is not responsible, however, for claims that are completely frivolous — the buyer is responsible for defending those claims and presumably should not have a difficult time in doing so.

The UCC also provides for **warranties against infringement**, for example, that the goods do not infringe on a patent. Such a warranty is given by a seller who is in the business of selling goods of the kind involved, unless the warranty is disclaimed. The warranty is not given, however, if it was the buyer who furnished the specifications for the goods. In such a case, the buyer must hold the seller harmless from any claim arising out of the seller's manufacture of the goods according to those specifications.[3]

(2) CISG Treatment

The United Nations Convention on Contracts for the International Sale of Goods (CISG) provides that a seller gives a warranty of title to the buyer similar to the warranty provided under the UCC.[4] The warranty protects the buyer from colorable claims, similar to the way that most courts interpret UCC §2-312. Again similar to the UCC, the seller may disclaim the warranty of title in the contract.

The CISG also provides a warranty against infringement on patents, trademarks or the like, but only if the seller knew or could not have been unaware of the claim. Even if the seller knew of the claim, there is no warranty if the buyer also knew or could not have been unaware of the claim.[5] The policy concern is that sellers are not in a position to easily know if their products violate a patent or other intellectual property right in all countries in which their goods might be sold. The buyer may be

---

[2]UCC §9-610.
[3]UCC §2-312(3).
[4]CISG Art. 41.
[5]CISG Art. 42.

in as good a position as the seller to know whether the product violates a patent in the buyer's country.[6]

B. Warranties of Quality

A seller may make express promises regarding the quality of the goods that will amount to **express warranties**. Both the UCC and the CISG have provisions governing such warranties. In addition, both the UCC and the CISG provide that warranties of quality will be implied in a couple of situations. One situation in which a warranty will be implied in some cases is that the goods will be fit for the ordinary purpose for which goods of the kind are used; the other is that the goods will be fit for the particular purpose of the buyer if the seller had reason to know of the purpose and that the buyer was relying on the seller to select suitable goods. We will first consider the topic of express warranties.

(1) Express Warranties

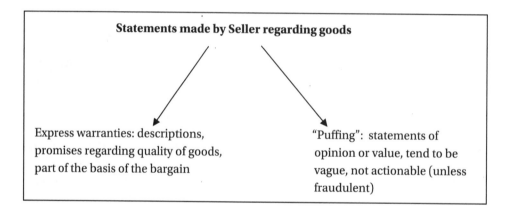

Statements made by Seller regarding goods

Express warranties: descriptions, promises regarding quality of goods, part of the basis of the bargain

"Puffing": statements of opinion or value, tend to be vague, not actionable (unless fraudulent)

The UCC requires that goods conform to any affirmation of fact or promise made by the seller with respect to the goods, any description of the goods and any sample or model that is shown to the buyer. In all cases, the UCC provides that such affirmations, promises, descriptions, samples, or models must be **"part of the basis of the bargain"** to be actionable.[7] The CISG is similar to the UCC in this regard, although the "part of the basis of the bargain" language is replaced by a provision that the goods must conform to descriptions "as required by the contract."[8]

Perhaps the most difficult issue in this area is to determine whether a statement made by a seller regarding the goods is an actionable statement of warranty or is instead what is referred to as **"puffery,"** which is not actionable. The UCC indicates that affirmations of the value of the goods or statements purporting to be merely the seller's opinion or commendation of the goods are not express warranties.[9]

---

[6]See Secretariat Commentary to Counterpart to Article 42 in 1978 Draft, http://www.cisg.law.pace.edu/cisg/text/secomm/secomm-42.html.
[7]UCC §2-313.
[8]CISG Art. 35.
[9]UCC §2-313(2).

For example, if a seller says "this car has never been in an accident" or "this car has a polymer finish," the seller is making definite statements about the car that would be considered express warranties. On the other hand, if the seller says "this car is a real beauty" or "you'll look great driving this car," such statements would typically be viewed as just being puffery or "sales talk" and would not be actionable.

It is not always easy to distinguish express warranties from puffery. The distinguished UCC scholars Professors White and Summers state that only a foolish lawyer is quick to distinguish between express warranties and puffery without first examining a number of factors.[10] Some of the factors that courts consider are the following:

1. the definiteness or lack of definiteness of the statement;
2. whether the statement goes to the quality of the product;
3. whether the seller was "hedging" at all;
4. whether the good is experimental;
5. the buyer's imputed or actual knowledge (as compared to the seller);
6. the nature of the defect; and
7. whether the statement is in writing.[11]

In terms of the definiteness of the statement, you should put yourself in the role of a judge and ask yourself whether you could tell whether the statement made by the seller was true or not. Many statements regarding goods are so indefinite that nobody can tell if they are true or not. For example, if a seller describes a car as "hot," who is to say whether that statement is true or not — that is, unless the seller is trying to say that it is stolen or has been sitting in the sun all day! Statements of warranty typically go to how well a good will perform, as compared to statements about whether the buyer is getting a good deal in purchasing the good at the price at which it is offered. For example, a statement that goods would not in the future be sold at a discount in retail stores was found not to be a statement of warranty as it did not go to the quality of the goods, but rather to whether the seller was selling at the lowest price.[12]

With regard to hedging, is the seller saying that a good "might" perform in a certain way, or is the seller saying the good "will" perform in a certain way? Obviously, the buyer should not rely as readily on statements that do not necessarily guarantee a certain level of performance.

The experimental nature of the good might cause a court to be less likely to find that a statement made by the seller is in the nature of a warranty, at least as long as the buyer understands that the good is experimental. This leads to the consideration of the buyer's imputed or actual knowledge. If the buyer is knowledgeable regarding the type of good being sold, a court will be less likely to find that statements made by the seller are actionable warranties — we expect experienced buyers to make decisions independently from a seller's sales talk. Also, if a buyer is buying from a merchant seller as compared to a private party, it is more likely that the buyer would rely on what the merchant seller says about the product.

The nature of the defect may also play a role — would it be obvious to a reasonable buyer? If the defect is obvious at the time the goods are sold, we would expect the

---

[10]White & Summers, *Uniform Commercial Code* §9-4 (5th ed.).
[11]*Federal Signal Corp. v. Safety Factors, Inc.*, 125 Wash. 2d 413, 886 P.2d 172, 25 UCC Rep. Serv. 2d 765 (1994).
[12]*Scheirman v. Coulter*, 624 P.2d 70 (Okla. 1980).

buyer not to pay much attention to any promises made by the seller that the goods will perform well. If, however, the defect was not obvious at the time the goods were sold but becomes obvious later, a court might be inclined to find a seller's statement that the goods will perform well to be a warranty, as it is easy to tell that the statement was false.

Finally, if a statement is in writing, it is more likely that the buyer will pay attention to it and it also shows that the seller really means what is being said. It also solves any proof problem as to what was said. In such cases, courts are thus more likely to find that the statement in writing is a statement of warranty.

Sidebar

THE MOVEMENT AWAY FROM "CAVEAT EMPTOR" ("LET THE BUYER BEWARE")

The law dealing with warranties of quality must be viewed against the old historic backdrop of *caveat emptor,* or "let the buyer beware." See Llewellyn, *On Warranty of Quality and Society,* 36 Colum. L. Rev. 699 (1936). In the old days, buyers were expected to look out for themselves, and the law gave little protection. Now, buyers are given significant protections from unscrupulous sellers, especially consumer buyers. There is still an element, however, of caveat emptor in that it is expected that sellers will engage in some sales talk or puffery that a reasonable buyer should probably ignore. Gullible buyers will not be protected from puffery that turns out to be false, unless the seller is involved in fraud, in which case the action is in tort and not in contract. See UCC §2-313, comment 8.

To demonstrate how courts might consider these factors, consider two cases in which a seller described a car as "reliable" or in "good condition." In one case, the seller was a merchant and in the other case the seller was a non-merchant. In both cases, the buyer was a non-merchant. The statement that a car is "reliable" or in "good contition" is indefinite—what is meant by reliability or good condition? How many times must a car break down before it is unreliable or in bad condition? Yet, a court held that the statement that a car was "reliable" was a statement of warranty in the case in which the seller was a merchant and another court held that the statement that the car was in good condition was not a statement of warranty in the case in which the seller was a non-merchant.[13] In the case in which the statement was held to be a warranty, it was also clear that the car was sufficiently defective that by just about anyone's definition it would not be considered "reliable." The two cases show the importance of focusing on the relative knowledge of the seller and buyer and the nature of the defect in the product itself, whether it is obvious that there was a problem.

Another case that demonstrates how what might be considered puffing in one context can be a statement of warranty in another is a case in which the seller informed the buyer that a certain cattle vaccine was "superior" to another brand.[14] Normally, whether one product is superior to another is a matter of opinion. In the cattle vaccine case, however, the court noted that the seller knew a lot more about the product than the buyer, who was a cattle rancher. The product was complex, so the buyer needed to rely on the seller's statements. In addition, when the new vaccine was used, many more cattle died than before, and when the old vaccine was used again, the death rate slowed. Thus, it was relatively easy for the court to determine that the vaccine at issue was not "superior" to the other one.

---

[13]*Compare Carpenter v. Chrysler Corp.,* 853 S.W.2d 346 (1993) (warranty) *with Guess v. Lorenz,* 612 S.W.2d 831 (1981) (opinion, not warranty).
[14]*Lovington Cattle Feeders v. Abbott Laboratories,* 97 N.M. 564, 642 P.2d 167 (1982).

If a statement is considered to be simply a statement of value or opinion, does that mean that the buyer has no remedy when it turns out that the statement is false? The commentary to §2-313 suggests that the buyer may still be able to sue in tort for fraud or misrepresentation. For example, assume that a seller tells a buyer that a watch being sold is much more valuable than the price that is being charged, but it turns out that the watch is actually worth a lot less. If the seller knowingly misrepresented the watch's value, the buyer could sue in tort, even though the statement regarding value was not a statement of express warranty under the UCC. Even though we would not expect people to take mere statements of value into account when contracting, we do not want people intentionally making misrepresentations of value and so liability is imposed in tort.

Even if a definite statement regarding a product is made, it must still be "part of the basis of the bargain." There is a question as to exactly how much of a showing the buyer must make regarding reliance on the statement in purchasing the good. The official commentary to UCC §2-313 suggests a rebuttable presumption test, that once a statement rising to the level of warranty has been made, it is presumed that it is part of the basis of the bargain unless the seller shows otherwise. The seller might be able to show that the statement was not part of the basis of the bargain if, for example, it was in advertising literature that the buyer never read. It might also not be part of the basis of the bargain if the buyer was very sophisticated regarding the good in question and thus paid no attention to statements made by the seller about it. For example, a statement about the medical condition of a horse to a veterinarian who can see that the horse is not sound would perhaps not be a statement of warranty as the veterinarian might make his or her own judgment about the horse independent of what the seller said.[15]

(2) The Implied Warranty of Merchantability

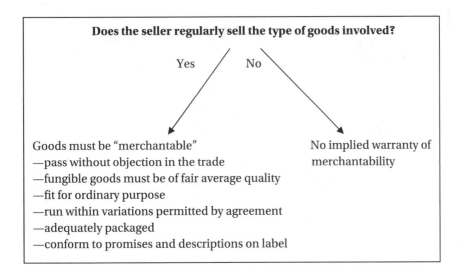

Does the seller regularly sell the type of goods involved?

Yes / No

Goods must be "merchantable"
—pass without objection in the trade
—fungible goods must be of fair average quality
—fit for ordinary purpose
—run within variations permitted by agreement
—adequately packaged
—conform to promises and descriptions on label

No implied warranty of merchantability

---

[15]See *Sessa v. Riegle*, 427 F. Supp. 760 (E.D. Pa. 1977), *aff'd*, 568 F.2d 770 (3d Cir. 1977).

The UCC provides that if a seller is a merchant with respect to goods of the kind involved in the sale, the goods must be merchantable. UCC §2-314(2) provides a number of requirements for a good to be merchantable, including the requirement that the goods "are fit for the ordinary purposes for which such goods are used." Basically, do the goods work in the manner that one would reasonably expect? Are they as safe as one would reasonably expect?

The ***implied warranty of merchantability***, if not disclaimed, is very important because it imposes strict liability on merchant sellers when goods do not work and harm either the user or the user's property. As noted previously, one reason why we care if UCC Article 2 applies to a transaction is because the implied warranty of merchantability provides for strict liability whereas the law governing service contracts applies a negligence standard. If, for example, a hair treatment burns the scalp of someone receiving a hairstyle, the stylist may be strictly liable under Article 2 but might not be liable if we consider the contract a service contract and find that the stylist exercised reasonable care.[16]

The first requirement for the implied warranty of merchantability to exist is that the seller be in the business of selling the goods of the kind involved. For example, let us assume that a company that is in the clothing business sells one of its used computers. The company is not in the business of selling computers. Although the seller is a merchant, no implied warranty of merchantability would exist in this transaction because the seller is not a merchant with respect to computers. The commentary to §2-314 suggests that casual and isolated sales of goods by a seller do not make that seller a "merchant with respect to goods of that kind."

What if a non-merchant seller knowingly sells goods with a major defect and does not tell the buyer about it? Nothing is said that would amount to an express warranty. Does the buyer have no remedy when the buyer discovers the defect? The commentary to UCC §2-314 suggests that the obligation to act in good faith and the policies underlying the implied warranty of merchantability would require "that known material but hidden defects be fully disclosed." So, it appears that the buyer could sue the seller for failure to disclose.

The implied warranty of merchantability is similar to the concept of ***strict tort products liability***. When personal injury or injury to property other than the goods themselves is involved, courts will look at (1) whether the goods were manufactured contrary to design, (2) whether there was a reasonable alternative design, and (3) whether adequate warnings were given, where reasonable risks of harm could have been reduced with reasonable instructions or warnings.[17]

Sidebar

RELATIONSHIP BETWEEN THE IMPLIED WARRANTY OF MERCHANTABILITY AND STRICT TORT LIABILITY FOR DEFECTIVE PRODUCTS

The famous torts scholar Dean William Prosser referred to warranty law as arising out of "the illicit intercourse of tort and contract." William Prosser, *The Assault upon the Citadel*, 69 Yale L.J. 1099, 1126 (1960). That makes the topic sound a lot more interesting than it really is! The point, however, is that there is a lot of overlap between tort and contract law in this area. The implied warranty of merchantability is imposed on parties by the law, just as the tort obligation not to sell unreasonably defective products is imposed by tort law. Sometimes, an action will lie both in tort and in contract. As will be discussed later at pages 149-150, *infra*, the tort action for strict liability for defective products is generally available in cases involving personal injury and property loss, while a plaintiff can sue under the UCC for breach of the implied warranty both in personal injury and property loss cases and in cases involving economic loss as well.

---

[16]See *Newmark v. Gimbel's Inc.*, 54 N.J. 585, 258 A.2d 697, 6 UCC Rep. Serv. 1205 (1969).
[17]*Restatement (Third) of Torts: Products Liability* §2.

An example of a court using strict product liability analysis to find a breach of the implied warranty of merchantability is *Commonwealth v. Johnson Insulation.*[18] In that case, the seller was found liable for installing asbestos without providing an appropriate warning. The court felt that the problems with asbestos were sufficiently known so that a warning should have been given. With regard to known dangerous products such as alcohol and cigarettes, even though harm is done to the buyer through use of such products, there is no breach of the warranty of merchantability assuming the goods were manufactured properly and warnings are given.[19]

If a patron of a casino cuts his or her hand when a defective glass containing a "free" cocktail breaks, can the patron sue the casino for breach of the implied warranty of merchantability? One issue that arises is whether there has been a "sale" and thus whether Article 2 should apply. At least one court has held that since the casino is giving the cocktails to people who are gambling, that there is a sale in that the cocktail is being given for value.[20] But is the glass containing the cocktail being sold? It is not, but one requirement for the good being sold to be merchantable is that it be adequately contained, and a glass that easily breaks in a consumer's hand would not be an adequate container for a beverage that is being sold.[21] So, there is a breach of the warranty of merchantability if the glass containing the cocktail is defective.

If a patron of a restaurant chokes on a chicken bone in a chicken salad, is there a breach of the implied warranty of merchantability? UCC §2-314 expressly states that the serving for value of food in a restaurant is a sale of goods for purposes of the implied warranty of merchantability, so it cannot be argued that the contract is for a service. Some courts will hold, however, that if the problem is with a substance in the food that is a natural substance, there is no liability.[22] Because a chicken bone would be a natural substance in a chicken salad, there would be no liability for breach of the implied warranty of merchantability. Other courts and the *Restatement (3d) of Torts — Products Liability* reject the natural/unnatural substance distinction and focus on the reasonable expectations of the buyer under the circumstances.[23] Would a reasonable person in the position of the restaurant patron expect to find a chicken bone in a chicken salad? Would a reasonable person expect to find a bone in a prepackaged salad? One could argue that a restaurant patron should be on the lookout for bones in a freshly prepared salad, while perhaps more care should go into preparation of salads for mass distribution.

UCC §2-314(2) also requires for merchantability that goods pass without objection in the trade, that fungible goods be of fair average quality, and that goods run within the variations permitted by the agreement. This all requires courts to examine any trade usage (industry practice) or course of dealing between the parties. If, for example, the contract calls for the sale of soybeans and the industry practice permits a certain percentage of spoilage, then the goods must be within that percentage.

The CISG provides that unless there is contrary agreement, goods must be fit for their ordinary purposes. Although there is no express requirement in the CISG that the seller must be a merchant for such an implied promise to exist, the CISG only applies to commercial transactions and it is likely that most international sales will

---

[18]425 Mass. 650, 682 N.E.2d 1323 (1997).
[19]See Owen, *Inherent Product Hazards*, 93 Ky. L.J. 377 (2004-05).
[20]*Levondosky v. Marina Assocs.*, 731 F. Supp. 1210, 11 UCC Rep. Serv. 2d 487 (D.N.J. 1990).
[21]UCC §2-314(2)(e).
[22]*Mexicali Rose v. Superior Court*, 1 Cal. 4th 617, 822 P.2d 1292, 4 Cal. Rptr. 2d 145 (1992).
[23]*Restatement (Third) of Torts: Products Liability* §7.

involve sales by merchants. Most courts and commentators suggest that the seller in an international sale is not responsible for any special governmental safety requirements in the buyer's country unless the seller is made aware of those requirements.[24]

(3) The Implied Warranty of Fitness for a Particular Purpose

Under the UCC and the CISG, a good must be fit for the particular purpose of the buyer if the seller had reason to know of the buyer's purpose and that the buyer was relying on the seller in selecting an appropriate good.[25] As is the case with the implied warranty of merchantability, this warranty can be disclaimed.

An example of an *implied warranty of fitness* would be a situation in which a buyer goes to a paint store and tells the seller that he or she is interested in painting an outdoor fence. The seller goes into the back of the store and produces a bucket of paint. There is an implied warranty of fitness that the paint will be suitable for painting the outdoor fence.

To demonstrate the difference between the implied warranty of merchantability and the implied warranty of fitness, assume that the seller gave the buyer paint that was actually manufactured for the purpose of painting indoors and was not suitable for painting outdoors. The paint is suitable for its ordinary purpose, which is painting indoors, and assuming that there are no problems with the labeling of the paint (meaning that it does not purport to be suitable for outdoor painting), there would be no breach of the warranty of merchantability. There is a breach, however, of the implied warranty of fitness for the buyer's particular purpose of painting outdoors. The buyer told the seller about the purpose, and the seller thus had reason to know of the buyer's reliance on the seller's expertise in providing suitable paint.

ELEMENTS FOR THE IMPLIED WARRANTY OF FITNESS

(1) Seller has reason to know Buyer's purpose in buying goods.

-and-

(2) Seller has reason to know that Buyer is relying on Seller's skill and judgment in selecting the goods.

It is quite possible that in a sale of goods, a warranty of merchantability, fitness and express warranties will all exist at the same time. For example, let us assume that the paint seller told the buyer that the paint was suitable for outdoor painting. Let us also assume that due to some manufacturing problem, the paint is not suitable for indoor or outdoor painting. There would in this circumstance be a breach of express warranty, implied warranty of merchantability, and implied warranty of fitness for a particular purpose. The UCC provides that warranties shall be construed as

---

[24]See *Medical Marketing International v. Internazionale Medico Scientifica*, 1999 WL 311945 (U.S.D.C. E.D. La. 1999).
[25]UCC §2-315 & CISG Art. 35(2)(b).

consistent with each other and are cumulative. If for some reason, they cannot be construed consistently, then the intention of the parties determines which warranty is dominant. In determining intention, exact or technical specifications displace an inconsistent sample or model or general language of description, a sample from an existing bulk displaces inconsistent general language of description, and express warranties displace inconsistent implied warranties other than in implied warranty of fitness for a particular purpose.[26]

To provide an example of how inconsistencies would be resolved, assume that the paint can in our hypothetical stated on the outside that it was suitable for indoor painting only. Nevertheless, the seller assured the buyer that it could be used outdoors. In this case, there are inconsistent express warranties and an implied warranty of fitness that contradicts the express warranty on the can. In this case, the implied warranty of fitness would trump the inconsistent express warranty on the can, as it is fairly clear that the intention of the parties was that the paint would be suitable for outdoor painting. The buyer is thus permitted to sue the seller for breach of the implied warranty of fitness, even though the description of the goods on the can is contrary to the buyer's intended use of the goods.

(4) Warranty Disclaimers

A seller may disclaim the implied warranty of merchantability or the implied warranty of fitness. The seller may not disclaim any express warranties that are made, although there may be some questions as to whether evidence of oral express warranties given before a written contract is executed will be admissible under the parol evidence rule (more on this later).[27] As an example, it is possible that during negotiations for the sale of a car, a seller will make definite statements about the car that amount to express warranties. The written sales contract will state that no warranties other than those contained in the written contract exist. If the seller's statement is not contained in the written contract, it could be viewed as attempting to disclaim the oral express warranty given by the seller. UCC §2-316(1) says that the seller cannot disclaim the express warranty, but the buyer may have a difficult time having it introduced into evidence under the parol evidence rule.[28]

The UCC provides rules on how the seller must disclose any disclaimer of implied warranties to the buyer.[29] One way for the seller to disclaim the implied warranty of merchantability is to use the word "merchantability," such as by saying **"there is no implied warranty of merchantability that goes along with this product."** The disclaimer of the implied warranty of merchantability can be oral. If it is in writing, the word "merchantability" must be used and it must be *conspicuous*. One way to exclude the implied warranty of fitness for a particular purpose is through a conspicuous provision in a written contract. The Code indicates that the following clause, if conspicuous, would effectively disclaim the implied warranty of fitness for a particular purpose: **"There are no warranties which extend beyond the description on the face hereof."**[30]

---

[26]UCC §2-317.
[27]UCC §2-316(1).
[28]For a discussion of the parol evidence rule analysis, see pp. 91-97, *infra*.
[29]See UCC §2-316.
[30]UCC §2-316(2).

What is meant by a "conspicuous" disclaimer is defined in UCC §1-201(b)(10). The test of conspicuousness is whether "a reasonable person against which [the warranty disclaimer] is to operate ought to have noticed it." To promote more consistent standards, the drafters of the UCC made the determination of conspicuousness one for the court as a matter of law, rather than a determination for the jury. Section 1-201(b)(10) gives some examples of conspicuous terms, such as "a heading in capitals equal to or greater in size than the surrounding text, or in contrasting type, font, or color to the surrounding text of the same or lesser size."

DISCLAIMERS UNDER UCC §2-316(2)

Implied Warranty of Merchantability — must use word "merchantability," if in writing, disclaimer must be CONSPICUOUS.
Implied Warranty of Fitness — must be in writing and must be conspicuous. Code suggests "THERE ARE NO WARRANTIES WHICH EXTEND BEYOND THE FACE HEREOF."

Another way to disclaim both the implied warranty of merchantability and the implied warranty of fitness for a particular purpose is for the seller to inform the buyer that the goods are sold *"as is," "with all faults"* or other language that "in common understanding" calls the buyer's attention to the fact that no implied warranties of quality accompany the sale.[31] Even though the Code does not expressly require it, courts have held that any such "as is" type disclaimer in writing must be conspicuous.[32]

In the 2003 approved amendments to UCC §2-316, the drafters make it more difficult to disclaim warranties in consumer contracts. Any disclaimer must be conspicuous and in a record. To exclude the warranty of merchantability, the record must state, "The seller undertakes no responsibility for the goods except as otherwise provided in this contract." To exclude the warranty of fitness, the record must state, "The seller assumes no responsibility that the goods will be fit for any particular purpose for which you may be buying these goods, except as otherwise provided in the contract." Sellers may still use "as is" language to disclaim implied warranties, but in consumer contracts, the "as is" language must be set forth conspicuously in a record.

If the buyer inspects the goods or refuses to inspect the goods, implied warranties are disclaimed with respect to any defects that an inspection ought to have revealed under the circumstances.[33] For the seller to put the burden on the buyer to inspect, the seller must demand that the buyer do an inspection.[34] Just a casual "Would you like to check out the goods?" is insufficient — the seller must put the buyer on notice that failure to examine the goods

---

[31]UCC §2-316(3).
[32]*Lumber Mutual Ins. Co. v. Clarklift of Detroit*, 224 Mich. App. 737, 569 N.W.2d 681 (1997).
[33]UCC §2-316(3)(b).
[34]UCC §2-316, official comment 8.

will result in the buyer assuming the risk of defects, which the examination ought to reveal. In terms of determining which defects ought to have been revealed, the expertise of the buyer and the normal method of examining goods under the circumstances must be considered. For example, if the buyer takes a car to an auto mechanic, more defects would likely be discovered than if the buyer is only allowed to examine the goods him- or herself and is not a professional mechanic.

Other ways that implied warranties are excluded are by ***course of performance, course of dealing, or usage of trade***.[35] In some situations, it is not customary for goods to be sold with any warranties of quality, it is a case of *caveat emptor* ("let the buyer beware"). Let us say that somebody buys a cheap watch at a swap meet. In a case like that, it could be argued that the trade usage is that goods are sold "as is," without any warranties of quality.

WAYS OF DISCLAIMING IMPLIED WARRANTIES UNDER UCC §2-316(3)

(1) Use language which in common understanding indicates that there are no warranties, such as "as is."
(2) Demand that the buyer inspect the goods before purchasing—warranties are disclaimed with respect to defects discovered or which should have been discovered through examination.
(3) Warranties are disclaimed if the buyer should expect to take risk of defect under course of performance, course of dealing or usage of trade.

Finally, another situation in which no implied warranties of quality would exist would be when the buyer gives precise and complete specifications to the seller regarding how the goods will be manufactured. In such a case, there is no implied warranty of fitness because the buyer is not relying on the seller's skill in designing the good. The express warranty that the goods will comply with the specifications would take priority over the implied warranty of merchantability.[36] In other words, if a buyer tells a seller how to manufacture goods and the seller does as it is told, the buyer has no right to complain when the goods don't work as well as the buyer wanted.

The CISG does not provide any specific rules, but does provide that almost any of its provisions, including any provisions requiring that goods conform to certain standards, may be altered by agreement.[37] It might be argued that if under choice of law analysis the UCC would fill gaps left by the CISG, the seller should have to follow UCC §2-316 if the seller wishes to disclaim liability under Article 35(2).[38] Under the CISG, the question is probably best phrased as to whether the buyer

---

[35]UCC §2-316(3)(c).
[36]UCC §2-316, official comment 7.
[37]See CISG Arts. 6 & 35.
[38]See Longobardi, *Disclaimers of Implied Warranties: The 1980 United Nations Convention on Contracts for the International Sale of Goods*, 50 Fordham L. Rev. 863 (1985).

reasonably understands that the seller is disclaiming responsibility for the goods being fit for ordinary or particular purposes. If a warranty is buried in a fine-print form in a language in which the buyer is not conversant, the buyer may be able to argue that the buyer did not reasonably understand that the seller was disclaiming responsibility for performance of the goods.[39]

(5) Privity Issues

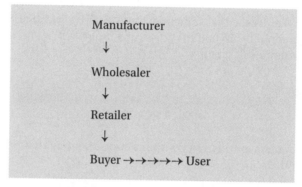

Historically, for party A to be able to sue party B for breach of contract, party A had to be in *privity* with party B. In other words, party A had to have contracted with party B, not somebody else. There were exceptions to this rule in cases in which contract rights were assigned or in which the person suing was the third party beneficiary of a contract between the defendant and some third person. In the sale of goods area, the question of whether privity is required arises in situations in which a manufacturer gives a warranty with respect to a product, but the product is not sold directly from the manufacturer to the ultimate user of the product. Can the ultimate user sue the manufacturer directly if the goods somehow do not conform to the manufacturer's warranty?

Privity questions are divided into two categories: *vertical privity* and *horizontal privity*. Vertical privity refers to the chain of distribution of the product. In the diagram shown earlier, the distribution from the manufacturer to the wholesaler to the retailer and finally to the ultimate buyer is a vertical privity chain. The question of whether the buyer can sue the manufacturer or the wholesaler is one of vertical privity. Questions of vertical privity focus on who the proper defendant is in a lawsuit. Horizontal privity focuses on the question of whether the user of the product can sue the retailer. The focus here is on who the proper plaintiff is in the lawsuit. Some cases may involve issues of both vertical and horizontal privity. For example, if a parent purchases a toy and gives it to a child who is injured by the toy, the question of whether the child can sue the manufacturer of the toy involves both horizontal and vertical privity questions because the child did not buy the good and the parent bought from the retailer and not directly from the manufacturer.

---

[39]See CISG Art. 8.

The UCC does not purport to answer all privity questions; many questions are left for the courts to decide as a matter of common law. The UCC does provide three alternatives to the states that deal with the question of who is entitled to sue for breach of warranty, basically a horizontal privity question. Under Alternative A, which is the alternative adopted by most of the states, a seller's warranty extends to any natural person who is in the family or household of the buyer or who is a guest in the buyer's home if it is reasonable to expect that the person may use, consume, or be affected by the goods. Such a person may sue the seller if the person is personally injured by breach of the warranty. Under Alternative A, a child injured by a toy purchased by the child's parents would be able to sue the seller of the good. Under Alternative B, the group of potential plaintiffs is extended to any natural person who may reasonably be expected to use, consume or be affected by the goods and who is personally injured. An employee who is injured on the job by equipment purchased by the employer would be able to sue the seller under Alternative B. Under Alternative C, the group of potential plaintiffs is extended to include entities other than natural persons, such as corporations, who may reasonably be expected to use, consume or be affected by the goods. Alternative C also extends liability to injuries other than personal injury. Under all three alternatives, the seller is not permitted to limit the operation of the rule, except that under Alternative C the seller can limit exposure with respect to damages resulting other than from personal injury to an individual.

The alternatives do not limit the ability of courts to expand liability beyond what is provided in the alternatives.[40] For example, in *Reed v. City of Chicago*,[41] the administrator of the estate of a prisoner who hanged himself with a special isolation gown sought to sue the manufacturer of the gown for breach of warranty because the gown was supposed to prevent such things from happening. The manufacturer raised lack of privity as a defense. The court looked first at Illinois' version of UCC §2-318, which was Alternative A. Under Alternative A, the decedent would not qualify as someone who could sue under the warranty as he was not a guest in the buyer's home (although a prisoner is sometimes called a "guest of the government"). The court noted, however, that Alternative A is not exclusive—courts are free to expand the group of plaintiffs who can sue. The court believed that for policy reasons, lack of

Sidebar

QUESTIONS OF VALIDITY AND OTHER GAPS IN THE CISG

The CISG states that except as expressly provided, it is not concerned with questions of contract validity. The CISG does not have rules dealing with mistake, duress, unconscionability, or other rules that might make an otherwise valid contract invalid. That does not mean that a contract formed under duress is enforceable under the CISG. What it means is that domestic law applicable by virtue of choice of law rules must be consulted. See CISG Article 7. Sometimes, as in the case of warranty disclaimers, it will be unclear as to whether the CISG supplies a rule or leaves a gap to be filled. As noted previously, it can be argued that whether a disclaimer is effective is a question of contract interpretation, not a question of validity, and the CISG has a rule for interpreting contracts under Article 8. There are no gaps. Or, it could perhaps be argued that UCC §2-316 is a rule of validity that should be used to invalidate any disclaimer that does not comply with its requirements. In thinking about whether §2-316 should be imposed in international sales, think about whether an international buyer will understand words like "merchantable" or "as is." That's why the better view is probably that disclaimers under the CISG should be treated as questions of contract interpretation. See John Honnold, *Uniform Law for International Sales under the 1980 United Nations Convention* §225 (3d ed. 1999).

---

[40]UCC §2-318, official comment 3.
[41]263 F. Supp. 2d 1123 (2003).

privity should not be a defense in that case. To give effect to the warranty, it was necessary to give the decedent's estate the right to sue. Otherwise, the manufacturer would not have been required to stand by its warranty, as no one would sue (i.e., the city wouldn't do it).

The bottom line is that in personal injury cases, lack of privity is rarely a defense to breach of warranty. As noted previously, courts liken breach of warranty actions in personal injury cases to the tort of strict product liability, and lack of privity is not a defense in those actions. Also, if the claim is one for breach of express warranty, courts will generally permit actions against manufacturers giving the warranty if the buyer was aware of the warranty at the time of sale (i.e., it was part of the basis of the bargain). The 2003 approved amendments to Article 2 make it clear that the ultimate buyer can sue a manufacturer for warranties given by the manufacturer (the so-called warranty in the box cases) if the warranties were part of the basis of the bargain, even if the goods were not purchased from the manufacturer directly.[42] The approved amendments also permit the ultimate buyer to sue a manufacturer for public advertisements if they constitute warranties (as compared to puffery) and are part of the basis of the bargain (i.e., the buyer knew about the advertisement and factored it into the decision to purchase the goods).[43]

Where lack of privity still has vitality as a defense is where the ultimate buyer of the goods seeks to sue the manufacturer for economic loss (as compared to loss from personal injury or property damage) due to breach of implied warranty. For example, assume that a bakery purchases a defective oven. The oven is purchased from a retailer, not directly from the manufacturer. Because of the defective oven, the bakery is required to close down and thus loses some profits. If the bakery were to sue the manufacturer for breach of the implied warranty of merchantability, the manufacturer would claim that there is a lack of vertical privity, and that the lawsuit is improper. The bakery's action would properly be against the retailer, which could be a problem if the retailer is insolvent.

F   A   Q

Q: Why should privity ever be required in a breach of warranty case?

A: Arguably, lack of privity is just a technical defense that prevents justice from being done. If a manufacturer makes a warranty regarding a product, the manufacturer should have to stand behind the product. This seems particularly true if the product is out in the stream of commerce injuring persons or property other than the goods themselves. On the other hand, once the goods leave the hands of the manufacturer, the manufacturer does not know what happens to the goods. The retailer could make alterations to the goods or could make statements to the buyer about the quality of the goods that the manufacturer would not make. The manufacturer does not know the buyer's purpose in using the goods, and if the manufacturer did know, a disclaimer of the warranty might be made. So, when it comes to implied warranties and economic loss, courts are more likely to require privity of contract in order for the plaintiff to sue the defendant. Courts will sometimes say that the buyer must choose its seller

---

[42]Amended UCC §2-313A.
[43]Amended UCC §2-313B.

wisely! See Holdych, *A Seller's Responsibilities to Remote Purchasers for Breach of Warranty in Sales of Goods Under Washington Law*, 28 Seattle U. L. Rev. 239 (2005).

Some courts in some situations will allow a buyer to sue for breach of implied warranty in economic loss cases even if there is no privity. One theory that is used to impose liability is that the ultimate buyer is a third party beneficiary of warranties given from the manufacturer to the party that sold the goods to the ultimate buyer. For this argument to work, the buyer must show that the manufacturer intended that any warranties it gave were for the benefit of the buyer. The third party beneficiary argument is particularly strong if the manufacturer is aware of the identity of the ultimate buyer and its intended use of the goods. In such a case it is clear that the manufacturer intended the ultimate buyer to benefit from any implied warranty. Such was the holding in *Touchet Valley Grain Growers v. Opp & Seibold General Construction, Inc.*[44] In that case the manufacturer worked together with a construction contractor in the design and installation of a grain storage building. Technically, the plaintiff buyer was in privity with the construction contractor and not the manufacturer of the components of the building, but the court held that the manufacturer was sufficiently involved in the entire transaction so that any implied or express warranties that were given to the construction contractor were really intended to run to the ultimate buyer of the storage building.

The CISG says nothing about privity. Article 4 of the CISG provides that it "governs only the formation of the contract of sale and the rights and obligations of the seller and the buyer arising from such a contract" (emphasis added). One can take from that language that the buyer can only sue its immediate seller under the CISG, not a remote party such as a manufacturer if the goods were bought from a retailer. When one thinks about it, it might be appropriate to require privity in an international sale as choice of law questions can be difficult—should the CISG apply if the buyer and the retailer are in one nation but the manufacturer is in another? The distinguished CISG commentator Professor John Honnold suggests, however, that if a manufacturer has been very involved in the sale, such as by advertising the goods directly into the market of the buyer and suggesting dealers from which the goods can be purchased, an action should exist against the manufacturer if the dealer is insolvent or is otherwise not available to sue.[45]

(6) The Magnuson-Moss Warranty Act and State Consumer Protection Law

Because of concern that the UCC does not provide sufficient protection to consumers, Congress enacted the *Magnuson-Moss Warranty Act* (Magnuson-Moss).[46] The

---

[44] *Touchet Valley Grain Growers v. Opp & Seibold General Construction, Inc.*, 119 Wash. 2d 334, 831 P.2d 724 (1992).
[45] Honnold, *Uniform Law for International Sales Under the 1980 United Nations Convention* §63 (3d ed. 1999).
[46] 15 U.S.C. §2301, et seq.

primary concern was that the UCC makes it too easy to disclaim implied warranties and that sellers of goods would on the one hand give a very limited express warranty while at the same time disclaim the implied warranties, thus leaving the buyer with less protection than if the seller had said nothing at all.

Magnuson-Moss applies to warranties covering consumer products, which are defined as goods which are "normally used for personal, family or household purposes."[47] Thus, while Magnuson-Moss is designed to protect consumers, it would apply to the sale of an automobile to a company for use in its business. The focus is not on the actual use of the good, but rather on whether the type of good is normally used by consumers.

Magnuson-Moss does not require that warranties be given, but does require that if a written warranty is given, it must provide certain information. The definition of "written warranty" includes any written promises or affirmations relating to the nature of the material or workmanship of the goods and also includes promises to remedy problems with respect to the goods.[48] The Federal Trade Commission, by regulation, has fleshed out the requirements of Magnuson-Moss regarding what is required to be disclosed in the written warranty, including exactly what is covered and what the warrantor will do in the event of a defect.[49]

One of the most significant requirements of Magnuson-Moss is that a warranty be conspicuously labeled either a "*Full Warranty*" or a "*Limited Warranty*."[50] If the warranty is labeled a "Full Warranty," it must comply with the Federal Minimum Standard for Warranties set forth in Magnuson-Moss. Under the minimum standard, the warrantor must, among other things:

(i) fix any defect within a reasonable time;

(ii) not limit the duration of any implied warranty;

(iii) not exclude or limit consequential damages for breach of warranty unless done so conspicuously on the face of the warranty; and

(iv) must permit the consumer to elect either a refund or replacement if the warrantor is unable to repair the defect within a reasonable number of attempts.[51]

Perhaps it comes as no surprise, then, that most warranties are labeled "Limited Warranties"! Take a look at products that you buy, and you will probably notice that the warranty is called a "Limited Warranty." If a Limited Warranty is given, the warrantor is not allowed to disclaim the implied warranties, but may limit the duration of the implied warranty to the duration of the written warranty. This limitation is permitted if (a) the duration of the written warranty is reasonable, (b) the limitation is conscionable, and (c) the limitation is set forth in clear and unmistakable language and is prominently displayed on the face of the warranty.[52]

In *Carlson v. General Motors Corp.*,[53] plaintiffs in a class-action suit sought a ruling that limitations on implied warranties in a Limited Warranty given on diesel engines were both unreasonable and unconscionable. The written warranty that was given expired after 24 months or 24,000 miles, and the limited warranties were limited to the duration of the written express warranty. The court stated that what this

---

[47]15 U.S.C. §2301(1).
[48]15 U.S.C. §2301(6).
[49]16 C.F.R. parts 700-703.
[50]15 U.S.C. §2303.
[51]15 U.S.C. §2304.
[52]15 U.S.C. §2308.
[53]883 F.2d 287 (4th Cir. 1989).

meant was that any problem with the engines had to arise within 24 months or 24,000 miles for the buyers to have any claim either under the express or implied warranties. In determining whether the warranty was of reasonable duration, the focus was on whether a reasonable buyer would expect the engines to run trouble-free for a longer period of time. In determining whether the limitation was conscionable, the bargaining process must be examined to determine if it was fair under the circumstances. In *Carlson*, there were allegations that the seller knew of problems with the engines that would likely arise after the warranty period and that the buyers did not have a meaningful choice in agreeing to the limitation. Although questions of reasonableness and unconscionability in this context can be decided as a matter of law, the court should give the plaintiff some opportunity to present facts to support its case. The court in *Carlson* thus held that the lower court had erred in deciding the case in favor of the sellers on demurrer.

Another protection given by Magnuson-Moss to even holders of Limited Warranties is the elimination of any privity requirement at least for suit on a written warranty.[54] If the manufacturer gives a written warranty, it can be sued under Magnuson-Moss even if there is no privity. Arguably, the buyer can sue the manufacturer also for breach of implied warranty despite no privity, although most courts hold that the ability of the buyer to do that depends on relevant state law.[55]

Magnuson-Moss encourages sellers giving warranties to establish informal dispute resolution mechanisms and provides certain minimum requirements for them. If such informal dispute resolution mechanisms are provided, buyers are required to comply with them before suing under Magnuson-Moss.[56] Assuming the buyer goes through the process and is not satisfied with the result or the warrantor does not establish an informal dispute resolution mechanism, the buyer may sue under Magnuson-Moss for any violation of the act and also for violation of any written warranty, implied warranty, or service contract.[57] The advantage to suing under Magnuson-Moss is that the buyer may be able to recover reasonable attorneys' fees.[58] The UCC does not provide for the recovery of attorneys' fees by a prevailing party — any such right to fees must be established in the sales contract.

Sidebar

LIMITING THE DURATION OF IMPLIED WARRANTIES

There is some question as to what is meant by limiting the duration of an implied warranty. This is because goods are either merchantable or not at the time they are delivered to the buyer — the warranty does not extend into the future. It may be that the defect will not be discovered until later, but whether goods are merchantable or not depends on their condition at the time of delivery. The statute of limitations on breach of implied warranty begins to run at the time of delivery. UCC §2-725(2). The court in the *Carlson* case discussed earlier held that limiting the duration of an implied warranty means that any problems must be discovered during the limited period. Another possible interpretation would be that the buyer may only pursue remedies under the express warranty during the period of limitation, but may pursue remedies for breach of implied warranty thereafter. That interpretation is more consumer protective. See Reitz, *Consumer Product Warranties Under Federal and State Law* 82, 86, 95 (2d ed. 1987).

---

[54]15 U.S.C. §2310(d).
[55]See *Mekertichian v. Mercedes-Benz U.S.A.*, 347 Ill. App. 3d 828, 807 N.E.2d 1165 (2004) (holding that Magnuson-Moss eliminates the privity requirement for suing on implied warranties, but recognizing that most courts find to the contrary).
[56]15 U.S.C. §2310(a).
[57]15 U.S.C. §2310(d).
[58]*Id.*

TABLE 4.1	Limited Warranty vs. Full Warranty Under Magnuson-Moss	
	Limited Warranty	Full Warranty
May seller disclaim implied warranties (assuming a written warranty is given)?	No	No
May seller limit duration of implied warranties?	Yes, to limit of express written warranty if limit is reasonable and conscionable	No
Must seller fix defects within a reasonable time or permit buyer to elect refund of price or replacement of goods?	No	Yes
Is privity required for actions on express, written warranties?	No	No
If the buyer wins a lawsuit under Maguson-Moss, may the buyer recover attorneys' fees?	Yes, in court's discretion	Yes, in court's discretion

Despite the existence of Magnuson-Moss, state legislatures do not believe that consumers are sufficiently protected. Many states have what are referred to as "lemon laws" that require sellers giving even "Limited Warranties" to replace defective goods or give buyers refunds if the sellers are unable to repair goods within a reasonable number of attempts. For example, in California, a "reasonable number of attempts" to repair a car is presumed to be four or more times within 18 months after the car was delivered to the buyer or 18,000 miles, whichever comes first.[59]

Sidebar

EXCERPTS FROM CALIFORNIA "LEMON LAW" — SONG-BEVERLY CONSUMER WARRANTY ACT

California Civil Code §1793.2(d)

(d)(1) Except as provided in paragraph (2), if the manufacturer or its representative in this state does not service or repair the goods to conform to the applicable express warranties after a reasonable number of attempts, the manufacturer shall either replace the goods or reimburse the buyer in an amount equal to the purchase price paid by the buyer, less that amount directly attributable to use by the buyer prior to the discovery of the nonconformity.

(2) If the manufacturer or its representative in this state is unable to service or repair a new motor vehicle, as that term is defined in paragraph (2) of subdivision (e) of Section 1793.22 to conform to the applicable express warranties after a reasonable number of attempts, the manufacturer shall either promptly replace the new motor vehicle in accordance with subparagraph (A) or promptly make restitution to the buyer in accordance with subparagraph (B).

---

[59]Cal. Civ. Code §1793.22(b).

However, the buyer shall be free to elect restitution in lieu of replacement, and in no event shall the buyer be required by the manufacturer to accept a replacement vehicle.

. . .

(C) When the manufacturer replaces the new motor vehicle pursuant to subparagraph (A), the buyer shall only be liable to pay the manufacturer an amount directly attributable to use by the buyer of the replaced vehicle prior to the time the buyer first delivered the vehicle to the manufacturer or distributor, or its authorized service and repair facility for correction of the problem that gave rise to the nonconformity. When restitution is made pursuant to subparagraph (B), the amount to be paid by the manufacturer to the buyer may be reduced by the manufacturer by that amount directly attributable to use by the buyer prior to the time the buyer first delivered the vehicle to the manufacturer or distributor, or its authorized service and repair facility for correction of the problem that gave rise to the nonconformity. The amount directly attributable to use by the buyer shall be determined by multiplying the actual price of the new motor vehicle paid or payable by the buyer, including any charges for transportation and manufacturer-installed options, by a fraction having as its denominator 120,000 and having as its numerator the number of miles traveled by the new motor vehicle prior to the time the buyer first delivered the vehicle to the manufacturer or distributor, or its authorized service and repair facility for correction of the problem that gave rise to the nonconformity. Nothing in this paragraph shall in any way limit the rights or remedies available to the buyer under any other law.

California Civil Code §1793.22(b)

(b) It shall be presumed that a reasonable number of attempts have been made to conform a new motor vehicle to the applicable express warranties if, within 18 months from delivery to the buyer or 18,000 miles on the odometer of the vehicle, whichever occurs first, one or more of the following occurs:

(1) The same nonconformity results in a condition that is likely to cause death or serious bodily injury if the vehicle is driven and the nonconformity has been subject to repair two or more times by the manufacturer or its agents, and the buyer or lessee has at least once directly notified the manufacturer of the need for the repair of the nonconformity.

(2) The same nonconformity has been subject to repair four or more times by the manufacturer or its agents and the buyer has at least once directly notified the manufacturer of the need for the repair of the nonconformity.

(3) The vehicle is out of service by reason of repair of nonconformities by the manufacturer or its agents for a cumulative total of more than 30 calendar days since delivery of the vehicle to the buyer. The 30-day limit shall be extended only if repairs cannot be performed due to conditions beyond the control of the manufacturer or its agents. The buyer shall be required to directly notify the manufacturer pursuant to paragraphs (1) and (2) only if the manufacturer has clearly and conspicuously disclosed to the buyer, with the warranty or the owner's manual, the provisions of this section and that of subdivision (d) of Section 1793.2, including the requirement that the buyer must notify the manufacturer directly pursuant to paragraphs (1) and (2). The notification, if required, shall be sent to the address, if any, specified clearly and conspicuously by the manufacturer in the warranty or owner's manual. This presumption shall be a rebuttable presumption affecting the burden of proof, and it may be asserted by the buyer in any civil action, including an action in small claims court, or other formal or informal proceeding.

Magnuson-Moss permits states to enact laws that provide more consumer protection than it affords and the UCC also yields to statutes that provide additional protection to consumers.

SUMMARY

- Both the CISG and the UCC provide that sellers give a warranty of good title to goods unless the warranty is clearly disclaimed. Most courts will find that the warranty of title protects the buyer from colorable claims to title in addition to legitimate claims.

- Unless the buyer furnished the specifications for the goods, the UCC provides the buyer with a warranty against infringement. The CISG provides a similar warranty but only if the seller knew or could not have been unaware of the infringement claim and the buyer did not know and could have been unaware of the claim.

- Under both the CISG and UCC, the seller will be responsible for statements made to the buyer regarding the goods that describe the goods or promise that they will perform in a certain way. Statements of opinion regarding the goods are not actionable warranties, however, such as "you meet the nicest people in a Honda." Such statements are considered puffery.

- Under both the CISG and UCC, goods must conform to any sample or model held out by the seller.

- If the seller is in the business of goods of the kind involved, the UCC provides for an implied warranty of merchantability that the goods will be fit for the ordinary purpose. The CISG provides a similar warranty.

- If the seller has reason to know of the buyer's purpose and that the buyer is relying on the seller's skill and judgment in selecting the goods, there is a warranty under both the CISG and the UCC that the goods will be fit for the buyer's purpose.

- The seller may disclaim the implied warranties of merchantability and fitness under both the CISG and UCC. The UCC generally requires such disclaimers to be conspicuous and that the seller use the word "merchantability" when disclaiming the implied warranty of merchantability or words like "as is." The CISG does not have formal requirements for disclaiming warranties.

- Historically, the buyer had to be in privity with the seller (i.e., have contracted with the seller) to sue for breach of warranty. The UCC and courts have lessened the privity requirement, especially in cases involving personal injury and express warranties (e.g., when the manufacturer puts a warranty in the box). It is now easier for buyers complaining of breach of warranty to sue manufacturers of goods even though the goods were bought from a retailer. Where lack of privity may still pose a problem for buyers is when suing a manufacturer for breach of the implied warranty of merchantability if the claim is for economic loss.

- The CISG does not have any rules that expressly deal with privity. If the manufacturer is heavily involved in promoting the sale through designated dealers, it can perhaps be argued that the manufacturer should be considered "the seller" and thus be found liable.

- The federal Magnuson-Moss Warranty Act requires that sellers selling goods that are normally used for consumer purposes conspicuously label written warranties as either being "Full" or "Limited." If the warranty is a "Full Warranty," it must comply with certain minimum standards, including requiring the seller to fix goods within a reasonable period of time. If it is a "Limited Warranty" (as most warranties are), there is no requirement under Magnuson-Moss that goods be repaired within a reasonable period of time. Even if the seller gives a "Limited Warranty," however, the seller is not allowed to disclaim implied warranties.

■ Because of the limited protections given to consumers under Magnuson-Moss, many states have adopted "lemon laws" that require sellers to either repair goods within a reasonable time or provide substitute goods or a refund.

CONNECTIONS

Choice of Law

The choice of law will determine whether the implied warranties given under Article 2 or under the CISG will exist in the contract. Assuming the transaction is a sale, the choice of law will determine what steps the seller must take if the seller wishes to disclaim the warranties.

Contract Formation

How the contract was formed may determine whether warranties are given. There will be an issue as to whether the buyer assented to any attempt to disclaim implied warranties, and whether the seller actually gave any express warranties. Does the contract consist of only the terms in the forms that the parties may have used, or does it also include oral statements made by the seller? This analysis may bring into play the parol evidence rule, which is discussed in the next chapter.

Unconscionability

Some attempts to limit the application of implied warranties may be determined to be unconscionable and therefore not enforceable. It may be determined that the seller, who typically is more sophisticated with respect to the goods, is unfairly taking advantage of the buyer in disclaiming implied warranties. The topic of unconscionability is considered in the next chapter.

Performance

Whether the seller has properly performed under the contract may depend on whether the goods conform to applicable warranties given by the seller, either express or implied. Failure of the seller to deliver goods that conform to applicable warranties may permit the buyer to reject the goods.

Remedies

The remedies available to the parties may depend on whether any warranties of quality or title were given and whether those warranties were breached. From the buyer's perspective, the law generally attempts to give an injured buyer the benefit of the bargain. If goods do not conform to warranties given, the law may give the buyer the difference between the value of the goods as warranted and the value of the nonconforming goods.

Other Contract Terms, Interpretation, and Unconscionability

5

There are many terms in a sales contract other than warranties of title or quality. The contract must provide for the time and method of delivery and payment. The contract must also provide for who bears the risk of loss if the goods are damaged. If parties do not expressly agree on these terms, the court must have a mechanism for fleshing out the contract. This chapter deals with other terms in the contract both as expressly agreed to by the parties and also as provided by law. This chapter also covers contract interpretation, including the treatment of parol evidence, and situations in which a court might choose not to enforce a contract or one or more terms of the contract on the basis of unconscionability.

OVERVIEW

A. COMPONENTS OF THE AGREEMENT

B. RISK OF LOSS

1. Cases in Which No Shipment Is Involved
2. Cases in Which Goods Are to Be Shipped
3. Risk of Loss — Breach

C. GAP FILLERS

1. Open Price Term
2. Output and Requirements Contracts
3. Provisions Dealing with Delivery and Payment

D. CONTRACT INTERPRETATION AND THE PAROL EVIDENCE RULE

1. CISG Rules of Interpretation
2. General Rules of Contract Interpretation and Construction
3. Parol Evidence Rule Analysis Under the UCC
4. The CISG Approach to Parol Evidence

E. UNCONSCIONABILITY

A. Components of the Agreement

The Uniform Commercial Code (UCC) defines "agreement" as the "bargain of the parties in fact as found in their language or by implication from other circumstances including course of dealing or usage of trade or course of performance."[1] The UCC gives the parties a lot of freedom to craft their own agreement—there are very few mandatory or forbidden contractual provisions. The UCC suggests that unless it states otherwise, all of the rules in the UCC may be varied by agreement.[2]

We have already seen some limitations on the ability of parties to contract freely. For example, if a seller wishes to disclaim implied warranties, the seller must conspicuously disclose any such disclaimer in the contract or it is unenforceable.[3] The UCC also indicates that obligations of **good faith**, reasonableness and care may not be disclaimed by agreement.[4] "Good faith" is defined, except as otherwise defined in UCC Article 5, as "honesty in fact and the observance of reasonable commercial standards of fair dealing."[5] Parties may, however, set standards by which the performance of those obligations will be measured, as long as not manifestly unreasonable.[6] Likewise, where the UCC states that an action must be taken within a reasonable time, the parties may agree on the time as long as it is not manifestly unreasonable.[7] The United Nations Convention on Contracts for the International Sale of Goods (CISG) is more relaxed or liberal than the UCC, stating that the parties may even exclude application of the CISG.[8]

It should be kept in mind, however, that the CISG does not deal with **rules of validity**.[9] That means that if for some reason an agreement between the parties would be invalid under applicable domestic law, it will not be enforced under the CISG. To give an easy example, a contract for the international sale of illegal narcotics would not be enforceable, even though not expressly prohibited by the CISG. Also, if an agreement were deemed unconscionable and thus unenforceable under applicable domestic sales law, it would not be enforced under the CISG.

The bottom line, then, is that the terms of the contract of sale consist mostly of whatever terms the parties expressly agree on, together with industry customs and customs between the parties that are not overridden by the express agreement. Both

---

[1] UCC §1-201(b)(3).
[2] UCC §1-302.
[3] See pp. 61-64, *infra*.
[4] UCC §1-302(b).
[5] UCC §1-201(b)(20).
[6] *Id.*
[7] UCC §1-205.
[8] CISG Art. 6.
[9] CISG Art. 4.

the UCC and the CISG also provide **gap filler** terms that enable courts to enforce agreements between the parties that are not complete, as has been previously discussed and will be discussed again later in this chapter. Remember that neither the UCC nor the CISG require parties to expressly agree on all details before an enforceable agreement exists.

B. Risk of Loss

An important term in the contract determines which party has the **risk of loss** when goods are damaged or destroyed. Is the seller or the buyer responsible? We start with the premise that initially, the risk of loss is on the seller. At some point, it passes to the buyer. The point at which the risk passes is subject to agreement between the parties, but if the parties have not expressly agreed, the UCC and the CISG provide default terms that fill the gap.

(1) Cases in Which No Shipment Is Involved

RISK OF LOSS — NO BREACH — UCC — GOODS PICKED UP BY BUYER

Seller Merchant

Contract	Goods Identified	Tender of Delivery	Buyer Takes Possession
		Risk of Loss on Seller	Risk of Loss on Buyer

Seller Non-Merchant

Contract	Goods Identified	Tender of Delivery	Buyer Takes Possession
	Risk of Loss on Seller	Risk of Loss on Buyer	

Generally speaking, unless the contract says to the contrary, goods are to be picked up by the buyer at the seller's place of business or residence.[10] If the parties are aware that the goods identified in the contract are in some other location, then the goods are to be picked up at that location.[11] In such a situation covered by the UCC, if the seller is a merchant, the risk of loss passes to the buyer when the buyer takes physical possession of the goods. If the seller is a non-merchant, the risk of loss passes to the buyer on tender of delivery.[12]

---

[10] UCC §2-308(a); CISG Art. 31(c).
[11] UCC §2-308(b); CISG Art. 31(b).
[12] UCC §2-509(3).

The parties by contract may define what is required by "tender of delivery." The UCC requires that tender be at a reasonable hour and that the goods be kept available for the period reasonably necessary to enable the buyer to take possession. Unless otherwise provided by the contract, the buyer must furnish facilities reasonably suited to receipt of the goods.[13]

To demonstrate the different treatment of merchant sellers from non-merchant sellers, consider a hypothetical sale of a car from a car dealer as compared to a sale from a private party. If a buyer contracts to purchase a car from a car dealer, the risk of loss will not pass to the buyer until the buyer actually picks the car up from the dealership and drives it away. If a buyer contracts to purchase a car from a private party who is not considered a merchant and the contract calls for the buyer to pick up the car on June 1, if the seller has made the car available for pick up on that date and it is not picked up, the risk of loss will pass to the buyer anyway. If the car is damaged or stolen, the buyer will have the risk.

F A Q

Q: Why distinguish between merchant and non-merchant sellers in allocating risk of loss?

A: When the UCC was first promulgated, the risk of loss provisions were controversial in that they allocated loss on the party that was most likely to have insurance in place rather than on the party who had "title" to the goods. This was a significant change in the law. A merchant seller is probably more likely to have insurance covering goods than a buyer, at least until the buyer actually takes possession of the goods. The same cannot necessarily be said when a non-merchant seller is involved. It should be noted, however, that under the 2003 amendments to Article 2, the distinction between non-merchants and merchants in this area is abolished, and the risk will pass in both cases on the buyer's receipt of the goods.

The risk of loss rule discussed previously applies only if the goods that were delivered conformed to the contract. Let's assume that in the car sale hypothetical that the car was not painted in the manner promised. After the buyer drove the car off the lot, the seller realized the problem and contacted the buyer, who then returned the car to the seller for repainting. The risk of loss remains on the seller in this case until the car is repainted and delivered again to the buyer.[14] Risk of loss in situations in which one of the parties is in breach of contract will be considered in more detail on pages 77-85, *infra*.

Sometimes the contract for sale will provide that title to goods will pass without the goods being moved. For example, assume that goods are located in a warehouse owned by a third party storage company and will remain there even after the sale. The storage company in such a case is a ***bailee***, that is, someone who is holding goods for the benefit of somebody else. The bailee will probably have issued a warehouse receipt covering the goods, naming the seller as owner of the goods. Such a warehouse receipt is known as a ***document of title*** because it indicates ownership in the

---

[13]UCC §2-503.
[14]UCC §2-510(1). See *Jakowski v. Carole Chevrolet*, 180 N.J. Super. 122, 433 A.2d 841 (1981).

goods. The document of title may be **negotiable** or **non-negotiable**, depending on how it is worded. This topic will be discussed in more detail on pages 192-194, but right now you should assume that possession of a negotiable document of title gives greater rights to the goods than possession of a non-negotiable document of title.

In terms of risk of loss in such cases, unless otherwise agreed in the contract between the buyer and seller, the risk of loss passes to the buyer when the buyer receives a negotiable document of title.[15] The risk of loss will also pass when the bailee (e.g., a warehouse operator) acknowledges the buyer's right to possession of the goods by notifying the buyer that the buyer has right to possession.[16] If the buyer receives a non-negotiable document of title, the risk of loss will pass after the buyer has had a reasonable time to present the document to the bailee; if the bailee refuses to honor the document or to obey the buyer's direction, the risk remains on the seller.[17]

GOODS IN POSSESSION OF BAILEE—DELIVERED WITHOUT BEING MOVED—UCC

Contract	Goods Identified	Negotiable Document of Title Delivered to Buyer
Risk of Loss on Seller		Risk of Loss on Buyer

Contract	Goods Identified	Bailee Acknowledges Buyer's Right to Goods
Risk of Loss on Seller		Risk of Loss on Buyer

Contract	Goods Identified	Non-negotiable Document of Title Delivered to Buyer	Reasonable Time to Present to Bailee*
Risk of Loss on Seller			Risk of Loss on Buyer

*Risk only passes if bailee honors document

To demonstrate how the risk of loss provision works when goods are in the hands of a bailee, consider the case of *Jason's Foods, Inc. v. Peter Eckrich & Sons, Inc.*[18] In that case, ribs were purchased by the buyer but were to remain in the warehouse in which they were held before the purchase. The warehouse operator simply adjusted its book account to indicate that the buyer owned the ribs rather

---

[15]UCC §2-509(2)(a).
[16]UCC §2-509(2)(b).
[17]UCC §§2-509(2)(c), 2-503(4)(b).
[18]774 F.2d 214 (7th Cir. 1985).

than the seller. Before the warehouse operator had notified the buyer that it held the goods for the buyer's benefit, the ribs were destroyed in a fire (not properly barbecued!). The court held that because the buyer had not received a negotiable document of title and had not been notified by the bailee that the goods were held for the buyer's benefit, the risk of loss did not pass and remained with the seller.

The CISG provisions regarding risk of loss in these cases are not the same as the UCC. In cases not involving shipment of goods, the buyer takes the risk of loss when the buyer takes over the goods, or, if the buyer does not do so in due time, from the time that the buyer is in breach of contract by not doing so.[19] If the buyer is to take over the goods at some place other than the seller's place of business, for example if the goods are in the possession of a warehouse operator, then the risk passes when delivery is due and the buyer is aware of the fact that the goods are at the buyer's disposal.[20]

CISG RISK OF LOSS RULES — CASES NOT INVOLVING SHIPMENT

Buyer Picks Up Goods at Seller's Place of Business

Contract	Goods Identified	Buyer Takes Possession
Risk of Loss on Seller		Risk of Loss on Buyer

Buyer in Breach in Not Picking Up Goods

Contract	Goods Identified	Buyer Breaches by Not Taking Possession
Risk of Loss on Seller		Risk of Loss on Buyer

Buyer to Take Delivery at Place Other than Seller's Business

Contract	Goods Identified	Delivery Due	Buyer Notified Goods at Disposal
Risk of Loss on Seller			Risk of Loss on Buyer

---

(2) Cases in Which Goods Are to Be Shipped

The sales contract will frequently call for the goods to be shipped by the seller to the buyer. In such cases, the seller will deliver the goods to a carrier for purpose of

---

[19]CISG Art. 69(1).
[20]CISG Art. 69(2).

shipment, for example, a trucking company. If the contract provides that goods are to be shipped by carrier, it is important to distinguish between *shipment contracts*, which only require the seller to deliver the goods to the carrier, and *destination contracts*, which require that the seller take responsibility to make sure that the goods are delivered to the buyer's place of business. Unless the contract expressly calls for the seller to take responsibility until the goods are delivered to the buyer, the law presumes that the contract is a shipment contract.[21]

Under a shipment contract, the risk of loss passes to the buyer when the seller *"duly delivers"* the goods to the carrier. "Due delivery" requires that the seller enter into a reasonable contract with a carrier for the shipment of the goods, obtain and promptly deliver to the buyer any document necessary for the buyer to obtain possession of the goods, and promptly notify the buyer of the shipment.[22] In terms of the reasonableness of the contract of shipment, the nature of the goods is important to consider. For example, if the contract involves the shipment of perishable goods, it may be necessary for the seller to arrange for delivery by refrigerated truck. In terms of the documents necessary, a carrier may issue a *bill of lading* when taking possession of goods and it may then be necessary to forward that document to the buyer so that the buyer can receive delivery of the goods from the carrier. A bill of lading represents the contract between the carrier and the seller calling for the carrier to deliver the goods to the person and place indicated. Bills of lading are discussed in more detail on pages 188-191, *infra.*

Under a destination contract, the risk of loss passes to the buyer when the goods are tendered at the destination so as to enable the buyer to take delivery of the goods.[23]

Risk of Loss for "Shipment Contracts" — No Breach — UCC & CISG

Contract	Identification of Goods	Goods Duly Delivered to Carrier*
Risk of Loss on Seller		Risk of Loss on Buyer

Risk of Loss for "Destination Contracts" — No Breach

Contract	Identification of Goods	Goods Delivered to Carrier	Goods Tendered at Destination
Risk of Loss on Seller			Risk of Loss on Buyer

*"Duly delivered" refers to making a proper shipping contract and giving notice to Buyer under UCC §2-504 & CISG Art. 32.

[21]See UCC §2-504 and its official commentary.
[22]*Id.* & UCC §2-509(1)(a).
[23]UCC §2-509(1)(b).

Parties will sometimes use shorthand shipping terms to indicate whether a shipment or destination contract is intended. For example, assume that the seller is located in Kansas City while the buyer is located in San Francisco. If the contract indicates "$500 F.O.B. Kansas City," this means that the price of the goods is $500, with the seller being obligated to deliver the goods to a carrier in Kansas City ("**F.O.B.**" means "free on board"). The buyer is obligated to pay in addition the cost of freight from Kansas City to San Francisco, and the risk of loss passes to the buyer when the goods are delivered to a carrier in Kansas City.[24] The F.O.B. Kansas City contract in this hypothetical is thus a shipment contract. If, on the other hand, the contract indicated "$500 F.O.B. San Francisco," this would mean that the price includes the cost of freight to San Francisco and the risk of loss would not pass until the goods were delivered to the buyer in that city. Such a contract would thus be a "destination contract."[25]

TABLE 5.1	Delivery Terms Defined by the UCC

Term	Duties of Seller Before Risk of Loss Passes
F.O.B. (Seller's place of business)	Make proper contract under UCC §2-504 and put goods into possession of carrier.
F.O.B. (Buyer's place of business)	Must tender delivery at named destination.
F.A.S. (vessel at named port) ("Free alongside"; UCC §2-319)	Must deliver goods alongside designated vessel in designated port, obtain and tender a receipt for the goods in exchange for which carrier issues bill of lading.
C.I.F. (named place) ("cost, insurance, and freight"; UCC §2-320)	Must deliver goods to carrier, pay the cost of shipment, and obtain insurance.
C. & F. (named place) ("cost and freight"; UCC §2-320)	Must deliver goods to carrier and pay the cost of shipment.
"Ex ship" (UCC §2-322)	Seller must discharge any liens arising out of the carriage. Risk does not pass until goods are properly unloaded.

Sometimes, particularly in international sales, the parties will use the shorthand shipping terms promulgated by the International Chamber of Commerce. These are referred to as the **INCOTERMS**. The contract may say something like "$400 **FCA**

---

[24]UCC §2-319.
[25]*Id.*

Hamburg INCOTERMS 2000," which would mean that the price of the goods is $400 Free Carrier from Hamburg according to the 2000 version of the INCOTERMS. The provisions of the INCOTERMS dealing with shipment of goods consist of what are called "F terms," "C terms," and "D terms." Under F terms, such as free carrier, the buyer arranges and pays for the shipment of the goods and the risk of loss passes from the seller to the buyer when the goods are delivered to the carrier. Under C terms, such as "*CIF*," the seller arranges and pays for the shipment, but the risk of loss still passes when the goods are delivered to the carrier. Under D terms, such as "*DAF*," ("delivered at frontier") the seller at its risk and expense must arrange for delivery of the goods at the agreed destination.

F   A   Q

Q: Are the INCOTERMS "law"?

A: The INCOTERMS are not "law" in that they are not adopted by any governmental body. They are not part of the CISG. Thus, they are unlike the UCC shipment terms such as FOB and CIF because the UCC is adopted by state legislatures. The INCOTERMS are promulgated by the International Chamber of Commerce, which is a private organization devoted to improving and promoting international commercial transactions. Parties are free to use the INCOTERMS or not use them as they wish. The INCOTERMS are not relevant unless the parties' contract uses them.

There are similarities and differences between the INCOTERMS and the UCC definitions of shipment terms. For example, both the INCOTERMS and the UCC use CIF and FOB. Under the INCOTERMS, however, FOB always refers to a shipment contract and CIF and FOB refer only to shipments by vessel. The INCOTERMS counterparts to CIF and FOB for shipments other than by vessel are CIP ("carriage and insurance paid to") and FCA ("free carrier").[26]

Although the UCC definitions of delivery terms and the ICC definition of the INCOTERMS will generally accurately describe what the parties mean when they use those terms, parties may have their own understandings as to what those terms mean. For this reason, the 2003 amendments to Article 2 delete all definitions of delivery terms, leaving it to the parties to define what they mean in the contract or leaving it to courts to determine the meaning based on custom and usage.

The CISG states that if the contract calls for shipment (called "carriage" in the CISG) of goods, the risk of loss passes when the goods are handed over to the first carrier for transmission to the buyer.[27] This is essentially the same as the rule under the UCC and presumes that contracts calling for shipment of goods are "shipment contracts" rather than destination contracts. The CISG also requires that the seller make a proper contract for shipment and if the goods are not clearly identified to

---

[26]For a more complete discussion of the INCOTERMS and to order publications fully describing them, see http://www.iccwbo.org/incoterms/id3042/index.html. For a comparison of the INCOTERMS to the UCC, see Spanogle, *Incoterms and the UCC Article 2—Conflicts and Confusion*, 31 Int'l Law. 111 (1997).
[27]CISG Art. 31(a).

the contract by markings on the goods, by shipping documents or otherwise, the seller must give the buyer notice of the consignment specifying the goods.[28] The parties may, of course, contractually agree to a destination contract, in which case the risk will remain on the seller until the goods are tendered at the destination, same as the UCC.

(3) Risk of Loss — Breach

The UCC provides other rules that apply in three specific circumstances in which one of the parties is in breach of contract: (1) where the buyer has a right to reject and has not as yet accepted the goods, (2) where the buyer rightfully revokes acceptance, and (3) where the buyer repudiates or is otherwise in breach with respect to conforming goods identified to the contract before the risk of loss passes to the buyer.[29]

We will discuss in more detail in the next chapter the options available to a buyer if a seller delivers goods that do not conform to the contract. For now, you should understand that if goods do not conform to the contract, for example there is a breach of warranty, the buyer may reject the goods within a reasonable time after tender of delivery has been made. In this situation, the risk of loss stays with the seller until cure or acceptance. Cure means that the repaired goods must be returned to the buyer. Let us assume that a buyer took home a car and discovered that it was defective on the ride home. The buyer notified the seller immediately that she was rejecting the car. If the car was stolen from the buyer before the seller could come pick up the car, the risk of loss would be on the seller assuming that the buyer took reasonable care of the car after rejecting it.

If after accepting goods a buyer discovers a serious problem with the goods that the buyer could not have reasonably discovered before the goods were accepted, the buyer may revoke acceptance of the goods. In this situation, the risk of loss remains on the buyer, but only to the extent of the buyer's insurance. So, let us assume that the buyer after accepting the car learns of a hidden, serious defect and rightfully revokes acceptance of the car by notifying the seller. The seller does not retrieve possession of the car from the buyer. If the car is stolen from the buyer and the buyer has insurance that covers the loss, the risk of loss is on the buyer. If buyer does not have insurance covering the car, the risk of loss is on the seller.

In the third situation in which the buyer is in breach before the risk of loss passes to the buyer, the risk of loss remains on the seller to the extent that the seller has insurance covering the goods. Otherwise, the risk of loss is on the buyer for a commercially reasonable time. What this means is that once a buyer repudiates its contractual obligations, the seller must within a commercially reasonable time make sure that it has insurance to cover any loss. So, assume that the parties contract for identified goods in a warehouse to be sold. Before the delivery date, the buyer repudiates the contract by calling up the seller and saying that the buyer will not be taking possession of or paying for the goods. The next day, the goods are destroyed in a fire. If the seller has insurance covering the loss, the risk is on the seller. If there is no effective insurance, the risk is on the buyer. If the fire happened a significant time after the repudiation and the seller did not have insurance, there would be a question

---

[28]CISG Art. 32.
[29]UCC §2-510.

as to whether a commercially reasonable time had elapsed. If so, the risk would be on the seller.

The CISG takes breach into account in allocating risk of loss in two situations. The first situation, discussed previously, is when the buyer is supposed to pick up the goods from the seller and fails to do so within the time indicated by the contract. In such a case, the risk of loss passes to the buyer when it is in breach in not taking over the goods.[30] The second situation is when a seller's act or omission causes loss or damage to goods after the risk of loss has passed to the buyer.[31] In such a situation, the buyer's obligation to pay the price for the goods is discharged. An example of this situation would be when a seller is obligated to deliver goods to a carrier for shipment and the seller damages the goods before they are loaded onto the carrier. Normally, the risk of loss would pass when the goods are delivered to the carrier,[32] but if the seller's conduct caused damage to the goods, the buyer may not be obligated to pay the entire price of the goods.

F   A   Q

Q: Why allow the breaching party to take advantage of the injured party's insurance under the UCC?

A: The UCC generally takes the position that the risk of loss should be on the party that is most likely to have insurance. There is no desire to punish breaching parties, other than requiring them to compensate the injured party for damages caused by the breach. Loss to goods may have nothing whatsoever to do with the breach. If a defective car is stolen, the defect didn't cause the loss — the theft caused the loss. If insurance is in place, the insurance covers the loss and there is no need to additionally charge the breaching party. Also, the Code requires parties in some situations to make sure that they have insurance in place, as in the situation in which a buyer repudiates before taking goods. There is an expectation that sellers will have insurance covering goods in their possession, and that buyers won't have insurance until they accept goods. By comparison, the CISG does not allocate risk on the basis of whether a party had effective insurance coverage.

C. Gap Fillers

Both the UCC and the CISG will supply terms to the contract if the parties have agreed to be bound without express agreement on all terms. These supplied terms are known as *gap fillers*. It is important to understand, however, that terms will be supplied only if the parties have agreed to be bound without having agreed to all terms. For example, if the parties have agreed on all terms except price and are

---

[30]CISG Art. 69(1).
[31]CISG Art. 66.
[32]See CISG Art. 67(1).

arguing over that term, there is no enforceable contract until the parties agree on an exact price or agree that they will be bound without agreement on price.

(1) Open Price Term

Both the UCC and the CISG provide a rule in the event that the parties have agreed to be bound without expressly setting a price.[33] One might wonder why parties would ever agree to be so bound, because price is one of the most fundamental terms of the contract. The reason may be that it is just understood that the price will be the prevailing price in the market at the time of contracting, or it may be that the parties do not want to set a price at the time of contracting and prefer the market price at the time of delivery.

The UCC price gap filler, UCC §2-305, provides that the price is a "reasonable price at the time of delivery if (a) nothing is said as to price; (b) the price is left to be agreed by the parties and they fail to agree; or (c) the price is to be fixed in terms of some agreed market . . . as set or recorded by a third person or agency and it is not so set or recorded." It should be emphasized, especially with regard to (b), that the price gap filler will apply only if the parties intend to be bound without having settled on the price. Postponement of agreement on the price means that no deal has actually been concluded. It is a question of fact whether the parties intend to be bound without having firmly agreed to price.

Section 2-305 has a couple of other rules dealing with the price. If the seller or buyer is allowed to unilaterally fix the price, that party must do so in good faith. Also, if a price fails to be fixed through fault of one of the parties, the other party may treat the contract as cancelled or may fix a reasonable price.

What is a "reasonable price"? If there is a market for the goods, it would seem that a market price would be reasonable most of the time, with reference being made to the market where the goods were to be tendered to the buyer.

Under the CISG, there is a question as to whether open price term contracts are enforceable. The rule providing the gap filler for price under the CISG, Article 55, applies only where a contract has been <u>validly concluded</u> without a price having been set. CISG Article 14 states that an ***offer*** has been made if a communication provides a means for determining the price. Arguably, a contract cannot be validly concluded without there being some agreement on price as there needs to be an offer and an acceptance for a contract to be formed. The Secretariat Commentary to the predecessor to Article 55 suggests that it applies only if the relevant nation has opted out of Part II CISG dealing with contract formation, which includes Article 14. Only a few Scandinavian countries have done this,[34] so under this analysis, Article 55 would rarely have any application. Other scholarly commentary suggests, however, that Article 55 should apply in other cases in which the parties intend to be bound without setting the price, at least if the contract is valid under domestic sales law determined by choice of law rules.[35] At the end of the day, the enforceability of open price contracts under the CISG is left to arbitral tribunals and courts — probably most of the time, it will be clear from the facts that the parties had some market price in mind at the time of contracting, and thus the issue will be avoided.

---

[33]UCC §2-305 & CISG Art. 55.
[34]Denmark, Finland, Norway and Sweden have opted out of Part 2 of the CISG. See http://www.uncitral.org.
[35]See, e.g., Honnold, *Uniform Law for International Sales Under the 1980 United Nations Convention* §§137.4-137.8 (3d ed. 1999).

Under CISG Article 55, assuming that a contract has been validly concluded without the setting of a price, the price is that generally charged for the goods in question at the time of the conclusion of the contract. ***Conclusion of the contract*** under the CISG is when the contract has been formed, for example by the receipt of an acceptance to an offer.[36] So, the approach under the CISG differs from that of the UCC, which sets price at the time of delivery. The CISG is assuming that when parties agree to a contract without setting a price, they are operating under the assumption that the current market price will apply. The UCC's assumption is that the parties are agreeing that the price will be the prevailing price in the future when the goods are delivered.

(2) Output and Requirements Contracts

Generally speaking, neither the UCC nor the CISG fill any gaps in the contract regarding quantity of goods. If the parties have not agreed on that term, the contract may be too indefinite to be enforced. The UCC does have, however, a provision dealing with ***output and requirements contracts***, §2-306. Under such contracts, the seller agrees to sell all of the product that it produces to a particular buyer or else the buyer agrees to purchase all of a certain product that it might require from a specific seller. For example, a contract pursuant to which a farmer agrees to sell all of the cotton that is produced from a specified acreage would be an output contract, and a contract pursuant to which a buyer agrees to buy all of the plastic bottles that it needs to package liquid soap from a seller would be a requirements contract.

Output and requirements contracts are arguably illusory because a seller could choose to have no output and a buyer could choose to have no requirements. UCC §2-306 provides, however, that output and requirements contracts impose a good faith obligation on the seller to produce in good faith and on a buyer to have requirements in good faith. The Code also provides that quantities must be reasonably proportionate to any stated estimates that are given and in the absence of estimates, comparable to prior output or requirements.

Courts and the official commentary to UCC §2-306 seem to focus, however, on the overall requirement of good faith. Parties may be allowed to reduce output or requirements to zero if the reason they are doing so is unrelated to the contract.[37] For example, if a buyer is having severe financial difficulty and is thus cutting back on its business, it would not be required to purchase as much product under a requirements contract. Likewise, if a farmer suffered a severe drought, the farmer would not be required to have as much output. By comparison, if a buyer opted to reduce its requirements just to avoid an unfavorable requirements contract, that would not be in good faith.

(3) Provisions Dealing with Delivery and Payment

As noted previously, under the UCC, unless the contract indicates otherwise, delivery is generally to occur at the seller's place of business.[38] Also, delivery is to be all at once, not in installments.[39] If the parties have not agreed on a time for delivery, it is to be in a

---

[36]CISG Art. 23.
[37]*Brewster of Lynchburg, Inc. v. Dial Corp.*, 33 F.3d 355, 24 UCC Rep. Serv. 2d 738 (1994).
[38]UCC §2-308.
[39]UCC §2-307.

	Chart Summarizing Significant Gap Filler Terms—	
TABLE 5.2	**Assume Parties Have Agreed to Be Bound with the Term Left Open and Agreement Is Enforceable**	

Term	UCC	CISG
Price	Reasonable time at the time of delivery. §2-305.	Price generally charged at the time the contract is concluded under comparable circumstances. Article 55.
Output and requirements contracts	To be determined in good faith by seller (output) or buyer (requirements), to be reasonably proportionate to any stated estimate and in absence of estimate to prior output or requirements. §2-306.	No provision.
Place of delivery	Seller's place of business, unless parties are aware at the time of contracting that goods are located elsewhere, in which case at location of goods. Documents delivered through normal banking channels. §2-308.	Same as UCC. Article 31.
Time for delivery	Reasonable time, in one installment. §§2-307, 2-309.	Reasonable time after conclusion of the contract, all goods must be delivered by that time. Earlier partial deliveries are acceptable if buyer not inconvenienced. Articles 33, 37.
Time and place for payment	Time and place at which the buyer is to receive the goods or document of title. §2-310.	Same as UCC. Articles 57, 58.

reasonable time.[40] UCC §1-205 indicates that whether a time is reasonable depends on the nature, purpose, and circumstances of the action. So, everything involved in the transaction must be examined. For example, if the contract calls for the goods to be delivered at a great distance, reasonable time for delivery might be greater than if delivery is at a short distance. If both parties are aware that the goods are urgently needed by the buyer, the time for delivery might be shorter. Obviously, where time is of the essence for delivery, it makes sense to provide a specific time in the contract!

Payment is due at the time and place at which the buyer is to receive the goods, unless delivery is made by delivering a document of title to the buyer, in which case payment is due at that time and place.[41]

The CISG is similar to the UCC in this area, except that it provides that if a seller has delivered some of the goods before the date of delivery, the seller may deliver the rest of the goods (i.e., in installments) up to the date of delivery under the contract, as

---

[40] UCC §2-309.
[41] UCC §2-310.

long as the buyer is not caused unreasonable inconvenience or expense.[42] The buyer is required to pay the price at the seller's place of business or, if the payment is against the handing over of goods or documents of title, at the place where the handing over takes place.[43] The price must be paid when the seller places the goods or documents controlling their disposition at the buyer's disposal.[44]

D. Contract Interpretation and the Parol Evidence Rule

(1) CISG Rules of Interpretation

The UCC does not have rules regarding contract interpretation, other than the ***parol evidence rule*** in UCC §2-202. We will discuss this in more detail shortly. The CISG, by comparison, does have a rule in Article 8 to aid courts and arbitral tribunals in determining the meaning of contractual terms. Under Article 8, the meaning of any statement in a contract is to be given the intended meaning of the person making the statement if the person hearing the statement knew of the meaning or could not have been unaware of it. If, however, the person hearing the statement did not know and could have been unaware of the intended meaning, the statement is to be "interpreted according to the understanding that a reasonable person of the same kind [as the person hearing the statement] would have had in the same circumstances." CISG Article 8 also tells courts and arbitral tribunals that in determining the intent of a party or the understanding that a reasonable person would have had, all relevant circumstances should be considered, including negotiations, any courses of dealing between the parties, trade usages, and any subsequent conduct of the parties.

To show how the CISG rules on contract interpretation work, assume that a seller in a common law country makes an offer to a buyer in a civil law country and states that the deadline for acceptance of the offer is June 1. The seller's intent is that this is a deadline for acceptance, but that the seller may revoke the offer at any time before then if the buyer has not yet accepted it. This intent is consistent with the law in the seller's country. The buyer on the other hand believes that the offer is irrevocable until June 1 because in the buyer's country, offers cannot be legally revoked before the time set for acceptance.

Under the CISG, if the buyer knew or could not have been unaware of the seller's intent, the offer is revocable. If, on the other hand, the buyer did not know and could be unaware of the seller's intent, whether the offer was revocable would be determined by asking whether a reasonable person in the buyer's position would have understood that it was revocable. If not, then the offer would be irrevocable. If the buyer was not that experienced in international transactions, a similarly inexperienced buyer in a country in which offers are generally irrevocable would have probably thought that the offer was irrevocable.

(2) General Rules of Contract Interpretation and Construction

Although the UCC does not have any rule similar to Article 8 of the CISG, that rule is similar to *Restatement (Second) of Contracts* §20 dealing with understanding of

---

[42]CISG Art. 37.
[43]CISG Art. 57.
[44]CISG Art. 58.

TABLE 5.3	Some Maxims of Interpretation and Construction	
Rule	**Explanation**	**Example**
Expresio unius est exclusion alterius ("the expression of one thing is the exclusion of another")	If a contract gives a list of items without stating "for example" or "including, but not limited to," the parties are understood to be excluding any item not listed.	A contract for the sale of "household items" lists a television, personal computer and sofa. It is assumed that the contract does not include a dining room set that isn't listed.
Ejusdem generic ("of the same kind")	If a contract lists specific items and a more general category, it is assumed that other items included are like the specific items.	A contract for the sale of a house includes "chairs, tables, a dining room set and other furnishings." Arguably, this would not include a television because it is not like the other items listed.
Construction that renders language surplusage or useless is to be avoided	There is an assumption that people contracting intend to give meaning to every word in the contract.	In UCC §2-207, subsection (1) says that additional or different terms may be in an acceptance. In subsection (2), the statute says that "additional" terms are to be considered as proposals for addition to the contract. That must mean that the drafters did not intend for "different" terms to be considered under subsection (2), or the term "different" would be surplusage in subsection (1). But see UCC §2-207, comment 3.
Construe the contract to provide a "fair bargain"	There is an assumption that parties intend to contract fairly so that neither party is taken advantage of.	If a contract calls for the sale of "chicken" at a certain price and the term chicken could mean broilers or stewing chickens, the court will assume that the parties intended stewing chickens if that is the only construction that would prevent a loss to the seller. See *Frigaliment Importing Co. v. B.N.S. Intl. Sales Corp.*, 190 F. Supp. 116 (S.D.N.Y. 1960).
Contra proferentem ("against the profferor")	Contracts, especially form contracts, will be construed against the party who drafted the term at issue.	If a seller provides a form contract calling for arbitration and it is ambiguous as to whether arbitration is to be binding, a court might find that the arbitration was not binding if such a construction would favor the buyer.

contract terms. It is likely that courts analyzing cases of misunderstanding of terms in sales contracts governed by Article 2 would probably use the general principles of contract interpretation applied in non-sales cases.

Table 5.3 provides some of the maxims of contract *interpretation* and *construction* that courts might use in trying to determine the meaning of the parties' agreement.[45] "Interpretation" refers to the court's attempt to determine what the parties meant when they used certain language in their contract. "Construction" refers to the legal effect that the court is willing to give to the terms of the contract.[46] For example, the rule *expresio unius est expresio alterius* ("the expression of one thing is the exclusion of another") is a rule of interpretation in that the court is assuming that the parties did not intend to cover items in their contract that are not specifically mentioned. The *contra proferentem* ("against the profferor") rule that construes ambiguous terms against the maker of the contract does not seek to determine the parties' intentions but rather imposes liability on the party who drafted the contract on the grounds that such party has a duty to draft terms in a clear, understandable fashion.

The first three rules in the table are also useful in interpreting statutes, such as the rule that language should be interpreted in such a manner as to avoid surplusage. Of course, it must be understood that these maxims will sometimes contradict each other and may be subject to more compelling arguments that are contrary to the maxims. For example, a construction that avoids surplusage may favor the party who drafted the contract, and so a court may need to choose between the maxims. Also, we previously discussed the ambiguity created in UCC §2-207 when the drafters referred to "additional or different" terms in an acceptance under subsection (1) but then stated that "additional" terms would be considered as proposals for addition to the contract under subsection (2).[47] Official comment 3 to §2-207 suggests that the drafters might have intended "additional" in subsection (2) to include "different," which would render the word "different" in subsection (1) to be surplus language. So, the maxims should be regarded as guides to interpretation and not necessarily decisive. At the end of the day, the court will try to determine each party's reasonable understanding of the terms of the contract.

(3) Parol Evidence Rule Analysis Under the UCC

As noted previously, the UCC does have a parol evidence rule, UCC §2-202. Under the parol evidence rule, if a written contract exists, evidence of a prior oral or written agreement and evidence of a contemporaneous oral agreement are inadmissible to contradict a term in the written contract that was intended to be the final expression of the parties with respect to that term. Evidence of a prior oral or written agreement and evidence of a contemporaneous oral agreement is also inadmissible to supplement the terms of a written agreement if that agreement was intended by the parties to be the complete expression of the parties' contract.

So, you should know to do the parol evidence analysis if you see (1) a written agreement between the parties and (2) one of the parties trying to introduce evidence of some agreement between the parties that was made before or at the same time as the written agreement that is not reflected in the written agreement. It is important to

---

[45]For further discussion see Farnsworth, *Contracts* §7.11 (4th ed. 2004).
[46]See Farnsworth, *Contracts* §7.7 (4th ed. 2004).
[47]See pp. 33-34, *supra*.

note that the parol evidence rule does <u>not</u> apply to modifications, that is, agreements made after the written contract that either change the terms of the written contract or add additional terms. Evidence of modifications will generally be admissible, although as previously noted, sometimes the modification may need to be evidenced by a writing.[48]

The theory behind the parol evidence rule is that when parties reduce their agreement to a final written form, they are superseding any prior agreements between them. If the parties had a prior understanding that is not evidenced in the writing, the assumption is that the parties no longer intend to be bound by that understanding. In doing the parol evidence analysis, the issue will be to what extent the parties intended the written contract to reflect the complete and final expression of their agreement.

In doing parol evidence analysis, you should look at (1) the type of evidence that the party is trying to introduce and (2) whether the evidence seeks to contradict the terms in the written agreement or seeks to supplement or explain it. With regard to the type of evidence, you should look at whether it is of an oral or written understanding or is evidence of course of performance, course of dealing, or usage of trade.

If you determine that the evidence might be inadmissible under the parol evidence rule, you should then examine the exceptions to the rule. These exceptions, discussed later, will allow evidence of prior agreements or contemporaneous oral agreements to be admitted even if they would otherwise be inadmissible under the rule.

(a) Evidence of Prior Written or Oral Agreements and Contemporaneous Oral Agreements that Contradict the Final Written Contract

Assume the parties have a written contract. One of the parties tries to introduce evidence that the parties had actually previously agreed to something that is contradicted by the written contract. For example, assume that the parties have a written contract that provides that delivery of the goods will be on May 1. The seller tries to introduce evidence that the parties had actually agreed before the written contract was signed that delivery would be on June 1. The evidence could be written or oral. The buyer raises an objection on the grounds of the parol evidence rule, and the court has to decide whether to admit the evidence of the prior agreement.

The parol evidence rule provides that evidence of alleged agreements made before the written contract or alleged oral agreements made at the same time as the written contract (i.e., contemporaneous with) that contradict the written contract should be excluded if the parties intended the written contract to be the final expression of their understanding with respect to the terms contained in the written contract. If a written contract was intended by the parties to be their final expression with respect to the terms in that contract, the written contract is said to be ***partially integrated***.

Returning to our example, let us assume that the parties have signed a contract that provides the quantity of goods to be sold, the price of those goods, and the delivery date of May 1. If we say that this written agreement is the final expression of the parties' understanding with respect to these terms, we say it is partially

---

[48]See pp. 42-44, *supra.*

integrated and no evidence of any prior agreement or contemporaneous oral agreement will be admitted to contradict these terms. If the agreement was not intended to be the final expression of the parties with respect to <u>all</u> terms in the contract (i.e., ***completely integrated***) then it may be possible to admit evidence of prior agreements regarding consistent additional terms, for example, warranties. Admission of evidence of prior agreements regarding consistent terms is discussed later.

In our example, if the court determines that the written contract was partially integrated, evidence of a prior agreement that the parties agreed that delivery was to be on June 1 will not be admissible under the parol evidence rule unless there is an applicable exception to the rule. It seems to make sense to say that if the parties put in writing that delivery would be on May 1, they intended to supersede any prior agreement that delivery would be on another date.

How does the court determine if the written agreement is partially integrated? The court will look to the detail of the agreement and will also look to the sophistication of the parties. If the parties are sophisticated and were negotiating a detailed written contract, one can assume that the written contract supersedes any prior contradictory agreement that the parties had. On the other hand, if the party seeking to introduce the evidence of the prior inconsistent agreement was not very sophisticated, perhaps it can be argued that the person did not understand the importance of the written contract and did not understand it to supersede any prior oral agreements that had been reached. Also, the party seeking to introduce the evidence may try to argue that the party was defrauded or that the written contract was drafted in error. Fraud and mistake are possible exceptions to the parol evidence rule, as will be discussed later in this chapter.

It is fair to say, however, that if an alleged prior oral or written agreement contradicts a subsequent written contract, there is a good chance that the evidence will be excluded on the basis of the parol evidence rule. It will probably be hard for the person trying to introduce the evidence to prove that the final written contract was signed without an understanding that any prior inconsistent agreements were superseded by the final written contract.

(b) Evidence of Prior Written or Oral Agreements and Contemporaneous Oral Agreements that Are Consistent with the Written Contract

The parol evidence rule also bans evidence of any prior agreement or contemporaneous oral agreement providing consistent additional terms if the written contract is considered to be the complete and final expression of the parties with respect to the entire agreement. This is what is referred to as a ***complete integration***.

For example, let's assume that the parties have a very detailed written contract providing for the sale of an airplane. The contract lays out the price, description of the plane, and the delivery date. The written contract also contains express statements of warranty. It has what is called a ***merger clause***, stating, "This contract contains all of the agreements between the parties regarding this transaction. There are no other agreements." The written contract says nothing about whether the seller will provide flying lessons to the buyer. Assume that the buyer wishes to introduce evidence that prior to the signing of the written contract, the seller had orally promised the buyer that the seller would provide flying lessons. This alleged promise is consistent with the written contract. Nevertheless, if a court were to determine that the written contract was completely integrated, it would exclude evidence of the alleged prior agreement of the seller to provide the buyer with flying lessons, unless the buyer could argue for an applicable exception to the parol evidence rule (discussed later).

How does a court determine if a written contract is completely integrated? As is the case with determining if a contract was partially integrated, courts will look at the level of detail in the written contract and the sophistication of the parties. Courts will look at the written contract to see if the contract contains a merger clause. The existence of a merger clause is generally considered not to be conclusive on the matter, however.[49] If the contract is detailed, contains a merger clause, was carefully negotiated, and was between sophisticated parties, the court is much more likely to exclude evidence of prior agreements under the parol evidence rule. If the contract is a form contract in which a stronger party imposed terms on a weaker party without much negotiation, the court is less likely to find that the written contract was partially or completely integrated. The commentary to UCC §2-202 provides a test, which is as follows: "If the additional terms are such that, if agreed upon, they would certainly have been included in the document in the view of the court, then evidence of their alleged making must be kept from the trier of fact."

F   A   Q

Q: What is the difference between a partially integrated contract and a completely integrated contract?

A: A partially integrated contract is the final expression of the parties only with respect to the terms that are in the written contract. It is possible that the parties had side agreements with respect to other terms that are not included in the writing. A completely integrated contract is the final expression of the parties with respect to all terms of the agreement. There are no side agreements. A complete integration will be more detailed than a partial integration and will probably contain a merger clause, saying that everything is in the written contract. Courts are more likely to find a complete integration if the parties are sophisticated, the agreement was carefully negotiated, and the contract is very detailed.

It is probably fair to say that courts are much more likely to admit evidence of terms that are consistent with the written contract than of terms that are inconsistent. It may be difficult in such a situation for the party seeking to exclude the evidence to convince the court that the written contract was completely integrated and that the evidence should thus be excluded.

(c) Evidence of Course of Performance, Course of Dealing, and Usage of Trade

The UCC has a special rule for the admissibility of evidence of course of performance, course of dealing, and usage of trade. Such evidence may be admitted to explain or supplement the written contract. The definition of "agreement" includes

---

[49] *Restatement (Second) of Contracts* §210, comment b takes the position that a writing cannot by itself prove its completeness.

course of performance, course of dealing and usage of trade along with any express agreements between the parties.[50]

We discussed these types of terms before and noted that "course of performance" is how parties are performing under a contract that calls for multiple performances, "course of dealing" is how parties have performed under prior contracts between them and "usage of trade" is how parties perform in the particular industry involved.[51] Course of performance, course of dealing, and usage of trade are to be construed in a manner reasonably consistent with the express terms of the contract if it is possible to do so. If it is not possible, then express terms control course of performance, course of performance controls course of dealing, and course of dealing controls usage of trade.[52] In any event, course of performance is relevant to show that a contractual term has been waived or modified.[53]

HIERARCHY OF TERMS — UCC §1-303

(1) Express Terms
(2) Course of Performance
(3) Course of Dealing
(4) Usage of Trade

All terms are to be construed as consistent where it is reasonable to do so. Even if not reasonable, course of performance may be relevant to show waiver of modification of express term.

An example of the use of trade usage and course of dealing to alter the terms of an otherwise integrated contract is presented in *Columbia Nitrogen Corp. v. Royster Co.*[54] In that case, the contract called for the delivery of a minimum quantity of phosphate each year for three years. When the market price for phosphate fell, the buyer refused to take the minimum quantity. When the seller sued for breach, the buyer attempted to introduce evidence of prior dealings between the parties (course of dealing) in which the buyer did not take the minimum quantity and trade usage that in this industry, the quantities in contracts were subject to adjustment based on market conditions.

The district judge excluded the evidence of trade usage and course of dealing under the parol evidence rule on the basis that it contradicted the plain meaning of the contract that required the buyer to take a minimum quantity of product. The appellate court reversed, holding that the **plain meaning rule** (i.e., that the court should exclude evidence inconsistent with what it determines to be the plain meaning of words under the contract) did not apply under the UCC, and that the evidence should have been admitted for the purpose of explaining what the parties intended under the contract. That there was a merger clause in the written contract was of no

---

[50]UCC §1-201(b)(3).
[51]UCC §1-303. See also pp. 22-23, *supra*.
[52]UCC §1-303(e).
[53]UCC §1-303(f).
[54]451 F.2d 3 (4th Cir. 1971).

consequence; the official commentary to §2-202 indicates that course of performance, course of dealing, and usage of trade can be excluded only by careful negation. If the parties wish to exclude evidence of any particular course of dealing or trade usage, they must specifically exclude it in the contract.

(d) Parol Evidence Rule Exceptions

There are some exceptions to the parol evidence rule such that courts will admit evidence of prior agreements or contemporaneous oral agreements even if we might say that the writing is partially or completely integrated. Although the UCC does not specifically provide for exceptions to the parol evidence rule, courts have applied common law exceptions in sale of goods cases. One type of evidence that is admitted despite the existence of the parol evidence rule is evidence that the parties had orally agreed that the enforceability of the written contract would be subject to some condition precedent. Oral conditions precedent to the contract could include such things as the obtaining of financing — for example, the contract for the sale of a car is conditioned on the ability of the buyer to obtain a suitable loan so as to purchase it. If the parties have orally agreed that the contract will have no effect unless financing is obtained, courts might admit evidence of such a condition unless the written contract makes clear that there are no conditions precedent. If the contract clearly indicates, however, that there are no conditions precedent to its enforceability, a court may nevertheless find evidence of a condition to be contradictory to the written contract and bar its admission under the UCC §2-202.[55]

Parol evidence will be admitted to explain ambiguous terms in the contract. It could be argued that if terms are ambiguous, the contract is not completely integrated because the parties could have had a side agreement to explain the ambiguity.

Courts will also admit evidence of fraud for the purpose of avoiding a contract. For example, in one case the court permitted the buyer to testify that an agent of the seller had fraudulently told the buyer that a car being sold had never been in an accident, despite the fact that the contract said nothing about this and had a provision indicating that no other representations or warranties had been made.[56] Courts are split on whether evidence of negligent misrepresentation should be admitted to avoid a completely integrated contract.[57]

One final area in which evidence might be admitted would be to show mistake of fact regarding the subject matter of the contract or the terms of the contract itself. For

---

[55]See *Bib Audio-Video Products v. Herold Marketing Associates*, 517 N.W.2d 68 (Minn. App. 1994).
[56]*City Dodge, Inc. v. Gardner*, 232 Ga. 766, 208 S.E.2d 794 (1974).
[57]*Compare Keller v. A.O. Smith Harvestore Products, Inc.*, 819 P.2d 69 (Colo. 1991) *with Rio Grande Jewelers v. Data General Corp.*, 101 N.M. 798, 689 P.2d 1269 (1984).

example, if a third party incorrectly drafted the contract and both parties mistakenly signed it, evidence of the mistake would be admitted to show the "scrivener's error." Again, the UCC does not specifically provide for such evidence to be admitted despite the parol evidence rule, but this would be an area where general principles of law and equity would supplement the Code.[58]

EVIDENCE THAT MIGHT BE ADMITTED EVEN IF CONTRACT PARTIALLY OR COMPLETELY INTEGRATED

(1) Course of performance, course of dealing, and usage of trade
(2) Condition precedent to enforceability of written contract
(3) Ambiguity
(4) Fraud (some courts permit evidence of negligent misrepresentation)
(5) Mistake regarding subject matter or contents of writing (scrivener's error)

Note: The only one of these exceptions mentioned in UCC §2-202 is the first one mentioned, but the others might apply by virtue of principles of common law and equity supplementing the UCC.

---

(4) The CISG Approach to Parol Evidence

As noted previously, the CISG specifically allows for courts to consider all evidence in determining the parties' intent, including evidence of prior negotiations. Courts and commentators have taken this to mean that the CISG does not have a parol evidence rule.[59] Parties can, however, by contract agree that evidence of prior agreements is not to be considered. A merger clause indicating that the written contract is the exclusive expression of the parties' understandings may be sufficient to cause a court to exclude evidence of prior verbal understandings.

E. Unconscionability

The UCC has a provision permitting courts to refuse to enforce any **unconscionable** contract or contractual clause.[60] Such contracts or clauses may be unenforceable in whole or in part.

Sidebar

PAROL EVIDENCE IN INTERNATIONAL SALES CONTRACTS

The CISG's lack of a parol evidence rule reflects the opinion of other legal systems that evidence of prior agreements might be useful in determining the parties' obligations under contracts. With language difficulties in international transactions, there may be a particular need to bring in evidence of what the parties were talking about before they signed the contract to determine what they intended. Remember also that under Article 8 of the CISG, the meaning of statements made by a party to a contract is to be determined based on that party's subjective intent if the other party knew of that intent or could not have been unaware of it. Parol evidence may be admissible to determine what that intent was.

---

[58]*Posey v. Ford Motor Credit Co.*, 141 Idaho 477, 111 P.3d 162 (Idaho App. 2005).
[59]*MCC-Marble Ceramic Center, Inc. v. Ceramica Nuova D'Agostino, S.p.A.*, 144 F.3d 1384 (11th Cir. 1998).
[60]UCC §2-302.

It is not easy to define what is meant by unconscionability — it's sort of like what Justice Potter Stewart said about obscenity, in that "you know it when you see it."[61] According to the official comments to the UCC, the purpose of the unconscionability rule is to prevent "oppression and unfair surprise." The test is "whether, in light of the general commercial background and the commercial needs of the particular trade or case, the clauses involved are so one-sided as to be unconscionable under the circumstances existing at the time of the making of the contract."[62] The determination is for the court as a matter of law, although the parties are to be afforded a reasonable opportunity to present evidence to the court to aid the court's determination. The rule reflects the view that courts may be in a better position than juries to evaluate a contractual provision in light of general commercial practices because courts see more cases than the typical juror.

Most courts and commentators suggest that for a contract or clause to be unconscionable, there must be both a procedural element and a substantive element. The procedural element goes to the fairness of the bargaining between the parties. In looking at the procedural element, courts focus on whether the contract was a form contract presented on a "take or leave it" basis, on the language used (is it "legalese"?), on the sales tactics of the seller and on the sophistication of the parties involved. The substantive element goes to the fairness or unfairness of the term.

The official commentary to §2-302 gives examples of contractual provisions that the drafters believed were properly held to be unenforceable. For example, a provision limiting the time within which complaints could be registered for latent defects was unenforceable where the defects could be determined only through microscopic examination.[63]

REQUIREMENTS FOR UNCONSCIONABILITY

(1) Procedural Element: Goes to the bargaining process and whether the buyer had a reasonable choice.

and*

(2) Substantive Element: Goes to the fairness of the term.

Unconscionability is a decision for the court, with parties being allowed to present evidence.

*Most courts require both elements, although some will focus on one or the other (generally the substantive element).

One of the earliest and most famous cases involving unconscionability is *Williams v. Walker-Thomas Furniture Co.*[64] In that case, the buyer of goods on credit (technically a "lease to own" arrangement) signed a contract that allowed the seller to

---

[61]*Jacobellis v. Ohio*, 378 U.S. 184 (Stewart, J., concurring).
[62]UCC §2-302, comment 1.
[63]*Id.*
[64]350 F.2d 445 (D.C. Cir. 1965).

retain an interest in all goods purchased over time until the amount due on all of the goods was paid off. If the buyer defaulted at any point, the seller could repossess all goods that had been purchased, no matter how long ago the goods had been purchased. This type of clause is called a "dragnet" clause, and was written in a way that was not easy to understand. When the buyer defaulted on payment for a stereo set purchased in 1962, the seller sought to repossess all goods purchased since 1957.

The appellate court held that the lower court should have considered whether the buyer had a meaningful choice—whether considering her level of sophistication she had a reasonable opportunity to understand the terms of the contract. In examining the fairness of the term, the court held that the lower court should evaluate it in light of "the mores and business practices of the time and place." The appellate court did not decide if the dragnet clause was unconscionable, but remanded to the lower court for further consideration of the issue. It is worth noting that subsequently, many state legislatures have limited the application of "dragnet" clauses in consumer sales contracts by outlawing them or requiring that payments be credited first to goods that have been purchased first, with paid off goods no longer being subject to repossession.[65]

Warranty disclaimers may also be questioned as being unconscionable. At least one court has held that warranty disclaimers can be unconscionable, even if presented in the conspicuous manner required by UCC §2-316.[66] In that case, the buyer suffered losses when equipment that was purchased did not perform in the manner that had been represented by the salesperson. In such a case, the court felt that it would be unfair for the seller to hide behind disclaimers in its form contract of sale that had been presented on a "take it or leave it" basis to the buyer, who was a farmer.

F   A   Q

Q: Is unconscionability only an issue in consumer contracts?

A: No. Some courts will also allow commercial buyers to raise it in certain cases. Such buyers may be small businesses or farmers compared to large corporate sellers. Form contracts are used, and there is little bargaining. For the most part, however, unconscionability is most useful for consumers.

In some cases, courts have invalidated the price that was charged on the grounds that it was unconscionably high. The cases tend to involve consumer buyers who are impoverished, and credit sales in which the high price is hidden by low monthly payments that are made over a long period of time. In one such case, the court held that the sale of a freezer with a retail value of $300 for $900 plus additional credit charges to welfare recipients was unconscionable.[67] Another court noted that if a contract price is at least 2½ times the fair market retail price of goods, that there is "a greatly increased probability" that the price will be found unconscionable.[68]

Another contractual term that is subject to scrutiny as possibly being unconscionable is an arbitration clause. Although generally enforceable, in some situations

---

[65]See Uniform Consumer Credit Code (UCCC) §3.303, which has been adopted in several states.
[66]*A & M Produce Co. v. FMC Corp.*, 135 Cal. App. 473, 186 Cal. Rptr. 114 (1982).
[67]*Jones v. Star Credit Corp.*, 59 Misc. 189, 298 N.Y.S.2d 264 (1969).
[68]*Remco Enterprises, Inc. v. Houston*, 9 Kan. App. 2d 296, 677 P.2d 567 (1984).

arbitration may force consumer buyers to pay large sums of money to initiate the arbitration process. Such a provision might discourage buyers from asserting their rights under the contract. An arbitration provision may also force buyers to arbitrate far from home. Assuming, however, that the provision does not prevent the buyer from having a reasonable opportunity to hold the seller responsible for promises made under the contract, the arbitration provision most likely will be upheld.[69]

The CISG does not have a provision dealing with unconscionability. As noted previously, the CISG gives parties great latitude in drafting contracts. The CISG also applies to commercial transactions only, meaning that parties can generally be expected to look out for themselves. The CISG does not, however, address questions of validity of the contract.[70] If U.S. law were to fill gaps in a transaction otherwise governed by the CISG, it is possible that an extremely one-sided contractual provision imposed by the stronger party on the weaker party could be found unenforceable on the basis of unconscionability.[71]

SUMMARY

■ Both the UCC and the CISG recognize the principle of "freedom of contract," generally permitting parties to vary the terms of the UCC or CISG. Exceptions under the UCC include the inability of parties to disclaim the covenant of good faith and fair dealing and any obligation to act reasonably. The CISG does not deal with rules of validity (e.g., unconscionability), so it is possible that some contractual provisions under the CISG will be unenforceable on the basis of public policy or unconscionability.

■ Unless the parties agree to the contrary, the risk of loss passes to the buyer when the buyer takes possession of the goods if the seller is a merchant. This rule applies in cases in which the goods are not being shipped or held by a bailee. If the seller isn't a merchant the risk passes when the seller makes tender of delivery. Under the amended version of Article 2, the risk passes when the buyer takes possession even if the seller isn't a merchant.

■ Under the CISG, in cases not involving bailees or shipment, the risk of loss passes when the buyer takes over the goods or is in breach of contract for not doing so.

■ In cases involving bailees who have issued negotiable documents of title under the UCC, the risk of loss passes to the buyer on delivery to the buyer of the document. If the bailee has issued a non-negotiable document, the risk passes when the buyer has a reasonable opportunity to present the document to the issuer, assuming the issuer honors the document. The risk of loss will also pass when the bailee acknowledges to the buyer its right to the goods.

■ Under the CISG, if the goods are somewhere other than the seller's place of business, the risk of loss passes when the buyer is notified that the goods are at the buyer's disposal.

---

[69]*Stenzel v. Dell, Inc.*, 2005 Me. 37, 870 A.2d 133 (2005).
[70]CISG Art. 4.
[71]CISG Art. 7.

- If the contract calls for the goods to be shipped, the risk of loss passes to the buyer under both the UCC and CISG if the contract calls for the delivery of the goods to a carrier at the seller's place of business. This type of contract is called a "shipment contract," and it is assumed that the contract is a shipment contract unless otherwise indicated.

- If the contract requires the seller to deliver the goods at the buyer's place of business, the risk of loss does not pass until goods are tendered at the destination. This type of contract is called a "destination contract."

- Parties will sometimes use shorthand shipping terms, like "FOB" or "CIF," to indicate if the contract is a shipment contract or destination contract. In international sales, the INCOTERMS are often used.

- If the seller delivers non-conforming goods to the buyer, the risk of loss remains on the seller under the UCC until the goods are accepted by the buyer.

- If the buyer rightfully revokes acceptance of goods, under the UCC the risk of loss is on the seller only to the extent that the buyer has inadequate insurance.

- If the buyer repudiates the contract before the goods are delivered to the buyer, under the UCC the risk of loss is on the buyer only to the extent that the seller does not have adequate insurance to cover the loss, and then only for a commercially reasonable time.

- Under the CISG, the risk of loss is on the seller if an act or omission of the seller causes loss to the goods, even if the goods have been delivered to the buyer.

- Under the UCC, if the parties intend to contract without having set a price, the price is a reasonable price at the time of delivery of the goods.

- Under the CISG, there is some question as to whether open price term contracts are enforceable. Assuming they are, the price is the price normally charged for such goods at the time the contract is concluded (i.e., is entered into).

- The UCC requires parties under output or requirements contracts to determine their output or requirements in good faith. Generally, the output or requirements must reasonably approximate any stated estimates or in the absence of any estimates, prior output, or requirements.

- See the chart on page 88, *supra* for a summary of other gap filler terms.

- Under the CISG, unless Party A knows or could not have been unaware of Party B's actual intent in making a statement, Party B's statements will be interpreted according to the understanding that a reasonable person in Party A's position would have had. This rule is similar to the *Restatement (Second) of Contracts* §20.

- The UCC has a parol evidence rule that limits the admissibility of prior agreements or contemporaneous oral agreements when there is an integrated writing.

- The CISG permits courts to consider prior agreements in determining the parties' intent. Most courts and commentators believe that there is no parol evidence rule in the CISG, although parties may by agreement state that parol evidence should be excluded.

- The UCC permits courts to refuse to enforce all or part of a sales contract on the basis of unconscionability. Unconscionability typically requires a procedural element (problems with the bargaining process) and a substantive element (terms unreasonably favorable to one side).

■ The CISG does not have a rule barring unconscionable terms, but as unconscionability is a rule of validity, it is possible that courts will apply it if the applicable law for gap filling purposes under choice of law principles is the UCC.

CONNECTIONS

Choice of Law
Determining which law applies to the transaction is important in determining the terms of the contract. The UCC is more liberal than the common law in terms of allowing parties to contract without having expressly agreed on all terms. The UCC also provides gap fillers to flesh out the terms of the agreement between the parties. If the CISG applies, it has its own set of gap fillers.

Contract Formation
How the contract is formed may determine the terms of the contract. Under the "battle of the forms," the terms may be contained in the first form that is sent (e.g., the purchase order) or in the last form that is sent (e.g., the order acknowledgment). If there is a failure to agree on terms and the parties perform anyway, the court will look to gap fillers to flesh out the terms of the parties' contract.

Warranties
Warranties of quality and warranties of title are very important terms of the contract. There may be questions, however, as to whether oral statements of warranty given by a salesperson are superseded by disclaimers that appear in the written contract. The buyer may face objections under the parol evidence rule that the alleged oral statements of warranty should be excluded. From the buyer's perspective, the buyer may wish to argue that warranty disclaimers are unconscionable if the seller imposed those disclaimers via a form contract.

Performance Under the Contract
In determining whether there is a breach and whether the buyer has a right to reject goods, we must understand whatever obligations the parties have agreed to undertake. If the buyer is not satisfied with the goods, the buyer may nevertheless be required to keep them and pay for them unless the buyer can point to some provision in the contract that the seller has breached.

Remedies
In calculating damages, we will see that the goal is to place the party in the position that the party would have been in if the contract had been performed. From the seller's perspective, we must determine the price that the buyer agreed

to pay for the goods. That will often be easy to do, but if the parties agreed to be bound without setting a price, we will need to consult the price gap filler provision to determine how much the buyer agreed to pay (i.e., a reasonable price at the time of delivery). From the buyer's perspective, we must determine what the seller agreed to sell in terms of quality and in terms of such issues as time of delivery.

Third Party Obligations

We must determine if the parties agreed to ship the goods and whether the parties agreed that the seller would take the risk of loss until goods were delivered to the point of destination. We must also determine if the parties agreed that the buyer would establish a letter of credit in favor of the seller to assure the seller that the price would be paid on proof of shipment.

Performance, Breach, and Excuse

Under the Uniform Commercial Code (UCC), tender of delivery of goods according to the terms of the contract gives rise to the buyer's responsibility to accept and pay for the goods, unless the parties have come to a contrary agreement (e.g., the buyer is allowed to pay over time).[1] Likewise, under the CISG the seller is required to deliver goods pursuant to the terms of the contract and the buyer is required to take delivery and pay the price as required by the contract.[2] This chapter deals with what happens when the seller fails to make a proper delivery or the buyer improperly refuses to pay.

O V E R V I E W

---

[1] UCC §2-507.
[2] CISG Arts. 30 & 53.

C. PERFORMANCE AND BREACH UNDER THE UCC

D. PERFORMANCE AND BREACH UNDER THE CISG

E. EXCUSE FROM PERFORMANCE — IMPRACTICABILITY AND FRUSTRATION OF PURPOSE

A. Prospective Non-Performance: Repudiation and Insecurity

Situations may arise in which it appears to one of the parties before the time of performance that the other party will not perform when that time comes. This may be because of statements made by the party (e.g., "I will not be delivering the goods") or because of circumstances that make it look like performance will not occur (e.g., news reports appear indicating that the buyer is about to file for bankruptcy). Both the Uniform Commercial Code (UCC) and the United Nations Convention on Contracts for the International Sale of Goods (CISG) have provisions giving remedies to parties in situations in which there is prospective non-performance.

(1) Repudiation

Under the UCC, if a party *repudiates* its contractual obligations in a way that substantially impairs the value of the contract to the other party, the injured party may act as though the contract has been breached.[3] That means, among other things, that the injured party may suspend its own obligations and cancel the contract. The injured party may, for a commercially reasonable time, wait to see if the repudiating party changes its mind. A repudiating party may retract its repudiation unless the injured party has cancelled, materially altered its position, or has otherwise indicated that it considers the repudiation final.[4]

The UCC does not define "repudiation," but the official commentary indicates that it can either come from action or words. An action which "reasonably indicates a

---

[3]UCC §2-610.
[4]UCC §2-611.

rejection of the continuing obligation" would constitute a repudiation.[5] For example, if a seller is obligated to deliver a specific painting to the buyer, news that the painting had been sold to somebody else would constitute a repudiation. Words can also constitute a repudiation, but it is important that the words reasonably indicate a refusal to perform under the contract. An attempt to negotiate for more favorable terms does not necessarily indicate a refusal to perform under the contract.[6]

(2) Insecurity and Demand for Adequate Assurance

If a party cannot tell whether the other party is repudiating or not, the party may nevertheless have ***reasonable grounds for insecurity***. In such a situation, the party is permitted to demand ***adequate assurance*** of performance.[7] Under the UCC, the demand for adequate assurance must be in writing. After the demand, the insecure party may, if commercially reasonable, suspend any performance for which the party has not already received a return. Performance may be suspended until adequate assurance is given. Failure of the other party to provide adequate assurance within a reasonable time, not to exceed 30 days after the demand for assurance, constitutes a repudiation of the contract.

To give a simple example, assume that a contract exists for the delivery of goods in installments. The buyer is late on payments for goods that have already been delivered, and the seller is concerned about not getting paid for future shipments. In such a situation, the seller would be on solid ground in demanding adequate assurance of future payment and in suspending delivery until the buyer paid for the goods that had already been shipped and promised to pay promptly for future shipments.

In some cases, it may be difficult to tell whether a party has reasonable grounds for insecurity and whether adequate assurance has been given. The official commentary to §2-609 provides some guidance. The questions are to be answered according to commercial standards and the obligation to act in good faith is relevant. A situation that the commentary suggests might give rise to reasonable grounds for insecurity, as noted previously would be one in which the buyer falls behind on its account with the seller. Another situation would be one in which the buyer discovers that the seller has been making defective deliveries to other buyers.[8]

As to the nature of adequate assurance, the commentary suggests that the grounds for insecurity and the reputation of the other party are relevant. If a seller has delivered defective goods, this may cause the buyer to be insecure regarding future shipments. If the seller is reputable, it may be enough that the seller promises to cure defects and take care to make certain that future goods will be conforming. If the seller is not reputable, it might be appropriate for the buyer to require the posting of a bond or some other form of guarantee.[9]

When in doubt as to whether the other party has repudiated the contract, it makes sense for an aggrieved party to demand adequate assurance rather than simply cancel the contract. This is because if the aggrieved party cancels and a court

---

[5]UCC §2-610, comment 2.
[6]*Id.*
[7]UCC §2-609.
[8]UCC §2-609, comment 3.
[9]UCC §2-609, comment 4.

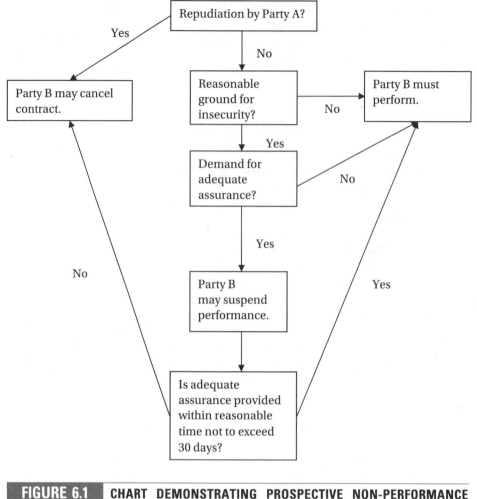

FIGURE 6.1   CHART DEMONSTRATING PROSPECTIVE NON-PERFORMANCE UNDER UCC

subsequently discovers that the aggrieved party did not have grounds to cancel, it is the aggrieved party that has repudiated instead.

(3) Repudiation and Insecurity Under the CISG

The CISG has similar provisions relating to prospective non-performance. In cases in which a party has reasonable grounds for insecurity, a party may suspend its performance and demand adequate assurance.[10] Unlike the UCC, the CISG does not provide that failure to provide adequate assurance within a certain time period constitutes a repudiation. A repudiation only occurs if it becomes clear that a party

---

[10]CISG Art. 71.

will in the future commit a ***fundamental breach***.[11] We will talk about this concept later,[12] but for now it's sufficient to say that the breach must be substantial, just as required by the UCC for a repudiation.

If enough time lapses after a demand for adequate assurance under the CISG, it may be clear that a fundamental breach will be committed, so the aggrieved party may then ***avoid*** the contract, a concept similar to cancellation under the UCC. For example, let's assume that a buyer has fallen behind in payments on an installment contract and the seller demands adequate assurance. The seller suspends delivery of goods. Several months pass, and it appears that the buyer is insolvent and has no intention of making the payments that are in arrears. The buyer has not responded to the request for assurance. At this point, the seller would likely be on firm footing in declaring the contract avoided so that the seller can sell the goods in question to another buyer.

B. Passage of Title from Seller to Buyer

The seller is required to tender conforming goods to the buyer. Remember that, unless disclaimed, the seller makes a warranty to the buyer that the seller will convey good title to the goods and that the goods will be delivered free of any security interest or other lien or encumbrance of which the buyer has no knowledge.[13] Here, we will talk about what it takes for the seller to comply with its obligation to deliver good title to the buyer.

(1) Title and the UCC

The UCC does not define "***title***," although it does talk about the passage of title. The requirement under the UCC warranty of title is that the buyer will take ownership of the goods free of any superior claims. Under UCC §2-403, a buyer obtains whatever title that the seller had; if the seller had good title, the buyer receives good title. If, on the other hand, the seller had no title, the buyer receives no title and is subject to the claims of the person who has good title.

For example, if somebody steals a diamond ring and sells that ring to a bona fide (i.e., "good faith") purchaser for value (a "bfp"), the bfp does not obtain any title whatsoever to the diamond ring. The thief had no title, and thus the buyer cannot obtain good title. The rightful owner of the diamond ring, the person from whom the ring was stolen, has a right to sue the bfp for its return. The bfp's only recourse would be to sue the thief in tort for fraud or for breach of warranty of title under the UCC.

> Rightful Owner of Goods ⟶ Thief ⟶ Bona Fide Purchaser
>
> **Bfp obtains no title.**

---

[11]CISG Art. 72.
[12]See pp. 125-127, *infra*.
[13]See pp. 52-54, *supra*.

(2) UCC Rules Regarding Voidable Title and Entrustment

The UCC has two exceptions to the rule that the buyer of goods obtains no greater rights than the seller. One is if the seller has what is called **voidable title** and the other is if the rightful owner of goods has **entrusted** them to the seller.

The UCC does not give an exclusive definition of voidable title. It gives three examples of when someone will be considered to have voidable title: (1) where the transferor of the goods was deceived regarding the identity of the purchaser, (2) where goods were sold for a check that was later dishonored (i.e., "bounced"), and (3) where delivery of goods was procured through fraud punishable as larcenous under criminal law.[14] The consistent thread of situations in which someone has voidable title is that in each case the rightful owner of goods voluntarily parted with possession of them, as compared to the situation of theft.

If someone has voidable title in goods, that person can give good title to a good faith purchaser for value.[15] So, for example, if somebody bought a diamond ring with a bad check, that person would be considered to have voidable title in the ring. This person, unlike the thief in the earlier example, could sell the ring to a bfp for value who would then have good title to the ring. The initial owner of the ring would have no right to get it back from the bfp. The initial owner's only recourse would be to sue the person who gave the bad check.

> Initial Owner ⟶ Person Buying with Bad Check ⟶ Bona Fide Purchaser for Value
>
> **Bfp gets good title, takes priority over initial owner.**

In an entrustment situation, goods are voluntarily delivered by the owner to somebody else. If a rightful owner knows that goods are in possession of somebody else and acquiesces in the possession of the goods, that is also considered an entrustment.[16] An example of an entrustment would be if the rightful owner of a diamond ring delivers it to a jeweler to have the setting repaired.

If a good is entrusted to a merchant who deals in goods of the kind involved, the merchant can convey all of the rights of the entruster to a **buyer in the ordinary course of business** ("biocob"). A biocob is defined by the UCC as a special type of good faith purchaser who buys goods from people who are in the business of selling goods of the kind involved.[17] For example, if you go into a hardware store and buy a wrench and are unaware that the sale violates the rights of anyone else, you would be a biocob. If, on the other hand, you buy a used car from a private party, you might well be a good faith purchaser for value, but you would not qualify as a biocob because the private party probably does not regularly sell cars. You can see that a biocob is thus given special protections.

So, let us assume that the rightful owner of the diamond ring brings it into a jewelry store for repair. The store repairs watches and rings, but also regularly sells them. If the jewelry store owner is unscrupulous, the person might sell the diamond ring in question to one of his or her customers. If the customer is unaware that the

---

[14]UCC §2-403(1).
[15]*Id.*
[16]UCC §2-403(3).
[17]UCC §1-201(b)(9).

sale violates the rights of the rightful owner of the ring, the customer would qualify as a biocob and would be able to defeat the rightful owner's claim to the ring. The rightful owner would only have a cause of action against the jewelry store for conversion.

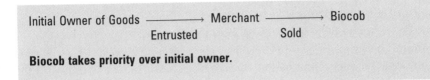

Initial Owner of Goods ⟶ Merchant ⟶ Biocob
        Entrusted   Sold

Biocob takes priority over initial owner.

(3) Title in Cases Covered by the CISG

The CISG does not have any provisions that deal with the passage of title. The CISG states that it does not deal with questions of rights in the property sold.[18] Thus, a choice of law analysis would have to be done in any international sale to determine whether a buyer of goods obtained a good title; domestic personal property and sales law would govern the question.[19] If the choice of law analysis resulted in application of the law of a UCC jurisdiction, then the analysis discussed previously would apply.

C. Performance and Breach Under the UCC

In analyzing performance and breach issues, it is important under the UCC to distinguish between contracts calling for the delivery goods in installments and contracts calling for the delivery of goods all at once. Unless the contract otherwise provides, goods are to be delivered all at once.[20] The UCC has different rules for installment contracts and non-installment contracts.

(1) Non-Installment Sales

In cases in which the goods are to be delivered all at once, the buyer's obligation to accept and pay for the goods is conditioned on the seller's tendering of goods that completely conform to the contract for sale in every way.[21] This rule is called the

> **Sidebar**
>
> **BUYERS IN THE ORDINARY COURSE OF BUSINESS**
>
> Buyers in the ordinary course of business (biocobs) are given special protections because they are useful for the economy. We want to encourage people to buy new products from stores because that leads to economic growth. People who buy goods from stores have no reason to believe that the store does not have good title to those goods. If someone buying goods from a store had to worry about having his or her title challenged, the person would not be as likely to make the purchase. On the other hand, if you buy a used good from a private party, you have reason to be suspicious regarding the private party's title to goods. It is more of a situation of *caveat emptor* ("let the buyer beware").

---

[18]CISG Art. 4.
[19]CISG Art. 7.
[20]UCC §2-307.
[21]UCC §2-601.

perfect tender rule. If the goods are delivered late or there is any breach of warranty, the buyer is entitled to *reject* the goods, that is, inform the seller that the buyer does not want them. As will be discussed shortly, the seller may have a right to *cure* defects (i.e., fix them), but until a perfect tender is made, the buyer need not accept or pay for the goods.

If the buyer wishes to reject the goods, the buyer must be able to point to a non-conformity with the contract. It is not enough that the buyer is not satisfied with the goods; there must be some breach of the contract of sale. If goods were sold without any warranties and do not work, the buyer does not have a right to reject because the buyer assumed all of the risk of performance with regard to the goods.

Q: Can I take my car back to the seller if I have a change of heart or just don't like it?

A: On more than one occasion, I have had a friend or colleague ask me if they could return goods just because they had a change of heart about the product (normally a car) or just didn't like it. Some sellers will have policies permitting returns of goods, no questions asked. Also, some states may have laws outside of the UCC that permit a "cooling off period" for certain types of transactions, permitting rescission within a specified period of time. Unless the seller has such a policy or the state has such a law, a buyer does not have a legal right to return a product that the buyer simply doesn't like, unless the buyer can point to a breach of warranty of some kind.

There is an issue as to what is meant by "conformity" of the goods. The commentary to UCC §2-106 notes that frequently course of dealing and usage of trade will permit leeway in performance. For example, it might be understood in the trade that a delivery of beans will contain some rocks or other foreign matter. It may also be the case that some industrial machines will be considered acceptable even if there are minor problems with them. So, a "perfect" tender does not necessarily mean that the goods must be perfect in every way!

(a) Acceptance and Rejection of Goods

When the buyer receives the goods, the buyer has a reasonable opportunity to inspect the goods before being obligated to accept the goods or pay for them.[22] This right may be waived by the contract, for example, in a situation in which the buyer is to pay against the delivery of documents of title which will arrive before the goods arrive.[23] Even in such a situation, however, the buyer may have a right to inspect the goods before technically accepting them.[24]

---

[22]UCC §2-513(1).
[23]UCC §2-513(3).
[24]UCC §2-606.

Simply taking physical possession of goods does not mean that the buyer has technically "*accepted*" them. With regard to some goods, it may be necessary for the buyer to use the goods for a brief time as part of the inspection process. If the buyer does not wish to accept non-conforming goods, the buyer must reject them within a reasonable time after tender of delivery by notifying the seller.[25] Failure to reject goods within a reasonable time after inspection will result in a technical acceptance, triggering the buyer's obligation to pay for the goods.[26]

If a buyer wishes to reject goods, the buyer is required to hold the goods with reasonable care to permit the seller to take them back.[27] If the buyer is a merchant and the seller has no agent or place of business where the goods have been rejected, the buyer is required to follow reasonable instructions of the seller regarding disposal of the goods, and if no instructions are forthcoming, must make reasonable efforts to sell the goods if they are perishable or threaten to decline in value speedily.[28] The buyer is entitled to be reimbursed for any expenses incurred in dealing with the goods and is given a *security interest*, or lien, on the goods to cover such expenses and any payments of the purchase price that have been made.[29]

F   A   Q

Q: Is "acceptance" of goods the same thing as "acceptance" of an offer?

A: Acceptance of goods and acceptance of an offer are generally two different concepts. Acceptance of an offer means that a contract has been formed, whereas acceptance of goods triggers the obligation of the buyer to pay for goods under a contract that already exists. It is true that sometimes acceptance of goods shows assent to an offer by the seller to sell goods to the buyer — acceptance of an offer can sometimes be by performance. But, it is also possible that the buyer will have "accepted" an offer by the seller to sell goods, thus forming a contract, and will subsequently have to decide whether to "accept" the goods that have been shipped. If the goods are rightfully rejected by the buyer, there is still a contract between the seller and buyer that has been breached by the seller's shipment of non-conforming goods.

If the buyer wishes to reject the goods, the buyer is required to state any particular defect that is ascertainable by reasonable inspection if the seller could have cured the defect or if both parties are merchants and the seller has made a request in writing for a full statement of all defects on which the buyer is relying. Failure of the buyer to state such defects precludes the buyer from relying on them to establish breach.[30]

---

[25]UCC §2-602.
[26]UCC §2-606.
[27]UCC §2-602(2)(b).
[28]UCC §2-603.
[29]UCC §2-711(3).
[30]UCC §2-605.

Duties of all buyers with regard to rejected goods, or goods with respect to which acceptance is revoked:

(1) Give seasonable notice of rejection within reasonable time.
(2) Take reasonable care of the goods.
(3) State in connection with the rejection any defect which is ascertainable by reasonable inspection if the seller could have cured the problem.

Additional duties of merchant buyers:

(1) If seller does not have an agent or place of business in market of rejection, follow reasonable instructions of seller. If no instructions received, make reasonable efforts to sell them for seller's account if goods are perishable or threaten to decline speedily in value.
(2) If seller is also a merchant, state all defects ascertainable by reasonable inspection if seller makes request for such a statement in writing.

If goods are rejected, the buyer may be required to permit the seller to cure the defect under two circumstances. The first is if the goods were delivered before the time for performance.[31] In such a case, the seller may seasonably notify the buyer of an intention to make a cure and then make a conforming tender within the time permitted under the contract. The second situation for cure exists when the seller had reasonable grounds to believe that the defective goods would be acceptable with or without a money allowance.[32] In that situation, the seller may cure by making a conforming tender within a reasonable time if the seller seasonably notifies the buyer.

(b) Revocation of Acceptance

If goods are accepted, it may subsequently become possible for the buyer to revoke acceptance of goods if a defect arises that *substantially impairs the value* of the goods to the buyer.[33] Note that this is a subjective test — the particular needs of the buyer are taken into account. The defect must have been difficult to discover before acceptance or else the seller must have given the buyer assurances that the defect would be cured and it was not cured. Perhaps the most frequent situation in which revocation occurs is after the seller has made numerous attempts to fix a problem and eventually the buyer throws up her or his hands and asks for her or his money back.

The version of Article 2 that is currently the law does not indicate that the seller has a right to cure after revocation of acceptance, only after a rejection. In many cases of revocation, the defect is very severe or the seller will have made many unsuccessful attempts to fix the goods. In such cases, it would not make sense to give a seller a right to cure. There may be some cases, however, in which a severe problem suddenly arises that substantially impairs the value of the good to the buyer, but the problem could be easily fixed. UCC §2-608(3) indicates that a buyer has the same duties with

---

[31]UCC §2-508(1).
[32]UCC §2-508(2).
[33]UCC §2-608.

regard to goods in revocation cases as in rejection cases, which could be taken to permit cure. The 2003 amendments to the UCC permit cure in cases in which the reason for revocation unexpectedly appears if the cure can be accomplished without undue hardship to the buyer. This right to cure does not exist, however, in consumer contracts.[34]

(c) Example of *Zabriskie Chevrolet*

To demonstrate how these rules work, it is useful to consider a famous case that is discussed or reproduced in many sales and contracts casebooks, *Zabriskie Chevrolet, Inc. v. Smith*.[35] The case involved a contract for the sale of a car. After delivery, the buyer's wife attempted to drive the car home from the dealership. After having driven 7/10 of a mile, the car stalled at a traffic light. The car stalled again within another 15 feet and thereafter stalled every time it was required to stop. Before reaching her destination, the buyer's wife was sufficiently distressed to call her husband, who then completed the 2½ mile journey by driving the car in its lowest gear.

Very upset with this turn of events, the buyer placed a stop payment on the check he had issued to the dealership and told the dealership that he was canceling the sale. The seller then had the car towed back to the dealership, where it was determined that the transmission was defective. The dealer took a transmission out of another car on its lot and used it to replace the defective transmission in the car plaintiff had purchased. The dealer then told the buyer what it had done and tendered delivery of the repaired car. The buyer refused to take it, asserting that the contract was canceled.

The seller sued the buyer for refusing to take the repaired car. One argument made by the seller was that the buyer had technically accepted the car by driving it away from the dealership. Acceptance of the car would then require the buyer to pay the price. The court held that the car had not been accepted because use of the car was within the buyer's reasonable opportunity to inspect the goods. The amount of time that a buyer has to inspect goods before acceptance depends on the complexity of the goods involved. A car is a complex good, so some driving needs to be done to make sure that the car is as promised. Driving the car 2½ miles was not excessive under these circumstances, and the buyer immediately notified the seller of rejection once the problems were discovered. So, the buyer had not "accepted" the goods and had properly rejected them.

The seller also argued that it had a right to cure the defect and that it had done so by replacing the transmission. An effective cure requires the seller to make a con-forming tender. Minor repairs may be permitted, but in this case the court held that replacing a factory-installed transmission with one taken from another car did not give the buyer what he had bargained for. The court also talked about how the purchase of a car was a major investment and that buyers had a right to the "peace of mind that flows from its dependability and safety." Because the buyer's faith in this car had been shaken, it appears that at a minimum the seller was required to tender a new car in substitution with a factory-installed transmission that worked. The court's discussion of the buyer's shaken faith has been referred to as the ***shaken faith doctrine***. Essentially, it stands for the proposition that in cases involving

---

[34]Amended UCC §2-508.
[35]99 N.J. Super. 441, 240 A.2d 195 (1968).

significant purchases with major defects, the seller is required to at least replace the goods and may not repair them. It could be taken as far as not permitting any cure in some cases (i.e., would the buyer ever feel safe in a car of the same type?).

Even if it were determined that the buyer had accepted the car in *Zabriskie Chevrolet* by driving it away from the dealership, the court held in the alternative that revocation of acceptance would be possible. There was no question that the car was defective; it had been represented as a "brand new car that would operate perfectly." There was also no question but that the defective transmission substantially impaired the value of the car to the buyer, and that the defect could not have been reasonably discovered before acceptance.

If the buyer's actions in *Zabriskie Chevrolet* were characterized as a revocation of acceptance, arguably the seller does not even have a right to cure because UCC §2-508 only speaks of that right after rejection of goods. Although the buyer has the same duties with regard to goods after revocation as he or she does after acceptance, that does not necessarily extend to permitting the seller an opportunity to cure. As previously noted, the 2003 amendments to Article 2 would permit cure in some cases of revocation, but not in cases involving consumer contracts.

(d) Use of Goods After Rejection or Revocation of Acceptance

One issue that has arisen in the courts is whether a buyer is allowed to use goods after a rejection or revocation of acceptance. It would seem that such use would violate the requirement that a buyer hold goods with reasonable care after rejection or revocation of acceptance. The UCC also provides that any act by the buyer inconsistent with the seller's ownership of goods constitutes an acceptance.[36]

Despite the statutory language that seems to forbid post rejection or revocation of acceptance use, some courts have permitted reasonable use of goods after rejection or revocation. Whether use is reasonable depends on the buyer's need for the goods and the conduct of the seller in responding to the buyer's legitimate complaints. In one case, a car had numerous defects, which the seller, after making some attempts at repair, ultimately refused to try to fix.[37] The seller also refused the buyer's demand for her money back. Because the buyer needed the car to drive to work, she drove it about 23,000 miles in the 1½ years between the time she attempted to revoke her acceptance and the time of trial. The court nevertheless permitted her to revoke her acceptance, holding that because she had a *security interest* in the car under UCC §2-711(3), she had a right to reasonably use it. She was put in a difficult spot by the seller's intransigence; it would be difficult for her to simply store the car and buy or rent another one during the time pending trial. Her use was reasonable under the circumstances. Any benefit that she derived in driving the car during this period could be offset against her recovery if the seller had attempted to prove any such benefit. The 2003 amendments to Article 2 would expressly permit reasonable use following rejection or revocation of acceptance.[38]

---

[36]UCC §2-606(1)(c).
[37]*McCullough v. Bill Swad Chrysler-Plymouth, Inc.*, 5 Ohio St. 3d 181, 449 N.E.2d 1289 (1983).
[38]Amended UCC §2-608(4).

F	A	Q

Q: Does the security interest given the buyer under UCC §2-711(3) justify use of the goods following a rejection or revocation of acceptance?

A: As previously noted, the UCC gives the buyer a security interest, or lien, on the goods to give the buyer protection for the money the buyer has paid to the seller and also to cover other expenses incurred in taking care of the goods after rejection or revocation of acceptance. If the seller does not reimburse the buyer, the buyer can sell the goods to satisfy the lien. That does not seem to include, however, any right to use the goods. Section 2-711(3) does not sanction use. Use of the goods causes them to depreciate, thus negatively affecting the seller's rights in them. It seems a bit of a stretch to say that the security interest permits use of the goods.

One other thing worth remembering is that just because we say that a buyer cannot reject or revoke acceptance of goods does not mean that the buyer has no remedy. Although acceptance of goods triggers the obligation to pay the price for the goods, the buyer might still be able to sue for damages for breach of warranty. We will discuss that remedy in the next chapter.

The next figure demonstrates the analysis one should go through in determining what options a buyer has when a seller delivers non-conforming goods. We start with a tender of non-conforming goods — there must be some kind of breach of the sales contract before the buyer can reject the tender. The buyer may reject or accept the goods.

Assume the buyer accepts the goods, which can occur if the buyer keeps the goods without objection outside the reasonable time the buyer has to accept. If a serious problem subsequently is discovered or if the seller fails in attempts to cure a defect, the buyer may be able to revoke acceptance of the goods. As noted previously, there is a question as to whether a seller ever has a right to cure after a revocation of acceptance. If it is determined that the seller does have such a right, and is able to make a cure, then the goods will conform to the contract and the buyer must accept them. If the seller either does not have a right to cure or is unable to cure, the buyer has rights under UCC §2-711, which includes a right to refund of the purchase price. We will discuss buyer's remedies in more detail in the next chapter.

Assuming the buyer rejects the goods, the question is whether the seller has a right to cure and is able to do so. If not, the buyer has remedies under UCC §2-711, which include *cancellation* of the contract, that is, calling the contract at an end because of breach. If yes, the buyer must accept the goods that now conform to the contract, although the seller may be liable for any damages caused by any delay in providing conforming goods.

The concept of "cancellation" under the UCC should be compared to *termination*. "Termination" occurs when a party ends a contract for reasons other than breach. For example, the contract may provide that the buyer may terminate a requirements contract on 30 days notice. The contract would then be terminated. Any right that the buyer might have with respect to defective prior deliveries and any obligation on the part of the buyer to pay the purchase price for goods delivered would be preserved, but all future obligations would be discharged. "Cancellation"

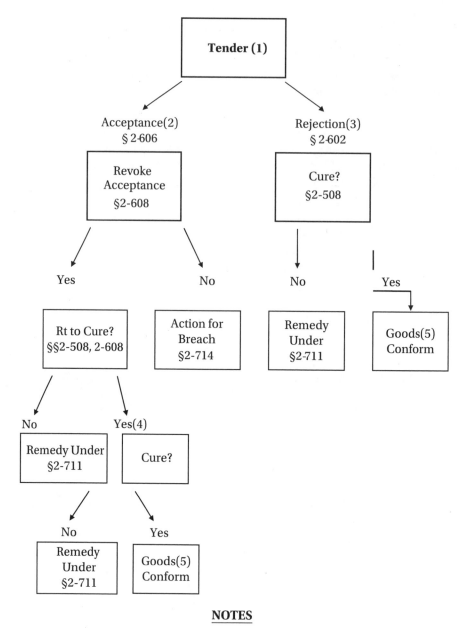

NOTES

(1) Before this chart has any effect, the seller must have tendered delivery of goods that do not conform to the contract, e.g., late shipment or breach of warranty.

(2) Possession does not necessarily equal "acceptance" of goods. The buyer has a reasonable opportunity to inspect. §2-606.

(3) After rejection, the buyer must comply with §§2-602-2-605, or the rejection may be considered ineffective and an "acceptance" will be deemed to have occurred.

(4) There is some question under existing Article 2 about whether a seller may cure after revocation.

(5) Even if the goods conform and are ultimately accepted after cure, the seller may still be liable for incidental or consequential damages due to delay. §§2-714, 2-715.

FIGURE 6.2   NON-CONFORMING GOODS — NON-INSTALLMENT SALES

occurs when either party ends the contract because of breach by the other. For example, if goods are defective and the seller does not cure the defect, the buyer may cancel. The canceling party retains any remedy for breach with respect to performance that has been rendered and also with respect to any future performance (e.g., if the seller was supposed to deliver goods in the future as in an installment contract, which we will next discuss).[39]

(2) Installment Sales

An *installment sales contract* under UCC §2-612 is one that either requires or authorizes the seller to deliver goods on more than one occasion. For example, if a buyer contracts to purchase 1,000 bushels per month of wheat to be delivered each month for six months, that would be an installment contract. If a contract is an installment sales contract and one of the installments does not conform to the contract, there is a question as to whether the buyer can reject the installment or else cancel the entire contract. Section 2-612 also addresses the question of whether a seller can cancel an installment contract if the buyer defaults on payments due.

(a) Rejection of Installments

In terms of the question of rejection of the installment, there is no perfect tender rule for installment contracts. Instead, the Code says that the buyer may reject an installment only if the non-conformity results in a substantial impairment in value that cannot be cured. Minor defects are not enough. The Code does not define "substantial impairment" in value, but commentators suggest that it is akin to the concept of "*material breach*" in contract law.[40]

Courts will more likely find a material breach if (1) the injured party has been significantly deprived of its reasonably expected benefit under the contract, (2) it is difficult to make the injured party whole through an award of damages, (3) the injured party will not suffer a significant forfeiture if the contract is canceled, (4) it is not likely that the breaching party will be able or willing to cure the breach, and (5) the party failing to perform is not acting in good faith.[41] Not all of these factors are required to find a material breach. If there is a sufficient deprivation of benefit to the injured party, a material breach may be found even if the breaching party is acting in good faith.

An example of a non-sales case in which a court applied the previously described material breach factors but found that there was no material breach is *Walker & Co. v. Harrison*.[42] In that case, plaintiffs had built and leased a sign to defendants for 36 months. As part of the lease, the plaintiff agreed to maintain the sign. Shortly after the sign was installed, it was hit by a tomato and some other maintenance issues were noted. When plaintiff did not respond to repeated requests by defendant that it come out and maintain the sign, defendant canceled the contract. After noting the *Restatement* material breach factors, the court held that plaintiff's failure to maintain the sign was not material and did not justify cancellation. One can see that if defendant were permitted to cancel the contract, the plaintiff would have

---

[39]See UCC §2-106.
[40]White & Summers, Uniform Commercial Code §8-3 (4th ed.).
[41]See *Restatement (Second) of Contracts* §241.
[42]347 Mich. 630, 81 N.W.2d 352 (1957).

suffered a forfeiture, as there were still about 32 months left on the contract and it does not appear that the defendant was substantially harmed by breach. The facts indicate that the plaintiff came out and cleaned the sign after defendant attempted to cancel.

Analogizing to an installment sales contract, if defects in goods are minor and the seller is willing to make a cure, the buyer will not be permitted to cancel the contract. The court must weigh the harm caused by the forfeiture that will be caused to the seller if the buyer is allowed to reject the installment or cancel the entire contract.

It is important to note that unlike the test for substantial impairment for revocation of acceptance, the test for substantial impairment in installment contracts cases is an objective one. The focus is on whether the seller had reason to know that the defect in question would cause a major problem for the buyer.[43] If the buyer has a particular concern regarding the goods in question, that concern needs to be communicated to the seller. In fact, the parties in their contract may define what would constitute a substantial impairment in value as long as there is some basis in reason for the definition.[44] For example, a contract could provide that potatoes being sold to a potato chip manufacturer need to be of a certain specific size and color to be acceptable.[45] Even then, the seller needs to be given the opportunity to cure, unless time is of the essence for deliveries. If timeliness of delivery is an important factor, it should be spelled out in the contract.

(b) Cancellation of the Entire Contract

If a non-conformity in an installment is sufficiently severe as to justify rejection, the next question is whether it substantially impairs the value of the entire contract. If so, the buyer may cancel the contract and is not obligated to take future shipments. In determining whether there has been a substantial impairment in the value of the entire contract, the cumulative effects of non-conforming shipments are to be considered. It may be, for example, that after four or five defective shipments, the costs and bother of dealing the defective shipments becomes sufficiently high that the buyer is justified in saying "no more." Keep in mind, however, that there is a concern for the impact of any cancellation on the seller; cancellation of a long-term supply contract may result in extreme forfeiture. The problem or cumulative effect of problems will have to be pretty severe before the buyer is allowed to cancel. In some cases, it may be better for the buyer to demand adequate assurance before taking any drastic measures.

F   A   Q

Q: Why is it more difficult for a party to get out of an installment contract than a non-installment contract?

A: The drafters of the UCC make it more difficult for a party to get out of an installment contract because of the danger of forfeiture. If a buyer is allowed to cancel, the seller will be out whatever money it has spent in preparing to supply

---

[43]UCC §2-612, comment 4.
[44]*Id.*
[45]*Hubbard v. UTZ Quality Food, Inc.*, 903 F. Supp. 444 (W.D.N.Y. 1995).

goods to the buyer over the time period of the installment contract. If a seller is allowed to cancel, the buyer may have made expenditures in reliance on having a steady supply of goods at the price indicated in the installment contract. In non-installment sales, the reliance of the parties on such contracts is not as great, so cancellation does not pose as much of a hardship on the breaching party.

UCC §2-612(3) also permits a seller to cancel an installment contract if the buyer's breach in not paying for or taking delivery of goods substantially impairs the value of the contract to the seller. The commentary to that section makes clear, however, that if the only concern is that the buyer won't pay in the future, the appropriate course of action is to demand adequate assurance. So, the failure to pay on the part of the buyer must be causing the seller some problem that is difficult to quantify in terms of damages, something in addition to the price of the goods themselves.

(c) Example of *Cherwell-Ralli, Inc. v. Rytman Grain Co., Inc.*

An example of a case in which a seller was allowed to cancel a contract for non-payment is *Cherwell-Ralli, Inc. v. Rytman Grain Co., Inc.*[46] The contract called for installment shipments of two certain types of meal. The buyer was almost immediately behind in its payments, with the arrearages sometimes being substantial. The buyer was supposedly concerned that the seller would not be able to perform under the contract because the market price of the goods had come to significantly exceed the contract price. In a conversation between the presidents of the buyer and seller, the buyer was assured that deliveries would continue as long as the buyer made payment. The buyer then sent a check to the seller for $9825.60 that was to pay for shipments through the preceding month.

Several days later, the buyer placed a stop payment on the check when it heard from one of the truck drivers (not an employee of the seller) that the delivery would be his last. After this, the buyer made no further payments and the seller made no further deliveries. The seller was forced to close its plant shortly thereafter because of stockpiling of excess material. The seller then sued the buyer for payments owed on goods that had been shipped.

The court held that the question of substantial impairment in value is one of fact, and that the record amply supported the lower court's finding that the buyer's refusal to pay constituted substantial impairment, justifying the seller's cancellation of the contract. It was not necessary for the seller first to demand adequate assurance, and the buyer had no right to suspend payment for goods that it had already received.

If one were to look at the material breach factors listed above and apply them to the *Cherwell-Ralli* case, one might think that cancellation by the seller was inappropriate because the seller could always sue for damages for the payments that had not been made. With regard to future shipments, the seller could suspend performance until adequate assurance was given by the buyer, which would reasonably require that payment be made in full for shipments already made. As the seller had to close its

---

[46]180 Conn. 714, 433 A.2d 984 (1980).

plant because of buyer's refusal to pay, it seems that this contract was one that was very important and that the buyer's conduct thus substantially impaired the value of the contract to the seller. Also, it appears that the buyer's conduct was not in good faith.

It should be noted that if a breach of an installment contract by one of the parties is not substantial, that does not mean that the injured party is without remedy. The injured party may be required to continue to perform under the contract, but can still hold the breaching party liable for any damages that are suffered. We will discuss damage remedies further in the next two chapters.

(3) Seller's Ability to Limit Buyer's Right to Reject or Revoke and to Recover Consequential Damages

The UCC permits parties to the contract to alter remedies available in the event of breach. The commentary to the Code suggests, however, that there must be at least "a fair quantum of remedy for breach of the obligations or duties outlined in the contract."[47] The commentary suggests that further limitations on remedies might be considered unconscionable. It is common in sales contracts, however, for sellers to limit the buyer's ability to reject or revoke acceptance of goods. It is also common for the seller to limit the buyer's ability to recover *consequential damages*.

The CISG appears to have no limit on the ability of the parties to agree that the buyer's remedies are limited. It should be kept in mind, however, that the CISG does not deal with the validity of contractual terms,[48] so in some cases, an extremely limited remedy may be found to be unconscionable under relevant domestic law and thus unenforceable.

In addition, under the CISG we have discussed how the statement of a party to a contract is to be interpreted according to the reasonable understanding of the other party, unless the intent of the party making the statement was known to the other party (or the other party could not have been unaware of that intent).[49] If a seller states that a buyer's remedy is limited to repair or replacement, would a reasonable buyer believe that the seller has unlimited attempts to make repairs before the buyer can obtain its money back? Perhaps not. The reasonable buyer might think that if the seller could not repair within a reasonable time period, that the buyer could get its money back or a replacement product.[50]

(a) Limits on Rights to Reject or Revoke

The apparent harshness of the perfect tender rule and the uncertainty about what constitutes a substantial impairment in value may cause the parties to define more carefully when a buyer may reject or revoke acceptance of goods. A contractual provision may state that the buyer's sole remedy is to permit repair or replacement of the goods. Such a provision in a contract, if enforceable, effectively means that the buyer cannot reject or revoke acceptance.

The UCC expressly countenances such a limitation, as long as the *limited remedy* does not fail of its essential purpose.[51] If it does fail of its essential purpose,

---

[47]UCC §2-719, comment 1.
[48]CISG Art. 4.
[49]CISG Art. 8.
[50]See John O. Honnold, *Uniform Law for International Sales* §§233-234 (2d ed. 1991).
[51]UCC §2-719.

the buyer is entitled to all of its remedies under the UCC, which would include the ability to reject (if the goods have not already been accepted) or revoke acceptance of goods.

This begs the question of what is meant by *"failure of its essential purpose."* What is the purpose of the limited remedy? From the seller's perspective, the purpose is to limit the seller's exposure. All that the seller is required to do is to repair the goods or perhaps replace them. From the buyer's perspective, however, the purpose is to have goods that conform to the sales contract. If the seller can repair the goods fairly expeditiously, then the buyer will get what the buyer bargained for. If the seller is unable to repair the goods after many attempts, then the buyer does not get what it bargained for, and arguably the limited remedy has failed.

Courts seem generally willing to uphold the seller's right to repair or replace under a limited remedy. Factors that a court will examine to determine if a limited remedy has failed will be the number of attempts at repair, the ability and willingness of the seller to make a repair, the experimental or complex nature of the good, and whether the transaction involves consumers or businesses. If a good is experimental or complex, the buyer should reasonably understand that it may be necessary for the seller to make more than a few attempts at repair. A commercial buyer can probably be expected to put up with repairs more than a consumer.[52]

Does a limited remedy of repair or replace fail of its essential purpose?

Factors to Consider:

(1) Number of attempts at repair
(2) Ultimate success of attempts to repair
(3) Willingness of seller to attempt repair.
(4) Is buyer a consumer or less sophisticated than the seller?
(5) Is the good experimental or complex, such that attempts at repair are to be expected?

An example of a situation in which a court found that a limited remedy failed of its essential purpose is *Chatlos Systems v. National Cash Register Corp.*[53] Technically the case involved a lease of goods, but the court treated it like a sale under Article 2 because Article 2A governing leases did not exist at that time. In that case, the lessor of a computer system promised that the system would perform six bookkeeping functions for the lessee. Eighteen months after the system was to be up and running, only one of the six functions was operating properly. This was the case despite the lessor's many good faith efforts to make the system work.

Despite the commercial nature of the transaction, the court ultimately determined that the contract's limited remedy failed of its purpose, and thus the lessee was allowed to sue for damages. The extended period of repair and the fact that the lessor ultimately appeared unable to make the goods come close to conforming to the contract guided the court in making its decision.

---

[52]These factors are discussed in *Riegel Power Corp. v. Voith Hydro*, 888 F.2d 1043 (4th Cir. 1989).
[53]635 F.22d 1081 (3d Cir. 1980).

It should be noted that in this area, state "lemon laws" may also limit the ability of a seller to rely on "repair or replace" limited remedies in consumer goods transactions. For example, in California, the state lemon law requires a manufacturer to replace the goods or refund the price if it is unable to repair goods to conform to applicable express warranties after a reasonable number of attempts.[54] For automobiles, the law presumes that a reasonable number of attempts have been made if, among other things, the same non-conformity has been subject to repair four or more times within 18 months from delivery to the buyer or 18,000 miles, whichever occurs first.[55] For automobiles, the buyer is also given the option of obtaining restitution rather than replacement.[56]

(b) Limits on Buyer's Rights to Recover Consequential Damages

UCC §2-719(3) expressly states that consequential damages may be limited or excluded unless the limitation is unconscionable. We will talk more about the ability of buyers to recover consequential damages in the next chapter. Consequential damages for breach of a sales contract would include such things as damages from personal injury if the goods caused such injury or lost profits if defects in the goods caused the buyer to lose business. For example, if a bakery purchased an oven that did not work and that caused it to lose sales, such a loss would be consequential damages. Also, if an airplane crashes because of a defective bolt, all of the damages resulting from the accident would be consequential damages.

Section 2-719(3) indicates that limitations on consequential damages are prima facie unconscionable in the case of personal injury in consumer goods cases. Such a limitation is not prima facie unconscionable if the loss is commercial. Although the Code and commentary do not speak to the issue, one would assume that focus should be on the bargaining process in terms of determining if the limitation on consequential damages should be viewed as unconscionable — did the buyer have a reasonable choice in entering into the contract, or was it on a "take it or leave it" basis?

Another issue in this area is whether a consequential damages limitation fails if an accompanying limited remedy of repair or replacement fails of its essential purpose. Some courts hold that a consequential damages limitation should be considered separately from the failure of a limited remedy — the Code drafters provided a separate section dealing with the enforceability of consequential damages limitations. Other courts focus on the language in §2-719(2) indicating that when a limited remedy fails, remedies under the UCC are available, and that includes consequential damages. It seems that courts are much more likely to uphold a consequential damage limitation when a limited remedy of repair or

> **Sidebar**
>
> **LIMITS ON CONSEQUENTIAL DAMAGES**
>
> Sellers wish to limit their liability for consequential damages because such damages may greatly exceed the purchase price the buyer pays for the goods. Such damages are also unpredictable, although as we will see, the Code only permits recovery of damages that are foreseeable. Some juries can foresee more damages than others, especially with the advantage of hindsight. It is said, "in California, on a clear day you can foresee forever!"

---

[54]Cal. Civ. Code §1793.2.
[55]Cal. Civ. Code §1793.22(b).
[56]Cal. Civ. Code §1793.2(d)(2).

replacement fails if (1) the transaction is a commercial transaction and (2) the seller has acted in good faith in trying to cure the problem. For example, in the *Chatlos* case discussed previously, the court was willing to uphold the consequential damage limitation even though the limited remedy was found to have failed of its essential purpose. The parties in that case had bargained at arm's length and the lessor had made a good faith effort to make the computer system conform to the contract. So, although the lessee could sue for damages relating to the loss in value of the defective computer system, consequential damages incurred in hiring additional employees were not available.

D. Performance and Breach Under the CISG

Under the CISG, when the seller makes delivery of goods that do not conform to the contract, the buyer is required to inspect them within a short period of time and give notice specifying any non-conformity within a reasonable period of time after discovery or when the buyer ought to have discovered the problem.[57] Failure to do this will deprive the buyer of a right to rely on the non-conformity in holding the seller responsible for breach, unless the seller knew or could not have been unaware of the problem or the buyer has some reasonable excuse for failing to give notice (such as failure of communications systems).[58] Similar to the UCC, the seller has a right to cure non-conformities unless the breach is so severe as to amount to a ***fundamental breach*** permitting the buyer to ***avoid*** the contract (more about this very shortly).[59]

The biggest difference between the UCC and the CISG in this area is that there is no perfect tender rule under the CISG. A buyer or a seller is able to cancel a contract (*avoid* the contract under CISG terminology) only if the breaching party has committed a fundamental breach or has failed to perform within a reasonable additional period of time for performance set by the injured party, called a ***nachfrist*** notice.[60]

(1) The Definition of "Fundamental Breach"

What is meant by fundamental breach? It is defined in CISG Article 25, and requires substantial deprivation of what the injured party was entitled to expect under the contract. In addition, the substantial deprivation resulting from the breach must have been reasonably foreseeable to the breaching party. The U.N. Secretariat Commentary to the predecessor section to Article 25 elaborates somewhat by stating that the monetary value of the contract, the monetary value of the harm caused by the breach, and the interference with the activities of the injured party are all relevant factors. As to whether the results of the breach must be foreseeable at the time of contracting or at the time of breach, the Commentary suggests that it is up to the tribunal deciding the case to decide based on the facts of the given case.

---

[57] CISG Arts. 38 & 39. See also CISG Article 43.
[58] CISG Arts. 39, 40, 43 & 44.
[59] CISG Art. 48.
[60] CISG Arts. 49 & 64.

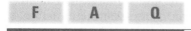

Q: Why is there no "perfect tender rule" under the CISG?

A: The CISG covers commercial contracts, not consumer contracts. A commercial buyer is in a better position than a consumer buyer to accept defective goods and then seek a remedy from the seller, for example by hiring a lawyer to file a lawsuit. Also, if a buyer were allowed to reject goods or cancel a contract for a minor reason, the seller would be put in a difficult spot if the goods were in a foreign country. It might be very costly to have the goods transported back home or difficult to resell them abroad. There is less chance of forfeiture in minor breach cases if the parties are still required to perform under the contract with the breaching party paying damages for breach or making repairs to the goods.

Cases and commentators focus on a number of factors in determining whether there has been a fundamental breach. One question would be whether the parties in the contract have defined what is fundamental. For example, have they agreed that the designated time of delivery is an essential condition to the buyer's obligation to accept and pay for the goods (often called "time is of the essence")? Have they agreed that the goods must be suitable for a particular purpose to be considered acceptable? Other factors include willingness of the breaching party to perform, ability of the breaching party to cure and adequacy of damages.[61] As you can see, these factors are similar to those considered in determining material breach or substantial impairment in value.

(2) The Example of *Delchi Carrier SpA v. Rotorex*

An example of a case in which a court found a breach to be fundamental is *Delchi Carrier SpA v. Rotorex Corp.*[62] In that case, Rotorex was required to deliver compressors to Delchi, which Delchi would then use in manufacturing air conditioning units. Over 90% of the compressors delivered were defective. After Rotorex made a couple of unsuccessful attempts to make them conform, Delchi demanded substitute compressors and Rotorex refused. Delchi then avoided the contract and sued for damages. The court noted that the breach was fundamental, permitting avoidance of the contract. Although there is not much reasoning on this issue, it is worth noting that there was a need for the seller to act promptly in providing conforming compressors because air conditioners are seasonal items; delays in providing conforming goods would result in delay in manufacturing and lost sales. Also, the seller was refusing to cure, and a very high percentage of the compressors were non-conforming.

An example of a case in which a breach was found <u>not</u> to be fundamental involved a contract for the sale of shoes from a manufacturer to a retailer. In that

---

[61]For a very good discussion of the factors taken into account in determining if a breach is fundamental, see Robert Koch, *The Concept of Fundamental Breach of Contract Under the United Nations Convention on Contracts for the International Sale of Goods*, in Pace, ed., *Review of the Convention on Contracts for the International Sale of Goods* 177-354 (1998). This discussion can be found online at http://www.cisg. law.pace.edu/cisg/biblio/koch.html.
[62]71 F.3d 1024 (2d Cir. 1995).

case, which was decided in Germany, deliveries were several months late, but the court held that because it had not been made clear to the seller that time was of the essence and because the buyer did not have an immediate need for the shoes, the breach was not fundamental and the buyer could not avoid the contract.[63] The buyer would be entitled to any damages that could be shown for breach.

(3) The Foreseeability Requirement for Fundamental Breach

On the foreseeability question, it can be argued that foreseeability should be determined at the time of contracting because it is at that time that the party decides to undertake the risks of performing. If the party is aware that a late delivery by one day will have catastrophic results for which that party will be liable, the party may decide not to enter into the contract. On the other hand, if the party subsequently becomes aware of the other party's special needs and it is not difficult for the party to perform exactly according to the contract, perhaps notions of good faith require exact performance on pain of finding fundamental breach in the event that such performance is not forthcoming. So this may explain why a "one size fits all" rule does not exist.[64]

> Factors in determining if breach is fundamental under CISG:
>
> (1) *Substantial deprivation* of what injured party was entitled to expect and
> (2) Substantial deprivation must have been *foreseeable* to breaching party.
>
> Factors in determining substantial deprivation: monetary value of contract, monetary value of harm, extent of disruption of injured party's activities, does contract define what is important (e.g., by saying "time is of the essence").
>
> Foreseeability: Is substantial deprivation reasonably foreseeable at time of contract? Is substantial deprivation reasonably foreseeable at time of performance and is it easy for breaching party to perform?

(4) The Concept of *Nachfrist*, or Extension, Notices

Another concept in the CISG that is different from the UCC is the concept of the *nachfrist*, or extension, notice. Either the seller or the buyer may give the other party a reasonable period of additional time to perform after a breach.[65] If performance is still not forthcoming after that time, then the contract may be avoided. Of course, there is a question as to what constitutes a reasonable period of time, and the question of what is reasonable probably is related to the concept of fundamental breach.

---

[63] Oberlandesgericht Dusseldorf 24 April, 1997, CLOUT abstract no. 275, http://cisgw3.law.pace.edu/cases/970424g1.html.
[64] These factors are discussed in the Koch paper cited previously; see note 61, *supra*.
[65] CISG Arts. 47 & 63.

To give an example of how a *nachfrist* notice would work, assume that a buyer was supposed to establish a letter of credit that would assure the seller that it would be paid once the goods were shipped. The letter of credit was supposed to be established within three weeks after the contract was signed. The buyer, because of financial difficulties, is unable to establish the letter of credit within the contract period. The goods are supposed to be shipped within a month. The seller might give the buyer an additional three weeks to establish the letter of credit, saying that unless the buyer is able to do so, the contract will be avoided. If it is determined that this was a reasonable period of extension, then the seller would be allowed to avoid the contract if the buyer cannot establish the letter of credit within the extension period.

If an injured party wishes to avoid the contract, the injured party must give notice of avoidance to the breaching party.[66] If the reason for avoidance is late delivery, the buyer must give notice of avoidance within a reasonable time after the buyer has become aware that delivery has been made.[67] With respect to any other breach, the buyer must give notice within a reasonable time after the buyer knew or should have known of the breach, or within a reasonable time after the expiration of any *nachfrist* period.[68] For sellers, if the reason for avoidance is late performance by the buyer, the seller must give notice before the seller has become aware that performance has been rendered.[69] In cases of other breaches by the buyer, the seller must give notice within a reasonable time after the seller knew or should have known of the breach or within a reasonable time after the expiration of any *nachfrist* period.[70]

It is important to note that even if a breach is not so substantial as to be fundamental, the injured party still had a right to damages or other remedies. These remedies will be discussed in the next two chapters.

The next figure demonstrates the options available to a buyer under the CISG if a seller delivers non-conforming goods. As noted previously, the buyer must give notice of any non-conformity within a reasonable time after the buyer discovers or should discover the non-conformity. Unless the buyer is excused from this requirement, failure to give such a notice prevents the buyer from relying on the non-conformity.

Assuming proper notice is given, the next question is whether the breach is fundamental. The factors that are important in determining if a breach is fundamental are discussed earlier in this chapter. If the breach is fundamental, the buyer may avoid the contract by giving notice to the seller. If the breach is not fundamental, the buyer may give the seller an extension of time within which to perform, known as a *nachfrist* notice. If the seller does not perform within this period of time, the buyer may avoid the contract. If the seller does perform, the buyer may not avoid the contract, although the seller may be responsible for any damages caused by the delay. The buyer's ability to recover damages and obtain other remedies is discussed in the next chapter.

---

[66]CISG Art. 26.
[67]CISG Art. 49(2)(a).
[68]CISG Art. 49(2)(b).
[69]CISG Art. 63(2)(a).
[70]CISG Art. 63(2)(b).

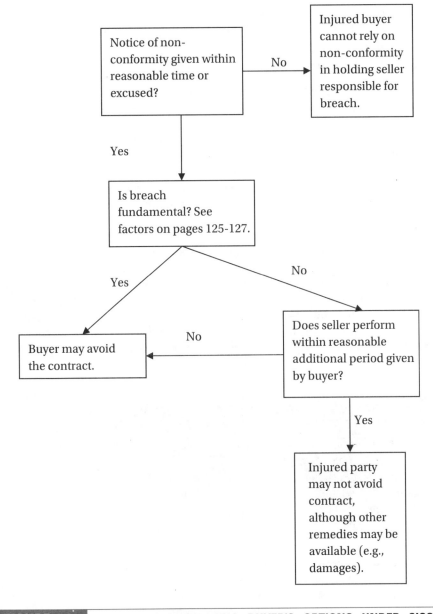

FIGURE 6.3 CHART DEMONSTRATING BUYER'S OPTIONS UNDER CISG IF SELLER DELIVERS NON-CONFORMING GOODS

E. Excuse from Performance — Impracticability and Frustration of Purpose

A seller who is not able to deliver goods under a contract may in rare cases be excused from performance under the doctrine of ***impracticability***. In other rare cases, the purpose of the contract may be substantially *frustrated*, thus permitting the buyer to be excused from taking delivery of goods and paying for them.

(1) Impracticability

The UCC has several provisions that deal with the topic of impracticability, §§2-613 and 2-615. Section 2-613 deals with situations in which there is a loss to goods that have been identified to the contract for sale. Section 2-615 deals with other situations in which the seller is unable to perform because of some event that makes performance impracticable.

Let's assume a contract for the sale of a specific antique gold watch. While the watch is still in the seller's possession, the watch is damaged, but not completely destroyed, when it falls to the ground during an earthquake. Assume that neither party is at fault.

Under UCC §2-613, when the contract requires for its performance goods that are identified when the contract is made and the goods are damaged or destroyed without fault of either party, if the loss is total, the contract is avoided. There is no liability to either party. If, on the other hand, the loss is partial, the buyer may inspect the goods and either terminate the contract or can demand that the seller make a due allowance from the contract price and then pay the reduced price for the goods. In the watch hypothetical, the buyer could demand to look at the watch and then either terminate the contract or insist that the seller make an allowance from the price to reflect the damage done to the watch.

REQUIREMENTS FOR EXCUSE UNDER UCC §2-613

(1) Contract must call for specific goods that have been identified to the contract at time it was made.
(2) Loss must occur through no fault of seller, fault includes negligence.
(3) If loss is not total, buyer must be given option of reduction of price or termination of contract.

Assume instead that a buyer contracts with a watch manufacturer to purchase one of its watches from stock. At the time of the contract, there is no specific watch that has yet been "*identified*" to the contract. Under UCC §2-501, goods are identified to the contract when the seller has designated which of the goods is intended for the buyer. Before the manufacturer has a chance to identify a watch to this contract, the manufacturer's warehouse burns down and almost all of its inventory is destroyed. Section 2-613 would not apply to this contract because the goods were not identified when the contract was made, so §2-615 must be examined instead.

Under §2-615, delay or non-delivery in whole or in part is not a breach if performance has been made impracticable by the occurrence of a contingency, the non-occurrence of which was a basic assumption on which the contract was made, or by compliance in good faith with any applicable foreign or domestic governmental regulation.

The two main elements of §2-615 are thus (1) impracticable performance and (2) caused by an event that non-occurrence of which was a basic assumption on which the contract was made. Foreseeability factors into this equation: If an event is foreseeable at the time of contracting, one cannot assume that its non-occurrence was a basic assumption on which the contract was made.[71]

Applying the rule to our contract for the sale of a watch, let's focus on the second factor first, whether the parties contracted under the assumption that there would be no fire that would destroy the seller's warehouse. Unless the seller caused the fire and unless a fire were foreseeable under the circumstances of this case, it is probably fair to say that this was an event the non-occurrence of which was a basic assumption on which the contract was made. The parties by contract may, however, impose risks of these events on either party — §2-615 will come into play only when the parties haven't been clear on whether a particular event might give rise to excuse for non-performance.

Assuming non-occurrence of the event was a basic assumption on which the contract was made, whether it is impracticable for the seller to deliver the watch to the buyer depends on how much inventory remains after the fire and how many other orders for purchase have been made or might be made by regular customers. Impracticability does not require impossibility of performance, but it is close. In cases in which the seller's capacity to perform is not entirely eliminated, the seller is allowed to make a reasonable allocation to its customers including regular customers not yet under contract.[72] The seller must notify the buyer of any delay or non-delivery and must notify the buyer of any estimated quota of delivery.[73] The buyer may then decide whether to accept the proposed delivery or terminate the contract.[74]

One area where litigation arises is in cases in which it becomes economically impracticable for the seller to perform, albeit physically possible. For example, assume that because of a war the cost of raw materials such as petroleum needed for a seller to perform under a contract goes through the roof. If the seller is required to perform under its contract, the seller will lose a lot of money. Assume that the war was not foreseeable — it was an event the non-occurrence of which was a basic assumption on which the contract was made.

At what point would a court say that the loss is sufficiently ruinous for excuse to be granted? How much of a loss should the seller be expected to take? The court in *Iowa Electric Light and Power Corp. v. Atlas Corp.*[75] refused to grant relief where the increase in seller's costs was 52.2% and the loss incurred by the seller was over $2.6 million. The court noted that cost increases of 50-58% are generally insufficient to grant relief. By comparison, relief was granted in *Aluminum Company of America (ALCOA) v. Essex Group,*[76] where the loss to the plaintiff would be $60,000,000 while the defendant would make a profit of the same amount. Official comment 6 to UCC §2-615 indicates that the court's analysis need not be "all or nothing" — it is possible for the court to come up with a middle ground result, perhaps adjusting the price so that both parties share some of the pain. The *ALCOA* case is an example of a court making an adjustment, but it seems that most of the times courts prefer "all or nothing," reflecting the difficulty of drawing lines of adjustment.

[71]UCC §2-615, comment 8.
[72]UCC §2-615(b).
[73]UCC §2-615(c).
[74]UCC §2-616.
[75]467 F. Supp. 129 (N.D. Iowa 1978).
[76]499 F. Supp. 53 (W.D. Pa. 1980).

Sidebar

HISTORY OF EXCUSE BASED ON IMPRACTICABILITY AND FRUSTRATION

It used to be that impossibility or frustration of purpose were not excuses for failure to perform under contracts except in rare circumstances. According to the late Professor E. Allan Farnsworth, the key cases in the modern evolution of impossibility and frustration doctrine were the English cases of *Taylor v. Caldwell*, 122 Eng. Rep. 309 (K.B. 1863) (impossibility) and *Krell v. Henry*, [1903] 2 K.B. 740 (C.A.) (frustration). In *Taylor v. Caldwell*, the contract called for a musical performance to occur in a music hall that was destroyed by fire without fault of the owner. The person who was to do the performance sued the music hall owner for expenses incurred in preparing to perform, but the court excused the music hall owner on the grounds that the continued existence of the music hall was a basic assumption on which the contract was made. In *Krell v. Henry*, Henry contracted to rent a room from Krell for the purpose of viewing the coronation of King Edward VII. The King developed appendicitis, and the coronation was postponed. Henry refused to pay rent for the room, and Krell sued. The court held that a basic assumption of the contract was that the coronation would occur, and the failure of the event frustrated the contract, thus excusing Henry. See Farnsworth, *Contracts* §§9.5 & 9.7 (4th ed. 2004).

The two cases evidence situations in which performance was either literally rendered impossible or the purpose of the contract completely frustrated. The evolution of the rules in this area has broadened the excuse to situations of impracticability and substantial frustration. Nevertheless, courts are reluctant to grant excuse under either doctrine. Remember, that if one party is excused, the other party may also be hurt, as in cases in which a buyer is relying on a steady supply of goods at a set price. If the seller is excused, the buyer will have to come up with another supplier at a higher price.

(2) Frustration of Purpose

The doctrine of ***frustration of purpose*** is an excuse that might be available to a buyer in the event that the reason for the purchase no longer exists. The UCC does not expressly provide for excuse on the basis of frustration—§2-615 only applies on its face to sellers. The official commentary suggests, however, that the policy underlying §2-615 might permit buyers to obtain relief on the grounds of frustration of purpose.[77] The doctrine of frustration may also be a general principle of law and equity that supplements the UCC under §1-103.

To be excused on the basis of frustration, a buyer would have to show that the known purpose of the contract was substantially frustrated and that the frustration was caused by an event the non-occurrence of which was a basic assumption on which the contract was made. There are not many cases in which a buyer can successfully prove both of these elements.

In one case, the court permitted the buyer to be relieved on the basis of frustration from a contract in which the buyer was obliged to purchase concrete medians for a road construction project.[78] The buyer had a contract with the state to perform this project, but the contract provided that if the state decided not to do the work, the buyer would have no recourse against the state for losses suffered. When the state decided to cancel the project, the buyer notified the seller that it would not be taking any more medians. The seller had not yet spent any money manufacturing or obtaining the medians. Nevertheless, the seller sued for the profits that it would have made on the job. The court excused the buyer, holding that the known purpose of the contract was to obtain medians for the cancelled project and the purpose was substantially frustrated by the state's decision not to go forward, an event the non-occurrence of which was a basic assumption of the sales contract.

It seems that one could question whether either element really existed in the case. Perhaps the medians could have been used on another project, which would mean that the purpose of

---

[77]UCC §2-615, comment 9.
[78]*Chase Precast Corp. v. John J. Paonessa Co.*, 409 Mass. 371, 566 N.E.2d 603 (1991).

the contract was not substantially frustrated (one could define the purpose as "the purchase of medians for road construction projects"). Also, because both parties were familiar with the fact that the state could cancel projects, the cancellation was foreseeable and thus non-occurrence of the event was not a basic assumption of the contract. It appears, however, that because the seller had not incurred any out-of-pocket expense, granting relief to the buyer might have been viewed as not imposing hardship on the seller. Why should the buyer be required to purchase medians that it did not necessarily need?

(3) CISG Excuse from Performance on the Basis of "Impediment"

The CISG also has a provision permitting a party to be excused from having to pay damages for breach if the breach is caused by "an impediment beyond his control and that he could not reasonably be expected to have taken the impediment into account at the time of the conclusion of the contract or to have avoided or overcome it or its consequences."[79] The term "impediment" is sufficiently vague as to permit courts and arbitral tribunals to engage in analysis similar to that undertaken by courts under UCC §2-615, and the issues are likely to be the same.[80]

SUMMARY

■ If a party repudiates its contractual obligations before the time for performance, the other party may treat the contract as being breached.

■ A repudiation may be by definite words, for example, "I will not perform," or by conduct indicating the contract will not be performed, for example, selling identified goods to somebody else.

■ A repudiation may be retracted unless the other party has declared a cancellation of the contract or has materially altered its position.

■ If a party has reasonable grounds for insecurity that the other party will not perform, the party may demand that the other party provide adequate assurance of performance. Failure to timely provide adequate assurance constitutes a repudiation.

■ The CISG has similar rules to the UCC on the topics of repudiation and adequate assurance. Under the CISG, the question is whether it appears that a party will commit a fundamental breach. If so, the CISG permits the injured party to avoid the contract.

■ The seller must deliver goods that conform to the requirements of the contract to avoid breach. If there is a warranty of title, the seller must deliver good title to the buyer.

■ Generally, the buyer receives only as good title as the seller had. A buyer of goods from a thief obtains no title to the goods, even if the buyer is a bona fide purchaser.

---

[79]CISG Art. 79.
[80]See Ziegel, *Report to the Uniform Law Conference of Canada on Convention on Contracts for the International Sale of Goods, Article 79*, found on the Internet at http://www.cisg.law.pace.edu/cist/text/ziegel79.html.

■ Someone with voidable title can deliver good title to a bona fide purchaser for value. An example of someone with voidable title is a person who buys goods with a bad check.

■ If goods are entrusted to a merchant, a buyer in the ordinary course of business from the merchant can obtain good title. An example of an entrustment would be leaving a watch with a jeweler to have it repaired.

■ The CISG does not deal with questions of title. Such matters are left to domestic law determined under choice of law rules.

■ The "perfect tender rule" applies to non-installment sales covered by the UCC. Under that rule, the buyer may reject part or all of any tender that does not conform to the contract of sale.

■ Acceptance of goods by the buyer triggers the buyer's obligation to pay for the goods. Acceptance occurs if the buyer fails to properly reject after having had a reasonable opportunity to inspect the goods.

■ A seller may cure a non-conforming tender if the time for delivery has not yet passed or the seller had reasonable grounds to believe that the goods would be acceptable with or without a money allowance.

■ If the seller wishes to cure, it must seasonably notify the buyer of its intention to do so and deliver conforming goods by the time set for delivery or else within a reasonable time thereafter.

■ If a buyer accepts goods and subsequently discovers a significant defect that substantially impairs the value of the goods to the buyer, the buyer may revoke acceptance of the goods.

■ If a buyer either rejects goods or revokes acceptance of them, the buyer must notify the seller of the rejection or revocation and hold the goods with reasonable care so that the seller can retake possession of them. In some cases, merchant buyers are required to resell goods for the seller if the goods threaten to decline in value. Some courts will allow reasonable use of the goods by the buyer if necessary for the buyer to avoid loss.

■ If the contract calls for goods to be shipped in installments, an installment may be rejected only if a non-conformity substantially impairs its value and it cannot be cured.

■ An installment contract can be cancelled only if breach results in a substantial impairment in the value of the entire contract.

■ Parties to a sales contract may limit the buyer's remedies in the event goods do not conform to repair or replacement. The limited remedy is not enforceable, however, if it fails of its essential purpose. A court might find a limited remedy has failed if the seller is unable to make a repair after numerous attempts.

■ Parties may limit the ability of the buyer to recover consequential damages unless such a limitation is unconscionable. Some courts will also find that a limit on consequential damages fails when a limited remedy of repair or replacement also fails.

■ Under the CISG, a party may avoid a contract if there has been a fundamental breach or if the other party has failed to perform within a reasonable *nachfrist* period (extension of time to perform). There is no "perfect tender rule" under the CISG.

■ A fundamental breach involves a substantial deprivation of the injured party's expectation under the contract that was foreseeable to the breaching party.

■ Both the seller and the buyer are permitted to give the other party an extension of time to perform (a *nachfrist* notice). If the period is reasonable, failure to perform within the period permits the injured party to avoid the contract.

■ Performance of a contract may be excused if performance is impracticable or if the purpose of the contract is substantially frustrated. Impracticability or frustration must generally be caused by events that were not foreseeable to the parties at the time of contracting (e.g., an embargo or a war).

■ Under the CISG, performance may be excused if failure is caused by an impediment beyond the control of the party failing to perform. As with the UCC, such an impediment must be something that was outside the control of the party seeking excuse and that could not reasonably have been anticipated.

CONNECTIONS

Choice of Law
The rules for performance differ depending on the law that applies. Under the common law of contract, a party generally cannot terminate unless there is a failure of an express condition to performance or a material breach. Under the UCC, the "perfect tender rule" permits a buyer to cancel a contract even for an insignificant breach if the seller does not cure the breach on a non-installment contract. On installment contracts, the buyer or seller cannot cancel unless the breach substantially impairs the value of the contract, which may be a concept akin to material breach. Under the CISG, a party cannot avoid a contract unless there is a fundamental breach, which again may be similar to the concept of material breach.

Contract Formation and Terms
In determining whether the parties have performed under the contract, we must determine the terms of the agreement. Determining the terms may depend on how the contract was formed. If the contract was formed through an exchange of forms, the terms in the first form (e.g., a purchase order) or in the last form (e.g., an order acknowledgment) may contain the terms of the contract, depending on application of UCC §2-207.

We must also determine whether warranties of quality or warranties of title were given and whether such warranties were breached. Even if the buyer is not satisfied with the goods, the buyer must be able to point to a term of the contract that was breached before the buyer may reject the goods and not pay for them. Some prior agreements may also not be enforceable under the parol evidence rule. In addition, some terms may not be enforceable as being unconscionable, such as warranty disclaimers.

Remedies

Whether a buyer can reject non-conforming goods or must accept them, the buyer may nevertheless have an action against the seller for damages. In the next chapter, we determine the amount of damages necessary to make the injured buyer whole. In addition, if the buyer wrongfully rejects goods or refuses to pay for accepted goods, the seller may be able to recover damages resulting from the buyer's breach or the price of the goods themselves. This calculation will be discussed more fully in Chapter 8.

Third Parties

If the parties have agreed that the goods are to be shipped and that the risk of loss passes when the goods are delivered to the shipping company delivering the goods, the buyer will have to accept and pay for goods even if they are damaged or destroyed in transit. The buyer may have a cause of action against the shipping company, which is discussed in Chapter 9. Even if the seller ships defective goods, a bank issuing a letter of credit may be required to pay on presentation of documents showing that the goods were shipped. The bank will have a right to be reimbursed by the applicant for the letter of credit, i.e., the buyer. The buyer will have to sue the seller for breach in delivering non-conforming goods.

Buyer's Remedies

7

In this chapter, we will consider the remedies available to the buyer in the event of the seller's breach. We have previously considered the buyer's rights to reject or revoke acceptance of goods. Here, we will focus on the ability of the buyer to recover damages and in some cases to obtain specific performance.

O V E R V I E W

A. UNDER THE UCC

1. Goods Not Accepted
2. Accepted Goods
3. Availability of Tort Remedies

B. BUYER'S REMEDIES UNDER THE CISG

1. Specific Performance
2. Price Reduction
3. Damages

C. THE STATUTE OF LIMITATIONS

REMEDIES AVAILABLE TO BUYER IF SELLER BREACHES THE CONTRACT UNDER THE UCC

If Goods Are Accepted	If Goods Are Not Accepted or Acceptance Is Revoked
Damages for loss resulting from breach — UCC §2-714	Refund of purchase price — UCC §2-711
Incidental & Consequential Damages — UCC §2-715	Difference between price of substitute goods and contract price — UCC §2-712 Difference between market price and contract price if buyer does not cover — UCC §2-713 Incidental & Consequential Damages — UCC §2-715 · Right to Claim Goods — UCC §2-502 Right to Specific Performance or Replevin — UCC §2-716

A. Under the UCC

We first consider the treatment of buyer's remedies under the Uniform Commercial Code (UCC). As the above table demonstrates, the UCC divides the remedies between situations in which the goods are not accepted, either because of failure to deliver in the first place or the buyer's rejection or revocation of acceptance, and situations in which the goods have been accepted. When considering UCC remedies, it is helpful to understand the overall policy of UCC remedies. That policy is to attempt to put the injured party in the position that it would have occupied but for breach.[1] The UCC does not generally provide for punitive damages. So, when trying to figure out the sometimes-complex language of the statutes describing the calculation of damages, keep in mind what the drafters are trying to accomplish.

(1) Goods Not Accepted

In the event that the seller fails to deliver goods or the buyer rightfully rejects or revokes acceptance, §2-711 provides the options available to the buyer if the buyer wishes to obtain damages. The buyer may either (a) make a reasonable substitute purchase, known as *cover*, or (b) obtain the difference between market price and the contract price for the goods, known as the ***contract/market differential.*** If the buyer covers, the Code clearly indicates that the contract/market differential is <u>not</u> available.[2] In both instances, the buyer may, in appropriate cases, also recover incidental and

---

[1]UCC §1-305.
[2]UCC §2-713, comment 5.

Sidebar

THE "EFFICIENT BREACH" THEORY

The UCC follows the rule from *Restatement (Second) of Contracts* §355 that punitive damages are not recoverable for breach of contract. They are available only in cases in which a tort has been committed. The great Justice Oliver Wendell Holmes, Jr., stated a version of this rule when he wrote, "[t]he duty to keep a contract at common law means a prediction that you must pay damages if you do not keep it — and nothing else." See Perillo, *Misreading Oliver Wendell Holmes on Efficient Breach and Tortious Interference*, 68 Fordham L. Rev. 1085 (2000) (quoting from Holmes). This rule is justified as protecting so-called efficient breaches. Under an efficient breach in a sale of goods case, a seller would breach its contract with the buyer so as to sell the goods in question to somebody who would be willing to pay more for them, with the injured party's damages from the breach being less than the profit that the seller would make on the substitute sale. Assume that a seller contracts to sell tables to Buyer #1 for $10 per table. The tables are not needed immediately. Buyer #2 has an immediate need for tables and is willing to pay $20 per table. The only way that the seller can produce tables for Buyer #2 is if it breaches its contract with Buyer #1. Assume that Buyer #1 can easily go elsewhere and buy comparable tables for the same price, with the delay in delivery not harming Buyer #1. The breach is arguably efficient and thus good for the economy because (a) the seller makes more of a profit than if it had performed its contract with Buyer #1, (b) Buyer #2 gets tables that it needed in a timely fashion, and (c) Buyer #1 is not harmed by the breach. There is a net gain for the parties concerned. The problem with the efficient breach theory is that it requires that the injured party be compensated for all damages suffered, and it is generally difficult to determine exactly how much damage is caused by a contract breach.

consequential damages, at least if there is no enforceable contractual provision limiting their recovery. If the buyer would prefer to obtain specific performance instead, the Code provides that this remedy is available in some cases, as we will discuss.[3]

(a) Cover

In cases in which (a) the seller does not deliver goods, (b) the seller delivers non-conforming goods and the buyer rejects them, or (c) the seller delivers non-conforming goods and the buyer ultimately rightfully revokes acceptance of them, UCC §2-712 provides that the buyer may make a reasonable substitute purchase of goods. The purchase must be within a reasonable time. If the buyer makes such a substitute purchase, the buyer is entitled to the difference between what the buyer paid and what the buyer was supposed to pay under the breached contract, plus incidental and consequential damages and less any expenses saved as a result of the breach.

BUYER'S COVER REMEDY — UCC §2-712

Cost of Substitute Goods − Contract Price on
Breached Contract + Incidental
Damages + Consequential Damages − Costs Saved
Because of Breach = Buyer's Recovery

---

[3]See pp. 145-147, *infra.*

For example, let's assume that the seller is supposed to deliver a certain model of car to the buyer for $25,000 but breaches by failing to deliver. The next day, the buyer purchases the exact same car for $28,000. Assume that additional shopping by the buyer for a substitute would have resulted in the buyer paying about the same price. Assume also that the buyer spent $20 in gas money driving around checking out other cars.

It appears that the buyer has made a reasonable substitute purchase within a reasonable time. The buyer could then obtain the $3,000 difference between the price of the substitute purchase and the contract price. The buyer is also entitled to any incidental and consequential damages. ***Incidental damages*** include "expenses reasonably incurred in inspection, receipt, transportation and care and custody of goods rightfully rejected, any commercially reasonable charges, expenses or commissions in connection with effecting cover and any other reasonable expense incident to the delay or other breach."[4] The $20 in gas money falls within reasonable charges in effecting cover, so this amount would be recoverable as an incidental damage. ***Consequential damages*** include "any loss resulting from general or particular requirements and needs of which the seller at the time of contracting had reason to know and which could not have been presented by cover or otherwise."[5] The facts of our simple hypothetical present no additional damages—we will consider consequential damages further when we talk about the contract/market differential. There is no evidence of any costs saved as a result of breach, so it looks as if the injured buyer would recover $3,020 in this case.

In determining whether a reasonable substitute purchase has been made, obviously a buyer cannot go out and buy a Rolls Royce and try to hold the breaching seller responsible for the difference between the price of the Rolls and an economy car. Courts do not require, however, that the buyer purchase the exact same good. For example, in some cases it might be permissible for the buyer to purchase a later-model car or a car with additional options if those are the only alternatives available.[6] The buyer's need for the goods in question is something that courts will consider in determining the reasonableness of a substitute purchase.

The reasonableness of the time period within which the substitute purchase was made will depend on market factors. In some situations, it may be difficult for the buyer to find a substitute product immediately, especially if market prices are rising. In such a case, a court might permit more of a delay in making the substitute purchase than in situations in which a substitute is readily available.[7]

(b) Contract/Market Differential—Buyer Does Not Cover

If the buyer does not purchase substitute goods, the buyer is permitted to recover the difference between the contract price and the market price at the time that the buyer "learns of the breach." The market is the place for tender unless the goods are delivered and rejected (or acceptance is revoked), in which case the market is the place of arrival.[8] To this amount is added any incidental and consequential damages, less any costs saved as a result of the seller's breach.

---

[4]UCC §2-715(1).
[5]UCC §2-715(2).
[6]See, e.g., *Mueller v. McGill*, 870 S.W.2d 673 (Tex. App. 1994).
[7]See, e.g., *Dangerfield v. Markel*, 26 UCC Rep. Serv. 419 (N.D. Sup. Ct. 1979).
[8]UCC §2-713.

BUYER'S CONTRACT/MARKET DAMAGES — UCC §2-713

Market Price — Contract Price on Breached Contract + Incidental Damages + Consequential Damages — Costs Saved Because of Breach = Buyer's Recovery

So, let us assume that the contract calls for delivery of goods "FOB Los Angeles" with the goods ultimately to arrive in New York. The contract price is $500. At the time the buyer learns of the breach, the market price for the goods in Los Angeles is $600 and $700 in New York. This would be a shipment contract, and remember that in a shipment contract the tender is made at the place of shipment.[9] So, if the seller never ships the goods, the relevant market for determining the contract/market differential would be Los Angeles and the buyer's damages would be $100 ($600 − $500). If the goods are shipped but are rejected in New York, the relevant market would be New York. Using the same numbers as before for market prices, the buyer's damages would then be $200 ($700 − $500).

A question may sometimes arise as to whether the buyer has actually made a cover purchase, in which case damages are calculated under UCC §2-712, or has not made one, in which case damages are calculated under UCC §2-713. This question may come up particularly in situations in which the buyer makes numerous purchases and sales of goods. For example, a commodities dealer might make many purchases and sales, so that it is difficult to determine which purchase (if any) is in substitution of a breached contract. An injured buyer may assert that there was no cover purchase and will try to recover the contract/market differential. The breaching seller may try to argue that there was a cover purchase at less than the relevant market price.

The official commentary to the 2003 amendments to UCC §2-713 indicates that the breaching party has the burden of proving that a purchase at less than the market price was in fact in substitution for the breached contract. It would seem that if the injured party is seeking to show a substitute purchase that the burden would be on the injured party.

Should the Buyer Be Limited to Actual Damages Suffered? If the buyer does not make a substitute purchase, a question might arise as to whether the buyer really lost anything as a result of the seller's breach. If the buyer is in the business of reselling goods that are purchased, the fact that the buyer did not make a substitute purchase when the seller breached may indicate that the purchase of additional goods proved unprofitable. The seller's breach may have actually saved the buyer from a loss. If that is the case, should the buyer be allowed to recover damages under the contract/ market formula in light of the UCC policy of trying to put the injured party in the position it would have occupied if there had been no breach without otherwise punishing the breaching party?

Some courts will not permit the buyer to recover under the contract/market formula if it is clear that the buyer suffered no damages as a result of the seller's breach.[10] Other courts view §2-713 as statutory liquidated damages, assuring the

---

[9]See pp. 80-84, *supra.*
[10]See, e.g., *Allied Canners & Packers, Inc. v. Victor Packing Co.*, 162 Cal. App. 3d 905, 209 Cal. Rptr. 60 (1984).

buyer of that measure of recovery in the event that the seller breaches unless the buyer actually makes a substitute purchase.[11] Given the uncertainty of determining if a buyer has in fact made a substitute purchase and given the uncertainty of determining actual damages suffered, it may make sense to view §2-713 as a measure of damages that will be available if the buyer does not cover no matter what the buyer's actual damages might be.[12]

Measurement of Damages When Seller Repudiates. Another issue that comes up in this area regards when the buyer "learns of the breach" if the seller repudiates. Assume that the date for delivery under the contract is August 1, and the seller calls on July 1 to say that it will not deliver. On July 1, the relevant market price is $10, on July 15 it is $15, and on August 1 it is $20. Which is the market price that should be used in calculating damages under §2-713?

Under the version of the UCC before the 2003 amendments, there is a question as to whether the date of repudiation, the date of delivery or some commercially reasonable time in between is the time to measure market price. The drafters answered this question only in cases in which the case comes to trial before the time for performance. In that event, the time for determining market price is the time that the buyer learns of the repudiation.[13]

In cases in which the case comes to trial after the time for performance, the time to measure the market price could be (1) the time the buyer learns of the repudiation, (2) the time of performance (the common law approach), or (3) a commercially reasonable time after the buyer learns of the repudiation. The UCC simply isn't clear on this question.

One could take the position that it would be appropriate to use the same rule to measure damages whether the case comes to trial before the time for performance or not. If that is the case, we would measure at the time the buyer learns of the repudiation. The problem with that approach is that it would render UCC §2-723 superfluous, and there is a fundamental rule of statutory interpretation that we try to interpret each statute as having meaning, that is, not superfluous. Because the drafters tell us that we measure damages at the time of repudiation when the case comes to trial before the time for performance, they must intend some other rule for other cases.

One could also take the position that the time to measure damages is at the time for performance. This is the traditional rule in non-sale of goods cases,[14] and is consistent with the rule governing seller's remedies, which indicates that damages are to be measured at the time and place for tender (not when the seller "learned of the breach").[15] The problem with this approach is that it permits a buyer to speculate at the seller's expense by waiting to see what happens with the market.[16] If the market price keeps going up, the buyer can wait until the time for performance and recover

---

[11]See, e.g., *Tongish v. Thomas,* 16 Kan. App. 2d 809, 829 P.2d 916 (1992). See Ellen Peters, *Remedies for Breach of Contracts Relating to the Sale of Goods Under the Uniform Commercial Code: A Roadmap for Article 2,* 73 Yale L.J. 199, 259 (1963).
[12]UCC §2-723.
[13]*Id.*
[14]See, e.g., *Bachewicz v. American Nat'l Bank & Trust Co.,* 126 Ill. App. 3d 298, 466 N.E.2d 1096 (1984).
[15]This approach was followed in *Hess Energy v. Lightning Oil Co.,* 338 F.3d 357 (4th Cir. 2003), which has a good discussion of this problem.
[16]See Jackson, *Anticipatory Repudiation and the Temporal Element of Contract Law: An Economic Inquiry into Contract Damages in Cases of Prospective Nonperformance,* 31 Stan. L. Rev. 69 (1968).

the full difference between the market price and the contract price at that time. If the market price falls below the contract price, the buyer can purchase substitute goods at the cheaper price and is better off than if the contract had been performed. The buyer does not have sufficient incentive to attempt to mitigate damages. In addition, this approach seems inconsistent with UCC §2-610, which allows an injured party to await performance by a repudiating party only for a commercially reasonable time.

The 2003 amendments to Article 2 choose a commercially reasonable time after the buyer learns of the repudiation as the time to measure damages, whether the case comes to trial before the time for performance or not.[17] The amendments also apply this rule to sellers in cases in which the buyer repudiates.[18] This approach probably most accurately reflects what a buyer or seller would do when learning of a repudiation by the other, that is, make a substitute purchase or substitute sale within a reasonable time after hearing that the seller or buyer had repudiated, respectively.

Incidental and Consequential Damages. In addition to recovering the difference between the market price and the contract price, the buyer is allowed to recover *incidental* and *consequential damages* under §2-713. Incidental damages were considered previously in the discussion of the buyer's cover remedy. Consequential damages are a broader measure of damages. The UCC provides recovery for "any loss resulting from general or particular requirements and needs of which the seller at the time of contracting had reason to know and which could not reasonably be prevented by cover or otherwise."[19]

The UCC rule with regard to consequential damages has been likened to the *Hadley v. Baxendale* rule limiting recovery of consequential damages at common law, focusing on the foreseeability of damages as a probable consequence of breach.[20] Comment 3 to §1-305 indicates that the term "consequential damages" is given the same meaning in the UCC that it has outside the Code. Section 2-715 also codifies the mitigation requirement of common law, stating that such damages are not recoverable if they could have reasonably been avoided. The requirement of certainty in proving damages is mentioned in comment 4 to §2-715: that while mathematical certainty in calculation is not required, the manner of measurement must be reasonable under the circumstances.

If a seller does not deliver conforming goods, what kinds of consequential damages might a buyer suffer? If the buyer is in the business of reselling the goods and cannot obtain substitute goods in time, it is likely that the buyer will suffer lost profits on resale of the goods. If the goods are to be used in the buyer's business as equipment, it would also be foreseeable that the business might be slowed in absence of the equipment or that additional employees might need to be hired. The types of damages recoverable would depend on the facts of the given case and what the seller knows regarding the buyer's need for the goods.

Subtraction of Expenses Saved as Result of Breach. Section 2-713, like §2-712, indicates that any expenses saved by the buyer as a result of the breach needs to be subtracted from damages. In the context of cover, one can imagine that if a buyer reasonably purchases a substitute product that is different from the product that was

---

[17]Amended UCC §2-713.
[18]Amended UCC §2-708(1)(b).
[19]UCC §2-715(2)(a).
[20]See White & Summers, *Uniform Commercial Code* §10-4 (5th ed.).

to be purchased under the breached contract, there could be some expenses saved as a result of the breach. For example, let's assume that the original contract called for the sale of a certain model of air conditioner that cost $500 to install. When the seller breached, the buyer was unable to purchase the same model, but reasonably purchased another model that cost $1,000 more. The substitute air conditioner cost only $250 to install, so $250 is saved on installation and should be subtracted from damages ($1000 − $250 = $750).

In the context of the contract/market differential, the Code is assuming that the buyer is buying comparable goods in the place of tender if the goods have never been delivered, or in the place of arrival in cases of rejection or revocation of acceptance. Let us assume that the buyer is in Los Angeles while the seller is in Chicago. If the contract is "FOB Chicago," that indicates that the tender of goods is to be in Chicago and that the buyer will pay the price of shipment from Chicago to Los Angeles. So, if the seller repudiates the contract and the buyer does not purchase replacement goods, is the cost of shipment from Chicago to Los Angeles "saved" as a result of the breach?

The answer to this question should be no. Because the assumption is that the buyer would go to Chicago to buy replacement goods and the contract/market differential is measured there, it must also be assumed that the goods would be shipped from Chicago to Los Angeles, and that the buyer would still have to pay for the shipment. Thus, the shipping cost would not be "saved" as a result of the seller's breach.[21]

When would expenses be saved under §2-713? If it is difficult to prove the market price at the place of tender, §2-723 permits proof of market price at other places that would be deemed reasonable substitutes. So, let us assume that it is difficult to prove the market price in Chicago. The market price in Los Angeles might be a reasonable substitute, and if so, the shipping costs would likely be less. The reduced cost of shipping should then be subtracted from the buyer's damages.

Example of Damage Calculation Under §2-713. To pull everything together, let us consider a contract for the purchase of 1,000 dress shirts by a department store chain at a discount price. The department store informs the seller that it intends to sell the shirts on sale during its annual Thanksgiving sale at its various locations with the hope that the sale will attract customers to the store to buy other items. Assume that the shirts are purchased at $15 per shirt and will be resold for $20. The delivery term of the contract is "FOB Dallas" and the buyer is in Kansas City. The cost of shipment of the shirts is $500. The seller does not deliver the shirts. By the time the buyer learns of the breach, it is too late to buy other shirts or comparable items for its Thanksgiving sale. The market price when the buyer learns of the breach for shirts in Dallas is $20 per shirt and in Kansas City it is $18. The department store claims that it lost profits of $8,000 on re-sales of the shirts and on other items that would have been sold if it had been able include the dress shirts in its Thanksgiving sale.

How should buyer's damages be determined under UCC §2-713? Because the term of the contract is "FOB Dallas," that means that the relevant market is Dallas. Dallas is the place of tender, and that is the relevant market since the goods were never shipped. So, the contract/market differential would be $20 minus $15 times the number of shirts being sold (1,000), or $5,000 (5 × 1,000). Should the $500 shipping

---

[21]*Id.* at §6.4.a.

charge be subtracted as a cost saved as a result of the breach? Because this is a hypothetical measure of damages and we are assuming that the buyer would go into the market of tender to make the substitute purchase, $500 would need to be spent anyway to get the shirts from Dallas to Kansas City. The $500 should not be subtracted from damages.

Should the buyer be entitled to damages for the profits that were lost as a result of not having the dress shirts for the sale? Because the seller was aware of the buyer's purpose in purchasing the shirts, it would seem that the lost profits were a foreseeable consequence of the seller's breach. The timing of the breach meant that it was not possible for the buyer to make a substitute purchase to prevent loss. The issue would be whether the lost profits could be shown with any reasonable certainty. In one similar case, a buyer was allowed to compare profits obtained from a prior year's sale with profits from the year when goods were not available to be resold because of a seller's breach.[22] If the department store can bring forth facts to show with reasonable certainty that it lost $8,000 in profits because of the seller's failure to deliver the dress shirts for the Thanksgiving sale, the court might grant recovery for those lost profits.

Should lost profits be awarded on top of the contract/market differential? In other words, should the department store be able to recover $8,000 (lost profits) plus $5,000 (the contract/market differential)? Permitting such a recovery would seem to give a double recovery for buyer. The lost-profit measure places the injured buyer in the position that it would have occupied if the seller had not breached (the department store claims it would have made an $8,000 profit on its Thanksgiving sale if the shirts had been delivered), so granting the contract/market differential on top of that would be unduly punitive. If the lost profits cannot be shown with certainty, then the contract/market differential would be available.

(c) Specific Performance, Replevin, and Right to Claim Identified Goods

Generally speaking, the UCC prefers that the buyer purchase substitute goods when a seller breaches and then obtain damages from the seller. The UCC permits the buyer to sue for *specific performance* where the goods are unique or in other special circumstances.[23] In determining whether circumstances dictate that specific performance be ordered, courts might look at the difficulty that a buyer would have in obtaining substitute goods.

For example, let us assume that a buyer contracts to purchase a car that will be produced only in limited edition. The car will be a collector's item, and it will be difficult to obtain. A court might grant specific performance of a contract in such a situation.[24]

Another situation in which a court might grant specific performance would be in the case of a long-term supply contract. At common law, courts were reluctant to order specific performance of contracts that required repeated performances because of the difficulty of supervising such contracts (see the Sidebar to this section for further discussion on this). Official comment 2 to §2-716 indicates, however, that if a contract for output or requirements involves a particular or peculiarly available

---

[22]See *Migerobe, Inc. v. Certina, U.S.A., Inc.*, 924 F.2d 1330 (5th Cir. 1991).
[23]UCC §2-716(1).
[24]*Sedmak v. Charlie's Chevrolet*, 622 S.W.2d 694 (Mo. App. 1981).

source or market, specific performance would be appropriate, even if the court is required to supervise such a performance.[25]

The UCC also permits the buyer to sue in ***replevin*** if goods have been identified to the contract if the buyer is unable to make a substitute purchase after a reasonable effort or the facts indicate that such an effort will be unavailing.[26] This may seem not to add much to the buyer's right to specific performance, since the buyer can also make an argument for that remedy if it is difficult to cover. The right of replevin is a legal remedy, however, as compared to specific performance which is equitable. So, there may be procedural advantages to suing in replevin as a jury trial would be possible.

An example of a case in which replevin would be available would be a contract for a painting by a famous artist, like Rembrandt or Van Gogh. The painting is identified to the contract at the time the contract is entered into — it isn't a contract for just any painting, it's for a specific one. Because these paintings are unique, it would not be possible to make a substitute purchase. Thus, the action for replevin would be appropriate, as would an action for specific performance.

WHY SPECIFIC PERFORMANCE IS NOT THE PREFERRED REMEDY

The UCC codifies the basic common law rule that specific performance is available only when the legal remedy of damages is inadequate (e.g., cannot be measured). Specific performance places a burden on the court to monitor the parties' conduct. If the court were to order that goods be delivered to a buyer, the court would need to schedule a future hearing to find out if the seller followed through. If not, it would be necessary for the court to sanction the seller and continue to monitor the situation. If the court awards damages, on the other hand, it is pretty much up to the plaintiff to try to collect it, although the court might help the plaintiff by allowing the plaintiff to examine the defendant under oath regarding the location of the defendant's assets (called a debtor's exam). Also, a specific performance order might chill an efficient breach — see the earlier discussion on page 139. The law would prefer that the injured buyer go out and buy substitute goods if the buyer can.

A third remedy available to a buyer who wants to obtain the goods that have been identified to the contract is the right to claim goods under UCC §2-502. Under that statute, if goods have been identified to the contract and the buyer has made a partial payment of the goods, the buyer may claim them by tendering the unpaid part of the purchase price if the goods were bought for personal, family, or household purposes and the seller repudiated or failed to deliver the goods under the contract. In other cases involving partial payment for identified goods, the buyer may claim them by tendering payment in full if the seller becomes insolvent within ten days after receipt of the first installment of the price. The latter situation will not come up very often, as it would have to be shown that the seller became insolvent (e.g., was not able to pay its debts when due) within a very short time window. The limitation on this remedy shows the preference of the drafters for injured buyers to go out and make substitute purchases instead of suing for the specific goods.

An example of a consumer buyer's right to claim goods under §2-502 would be if a consumer has made a deposit on an identified piece of furniture that the seller is supposed to deliver to the buyer. If the seller refuses to deliver the furniture, the consumer would have a right to claim the furniture by tendering the balance of the purchase price. Note that the buyer probably could not recover under a specific

---

[25]See *Copylease Corp. of America v. Memorex Corp.*, 408 F. Supp. 758 (S.D.N.Y. 1976).
[26]UCC §2-716(2).

performance or replevin theory as it would probably be possible for the buyer to obtain substitute furniture on the market, unless the furniture was a rare antique.

(2) Accepted Goods

If a buyer accepts non-conforming goods, the buyer is obligated to pay the price for them. The buyer is not without remedy, however. The buyer can sue the seller for damages caused by the non-conformity, including consequential damages if any. The buyer has the burden of proof to show non-conformity once the goods are accepted.

(a) Notice Requirement

UCC §2-607 requires the buyer to notify the seller within a reasonable time after the buyer discovers or should have discovered the breach or the buyer is barred from any remedy. The notice need not be formal and need not necessarily demand anything—it is enough for the buyer to "let the seller know that the transaction is still troublesome and should be watched."[27] There is no requirement that the buyer give the seller a complete listing of all objections that the buyer has with the seller's performance.

One could even argue that a lawsuit filed within a reasonable time after the buyer discovers or should have discovered the breach is satisfactory notice. Not everyone agrees with this position, however.[28] It is probably prudent before a lawsuit is filed for the buyer to first give a notice to the seller of the breach and try to work things out.

(b) Measurement of Damages

Assuming that proper notice of breach is given, the UCC provides the buyer is allowed to "recover as damages for any non-conformity of tender the loss resulting in the ordinary course of events from the seller's breach as determined in any manner which is reasonable."[29] The Code suggests that one way to measure damages would be to award the buyer the difference between the value of the goods as warranted and the value of the goods as they are at the time and place of acceptance.[30] This is not, however, the exclusive measure of damages—the court has leeway to measure them in any reasonable manner. In addition, consequential and incidental damages are available.

BUYER'S DAMAGES FOR ACCEPTED GOODS—UCC §2-714

Value of Goods as Warranted – Value of Defective Goods at Time and Place of Acceptance + Incidental Damages + Consequential Damages = Buyer's Recovery

or

Cost of Repair + Incidental Damages + Consequential Damages = Buyer's Recovery

or

Other reasonable measure of damages to put Buyer in position it would have occupied if contract had been performed

---

[27] UCC §2-607, comment 4.
[28] See *Aqualon Company v. MAC Equipment, Inc.*, 149 F.3d 262 (1998).
[29] UCC §2-714(1).
[30] UCC §2-714(2).

How does one go about measuring the difference between the value of goods as promised and the value of defective goods? With respect to the value of the goods as promised, one could take the position that the contract price shows what the parties thought the goods would be worth if the goods conformed to the contract. That is not necessarily the case, however. It is possible that the buyer got a really good deal in terms of the price charged, and the market value of the goods as warranted is considerably more than the contract price. For example, let us assume that the seller agreed to sell the buyer a piece of equipment for $50,000 and that the market price for comparable equipment is $60,000. In determining the value of the goods as warranted, $60,000 should be used if we are trying to give the buyer the benefit of the bargain.[31] Assuming a court determines that because of defects the value of the goods at the time and place of acceptance is $20,000, the buyer should recover $40,000 ($60,000 − $20,000), plus incidental and consequential damages. That being said, the contract price is probably as good a measure as any most of the time, and a buyer who wants a greater measure of damages will have the burden of proving that the goods as warranted are worth more than the contract price.

Perhaps a more difficult question is how one goes about valuing defective goods. There typically isn't much of a market for defective goods, especially goods that have the specific defect of the goods in question. A better way to measure damages may be to simply focus on the cost of repair, if that is something that can be determined with reasonable certainty. Otherwise, some speculation will have to occur regarding the value of the defective good.

To give an example of using repair or replacement cost as a way of calculating damages under UCC §2-714, assume that a seller contracts to install custom cabinets for $40,000. It is very difficult to determine the market value of these cabinets because they are custom designed and installed. The cabinets turn out to be seriously defective after they are installed due to the use of inferior materials. It would cost $44,000 to rip out the defective cabinets and install new ones that conform to the sales contract. A court might in such a circumstance award the $44,000.[32]

Consequential and incidental damages are awardable just as they are in the cases in which the goods are not delivered. As is the case with situations in which the buyer covers or recovers the contract/market differential, an injured buyer may suffer lost profits when a good does not perform as well as it should. For example, if a commercial oven is installed in a bakery and turns out not to work properly, the bakery might be allowed to recover any profits that it can prove with reasonable certainty it lost because of inability to produce sufficient baked goods for its customers. Another type of consequential damage that is seen in cases in which goods are accepted is personal injury. If a defective car catches fire and burns the buyer, the buyer's injury is a consequential damage from breach. The seller may be liable in both tort and in contract (more on tort recovery shortly). The UCC provides that consequential damages includes "injury

---

[31]See, e.g., *Chatlos Systems v. National Cash Register*, 670 F.2d 1304 (3d Cir. 1982), where the court allowed a recovery of substantially more than the contract price because of the view that the buyer was promised a really good deal and the goods delivered did not perform.

[32]See *Gem Jewlers v. Dykman*, 160 A.D.2d 1069, 553 N.Y.S.2d 890 (App. Div. 1990).

to person or property proximately resulting from any breach of warranty."[33] This should be contrasted with the foreseeability test that is used for other types of consequential damages, such as lost profits.

The Code does not give much guidance on what is meant by **proximate cause**, other than by suggesting that if a buyer discovered or should have discovered a defect in the goods that would have caused the injury and then used the goods anyway, the defect would not be considered to be the proximate cause of loss (the buyer's use is the proximate cause).[34] Unlike §2-715(2)(a), subsection (2)(b) has no requirement that the harm be foreseeable. If the injury caused was something that was not at all within the contemplation of the parties as being possible, a court might be tempted to use the rule from tort law that says, "The actor's conduct may be held not to be a legal cause of harm to another where after the event and looking back from the harm to the actor's negligent conduct, it appears to the court highly extraordinary that it should have brought about the harm."[35] So, foreseeability may factor in the analysis to some extent, but not to the extent that it does in determining liability for economic loss.

(3) Availability of Tort Remedies

As the discussion in the previous paragraph indicates, there is overlap between tort and the UCC when it comes to the recovery of damages for defective products. When a product is defective, a buyer might be able to sue under a theory of strict liability, negligence, or maybe even fraud. The buyer may prefer to sue in tort in some cases because the measurement of damages may be different. Also, actions in tort require no privity of contract and there are no technical notice requirements. The statutes of limitation are different, so an action in tort might sometimes be available when the action under the UCC is not, and vice versa. Perhaps the greatest reason why a buyer might like to sue in tort is because punitive damages might be available, while they generally are not in a breach of contract case.

So, when does the buyer have the option of forgoing the contract action and suing in tort? If there is a tort independent of the contract breach, a tort action is available.[36] For example, if someone was fraudulently induced to enter into the contract, that would be a tort independent of the contract breach, so a tort cause of action would be possible. In other situations, courts have taken different approaches on the question of when the action in tort is possible. The majority approach is to ask whether the contract breach caused injury to person or property other than the good itself, or simply caused economic loss to the buyer (the so-called **economic loss rule**).[37] If, for example, a defective car catches on fire and burns the buyer, the personal injury would permit the buyer to sue the seller in tort. If, on the other hand, the car burned but did not cause any personal injury or injury to other property, then the action would have to be for breach of

---

[33]UCC §2-715(2)(b).
[34]UCC §2-715, comment 5.
[35]*Restatement (Second) of Torts* §435.
[36]*Robinson Helicopter Co. v. Dana Corp.*, 23 Cal. 4th 979, 102 P.3d 268, 22 Cal. Rptr. 3d 352 (2004).
[37]The three approaches discussed here are described in *East River Steamship Corp. v. Transamerica Delaval, Inc.*, 476 U.S. 858 (1986), in which the U.S. Supreme Court states its view that the "economic loss rule" is the majority approach.

contract under the UCC. Other courts will permit a tort action if the defect <u>could</u> have caused personal injury or property damage, even if it did not in the particular case.[38] Yet other courts do not distinguish between cases in which personal injury is caused and cases in which it is not caused, permitting the tort cause of action at the buyer's option.[39] This last approach seems to be the least popular approach now.

The recent case of *Robinson Helicopter Co. v. Dana Corp.*[40] demonstrates the approach of the California Supreme Court to the issue of when a tort cause of action is available. In that case, the seller of a component part used in the manufacture of helicopters allegedly intentionally misrepresented that the part was being manufactured according to the specifications of the contract. In fact, the manufacturer had changed the way it was making the component. The component then proved to be defective, and had to be replaced at a cost of approximately $1.5 million. Fortunately, the problem was discovered before any helicopters crashed, although they apparently could have. Thus, the only damage suffered by the buyer was economic — the cost of replacing the defective part in all helicopters it had manufactured and sold. The court recognized the economic loss rule as being applicable in California, but held that the misrepresentation that the goods were being manufactured in accordance with specifications was an independent tort, thus permitting an action for fraud. Punitive damages could thus be recovered, which in the court below had been determined to be $6 million.

Q: Why make a distinction between economic loss cases and cases involving personal injury or damage to property other than the goods themselves?

A: There is a concern that permitting tort actions in all cases will result in an increase in liability for sellers and that might result in a chilling effect on commerce. If the only problem suffered by a buyer is economic, the buyer should have to live with the contract the buyer made. If, on the other hand, the goods are harming persons or property, there is a policy against having such goods in the stream of commerce. Thus, it is appropriate to permit an action in tort, which increases the liability of sellers of such goods. On the other hand, do we want to encourage sellers to engage in the kind of conduct allegedly engaged in by the seller in *Robinson Helicopter*? Even if loss is only economic, we might want to punish sellers who intentionally defraud buyers.

---

[38]See, e.g., *Northern Power & Engineering Corp. v. Caterpillar Tractor Co.*, 623 P.2d 324 (Alaska 1981).
[39]See, e.g., *Lloyd F. Smith Co. v. Den-Tal-Ez, Inc.*, 491 N.W.2d 11 (Minn. 1992).
[40]23 Cal. 4th 979, 102 P.3d 268, 22 Cal. Rptr. 3d 352 (2004).

B. Buyer's Remedies Under the CISG

Remedies Available When Contract Avoided	Remedies Available When Contract Not Avoided
Difference between price of substitute goods and contract price — Art. 75	Specific performance, including substitute goods and repair — Art. 46
Difference between market price and contract price if substitute goods not purchased — Art. 76	Price Reduction — Art. 50
Consequential and Incidental Damages — Art. 74	Consequential and Incidental Damages — Art. 74
Interest — Art. 78	Interest — Art. 78

(1) Specific Performance

Unlike the UCC, the United Nations Convention on Contracts for the International Sale of Goods (CISG) demonstrates a preference for specific performance. The buyer is allowed to demand that the seller perform its obligations under the contract.[41] If goods were delivered that are so non-conforming as to amount to a fundamental breach, the buyer may demand substitute goods.[42] The buyer may also demand that the seller repair non-conforming goods as long as it is reasonable to do so.[43] One situation where it would not be reasonable would be if the cost of repair were high in comparison to the value of the goods.

The buyer's right to demand specific performance under the CISG may not mean that much, however, if the case is litigated in a common law country like the United States, where damages is the preferred remedy. Article 28 provides that a court is not required to enter an award for specific performance unless the court would do so under its own domestic law. So, if a case is litigated in a UCC jurisdiction, the ability of a buyer to obtain specific performance will depend on whether it could do so under the UCC.

(2) Price Reduction

Another difference between the CISG and the UCC is the existence of the price reduction remedy under CISG Article 50. Under this remedy, which comes from civil law countries, in a case of non-conformity the buyer may reduce the price by multiplying it by a fraction, the numerator of which is the actual value of the goods at the time of delivery and the denominator of which is the value that the goods would have had at that time if they had been as warranted. This remedy is available whether

---

[41] CISG Art. 46(1).
[42] CISG Art. 46(2).
[43] CISG Art. 46(3).

the buyer has paid the price or not; if the buyer has paid the price, it can sue the seller for a refund.

PRICE REDUCTION — CISG ARTICLE 50

$$\text{Price of Goods} \quad \times \quad \frac{\text{Value of Defective Goods at Time of Delivery}}{\text{Value of Goods as Warranted at Time of Delivery}}$$

In some cases, the price reduction remedy will actually put the buyer in a better position than if the contract had been performed. For example, let us assume that the contract price for goods is $110, and let us assume that the market price falls so that at the time of delivery, the goods as warranted would be worth only $100. Let us assume also that the goods are defective, and that it would cost $10 to repair them. We can then value those defective goods at the time of delivery as being $90. So, a price reduction under Article 50 would result in a reduced price of $99 (price ($110) × value as defective ($90)/value as warranted ($100)). The price would thus be reduced by $11 ($110 − $99). Because it costs only $10 to fix the goods, the injured buyer would have an extra $1 and would thus be in a better position than if the contract had been performed. If you add a few zeros to the numbers in the hypothetical, you can see that this benefit could sometimes be substantial!

(3) Damages

An injured buyer may also sue for damages under the CISG.[44] If the buyer has received the goods and has opted not to avoid or cannot avoid because the breach was not fundamental, damages under the CISG will be measured in a manner similar to UCC §2-714.[45] This is true even if specific performance or price reduction is sought, assuming that those remedies do not make the injured buyer whole.[46] The goal of damages under the CISG is to put the injured party in the position it would have occupied if the contract had been performed, so the calculation of damages will be similar to that under the UCC.[47] Assume for example that a buyer seeks specific performance under the CISG. The buyer can also prove with reasonable certainty that it lost profits of $1,000 because of delay on the part of the seller in delivering. These damages were foreseeable at the time of contracting. If the court orders specific performance, it should also award the $1,000 in lost profits.

In the event that a buyer chooses to avoid the contract, the buyer may make a reasonable substitute purchase and obtain the difference between the price of the substitute purchase and the contract price.[48] For example, assume that the buyer avoids the contract and makes a reasonable substitute purchase of the same goods for $100. If the contract price was $90, the buyer would recover $10 ($100 − $90). If the buyer does not make such a substitute purchase, the buyer is entitled to the

---

[44]CISG Art. 74.
[45]See discussion on pp. 147-149.
[46]CISG Art. 45(2).
[47]CISG Art. 74.
[48]CISG Art. 75.

difference between the market price and the contract price at the time of avoidance if the buyer did not take over the goods, and at the time the goods were taken over if the buyer avoided the contract after taking them over.[49] The relevant market is where the delivery was to have been made.[50] For example, assume that at the time the buyer avoids the contract, the market price of the goods at the place the goods were to be delivered is $100. The buyer does not purchase substitute goods. If the contract price is $90, the buyer may recover $10 ($100 − $90).

In addition to obtaining specific performance, price reduction, the difference between the price of substitute goods and the contract price or the difference between the market price of substitute goods and the contract price, a buyer may also recover incidental or consequential damages under the CISG.[51] Article 74 allows specifically for such damages, including loss of profits, if foreseeable as a possible consequence at the time the parties contracted. Arguably, this is a lesser standard of foreseeability than under the UCC, where courts generally focus on whether economic loss damages were foreseeable as a probable consequence.[52] Foreseeability is determined, however, "in the light of the facts and matters of which [the breaching party] . . . knew or ought to have known" at the conclusion of the breach of contract, so the difference between the UCC and common law rule and the CISG rule may not be that great at the end of the day.[53] So, let us assume that a buyer makes a reasonable purchase of substitute goods for $10 more than the contract price. During the time it took for the buyer to make the substitute purchase, the buyer lost $20 in profits because it did not have sufficient inventory to resell. Assume that the buyer's actions were reasonable in all respects and that it was foreseeable to the seller that the failure to deliver would cause lost profits to the buyer. The buyer may then recover $10 (the difference between the cost of substitute goods and the contract price) plus $20 (the lost profits), equaling $30.

Similar to the UCC and the common law of contracts, the CISG imposes an obligation on the injured party to take reasonable steps to avoid damages, that is, to mitigate them.[54] For example, if a buyer could have reasonably obtained substitute goods but chose not to do so, the buyer cannot obtain lost profits that could have reasonably been avoided if the buyer had gone out and purchased substitute goods.

The CISG also permits the injured party, whether it be the seller or the buyer, to recover prejudgment interest on any sum owed to the injured party. The ability of the injured party to recover interest is discussed more fully under the topic of Seller's Remedies, pages 172-173, *infra*.

C. The Statute of Limitations

The ***statute of limitations*** for breaches of contracts covered by UCC Article 2 is four years after the cause of action has accrued. The parties may reduce the period to not less than one year, but may not extend it.[55] Amended UCC §2-725 extends the

---

[49]CISG Art. 76.
[50]CISG Art. 76(2).
[51]CISG Art. 45.
[52]See p. 143, *supra.*
[53]See Farnsworth, *Damages and Specific Relief*, 27 Am. J. of Comp. L. 247 (1979), reproduced at http://www.cisg.law.pace.edu/cisg/biblio/farns.html.
[54]CISG Art. 77.
[55]UCC §2-725.

limitation period to the later of four years after the cause of action accrued or one year after the breach was or should have been discovered, but in no event longer than five years after the cause of action accrued.

This begs the question of when the cause of action accrues. Section 2-725(2) indicates that the cause of action accrues when the breach occurs, regardless of the injured party's knowledge of the breach. For breach of warranty, the breach occurs when tender of delivery is made, unless the warranty <u>explicitly</u> extends to future performance of the goods. In such a case, the cause of action accrues when the breach is or should have been discovered.

For breaches of the implied warranty of merchantability and fitness, the cause of action would accrue at the time of tender of delivery because those warranties do not explicitly extend to future performance. For express warranties, there may be some question as to whether the warranty extends to future performance. Most courts require that the warranty make reference to some time period to explicitly extend to future performance. For example, in one case a warranty was given that a particular adhesive would work as well on filon as it did on aluminum.[56] The appellate court reversed the trial court in finding that this was not a warranty that explicitly extended to future performance, even though the adhesive worked for five years on aluminum.

One issue that has come up is whether someone who is suing on an indemnity theory is barred from suing a seller of goods if the statute of limitations has run. To give an example, assume that a contractor purchases a product that it uses in constructing a building. The product is warranted as being merchantable. Assume that five years later, the owner of the building discovers that the product has caused structural damage to the building, and thus sues the contractor for negligence in constructing the building. The contractor would like to sue the seller of the defective product for indemnity. The statute of limitations for the indemnity action does not accrue until the indemnitee has actually discharged the obligation being indemnified, meaning when the contractor pays the owner of the building. On the other hand, the UCC statute of limitations for breach of warranty has run. Can the contractor proceed with the indemnity action against the seller of goods?

There is a split of authority on the question of whether the indemnity action can be brought if the claim for breach of warranty is time barred. The majority of courts would permit the indemnity action to be brought,[57] and the 2003 amendments to §2-725 are in accord with this approach. The amendments, which add a §2-725(2)(d) on this point, indicate that if a buyer has a cause of action

S i d e b a r

THE POLICY OF FINALITY

The statute of limitations under the UCC may seem harsh in that it could bar an action before a buyer even knew that one existed. Latent defects in goods may not rear their ugly heads until after the four-year limitation period. Some goods can generally be expected to work for more than four years. As one court put it, however, §2-725 "serve[s] the important function of providing a point of finality for businesses after which they c[an] destroy their business records without the fear of a subsequent breach of contract for sale or breach of warranty suit arising to haunt them." *Ontario Hydro v. Zallea Sys.*, 569 F. Supp. 1261, 1266 (D. Del. 1983). Arguably, permitting a party to sue on an indemnity action when a direct suit for breach of warranty would be barred undercuts this policy, but there is also concern for imposing liability on the party that really ought to pay.

---

[56]*Western Recreational Vehicles v. Swift Adhesives*, 23 F.3d 1547 (9th Cir. 1994).
[57]See, e.g., *Kohl's Dept. Stores v. Target Stores*, 290 F. Supp. 674 (E.D. Va. 2003).

for indemnity, the cause of action accrues when the claim is asserted against the buyer.

For international sales, UNCITRAL has promulgated the Convention on the Limitation Period in the International Sale of Goods (CLPISG), which also provides a four-year period and which considers similar issues to the UCC regarding the time that the cause of action has accrued.[58] For example, generally the cause of action accrues at the time the breach occurs, which in cases involving non-conforming goods is when the goods are handed over to the buyer.[59] If, however, the seller warranties that the goods will perform for a specified period of time, the breach occurs at the earlier of (1) the buyer's notification to the seller of the non-conformity or (2) when the specified period of time for performance expires.[60]

Under choice of law principles, ordinarily the forum state will apply its own statute of limitations, although it may apply the shorter statute of limitations of a jurisdiction that had a closer relationship to the transaction and the parties. *Restatement (Second) of Conflict of Laws* §142. Thus, if an international sale of goods case is litigated in a U.S. state that has adopted the UCC, the UCC rule or the shorter statute of limitations of the jurisdiction more closely related to the transaction will apply unless the other nation involved has also acceded to the CLPISG. As is the case with the CISG, the United States has declared that its citizens will be bound to the CLPISG only if the nation of the other party involved in the transaction has also acceded to it.

SUMMARY

Buyer's Remedies Under the UCC

■ If the seller breaches by not delivering or if the buyer justifiably rejects the goods or revokes acceptance of them, the buyer may cover by purchasing substitute goods. If the substitute purchase is a reasonable one made within a reasonable time, the buyer may recover the difference between the cost of the substitute goods and the contract price, together with incidental and consequential damages minus any costs saved as a result of breach.

■ If the buyer does not make a reasonable substitute purchase, the buyer may recover the difference between the market price for substitute goods and the contract price at the time the buyer learns of the breach, together with incidental and consequential damages minus any costs saved as a result of breach.

■ The market price is determined at the place for tender unless the goods are rejected or acceptance is revoked at the place of arrival, in which case the market price is determined at the place of arrival.

■ In cases in which the seller repudiates, the time for measuring damages is the time the buyer learns of the repudiation if the case comes to trial before the time for performance. Otherwise, courts split on whether it should be measured then, at

---

[58]The CLPISG was promulgated in 1974 and amended in 1980 to make it conform to the CISG. The CLPISG, as amended in 1980, has been acceded to by 18 nations, including the United States. Some of the nations that adopted the 1974 CLPISG have not adopted the 1980 amendments. For a complete listing, see http://www.uncitral.org under the link "status of texts."
[59]CLPISG Art. 10.
[60]CLPISG Art. 11.

the time for performance, or at a commercially reasonable time after the buyer learns of the repudiation. The amendments to Article 2 choose a commercially reasonable time after the buyer learns of the repudiation.

■ Incidental damages are damages incurred by the buyer in dealing with the goods after breach or in attempting to mitigate damages.

■ Consequential damages are a broader category of damages, such as lost profits resulting from the seller's breach, which are recoverable to the buyer if they were reasonably foreseeable as a probable consequence of breach at the time of contracting, are not reasonably avoidable, and can be shown with reasonable certainty.

■ An injured buyer can obtain specific performance for non-delivered goods if the goods are unique or in other special circumstances, such as inability to cover.

■ An injured buyer can obtain replevin for goods identified to the contract if it is difficult to obtain substitute goods.

■ An injured buyer can obtain goods that are identified to the contract if the buyer has made a down payment for the goods before the seller refuses to deliver and (a) the goods are consumer goods or (b) the seller becomes insolvent within ten days after receipt of the first installment on the price.

■ The buyer is required to give notice of breach within a reasonable time after the buyer knows or should know of the breach or is barred from any remedy.

■ If the buyer accepts goods that are defective, the court may measure damages in any manner that is reasonable, such as the difference between the value of the goods as accepted and the value of the goods as warranted at the time and place of acceptance. Cost of repair may be another reasonable way of measuring damages.

■ Consequential damages and incidental damages are also allowable in cases in which the goods are accepted.

■ Sometimes an action in tort is also available in cases in which goods are defective. Generally, either an independent tort is required (e.g., fraud in the inducement), or else the loss must be to person or property other than the goods themselves (e.g., the goods personally injure the buyer).

■ The statute of limitations is four years from when the cause of action accrues. For implied warranties, the cause of action accrues at the time of delivery. For warranties that explicitly extend to the future, the cause of action accrues when the breach occurs or should have been discovered.

Buyer's Remedies Under the CISG

■ Unlike the UCC, the CISG generally permits a buyer to elect specific performance as a remedy, although courts in common law countries like the United States may refuse to grant specific performance if they would not do so under their own domestic law (e.g., the UCC).

■ The buyer is allowed to reduce the price if goods do not conform to the contract. The price is multiplied by a fraction, the numerator of which is the value of the goods as delivered and the denominator of which is the value of the goods at the time of delivery if they had been as warranted.

- Similar to the UCC, the buyer may recover the difference between the price paid for substitute goods and the contract price if the substitute purchase is reasonable.

- Similar to the UCC, the buyer may recover the difference between the market price and the contract price for substitute goods if the buyer avoids the contract but does not purchase substitute goods. Market price is determined at the time of avoidance of the contract and at the place that delivery was to be made.

- Consequential damages are recoverable if reasonably foreseeable as a possible result of breach.

CONNECTIONS

Choice of Law

The choice of law determination is important because the remedies available may differ depending on whether the common law, UCC, or CISG apply. All three laws generally award damages on the expectation principle, namely that we try to put the injured party in the position that the party would have been in but for breach. The CISG may be a bit more liberal than the UCC or common law in awarding consequential damages as the foreseeability test seems less restrictive (i.e., foreseeable as a possible consequence compared to foreseeable as a probable consequence). Also, the CISG is more liberal in permitting specific performance than the UCC or the common law. That difference is not significant if the case is litigated in the United States, as the CISG yields to domestic law on the question of specific performance. The UCC may be a bit more liberal than common law in permitting specific performance in cases of long-term supply contracts.

Contract Formation and Terms

As the purpose of contract remedies is to put the injured party in the position that person would have occupied if the contract had been performed, we need to determine what exactly was promised to the injured party. The terms of the contract may depend on how the contract was formed. If the parties exchanged forms containing varying terms, we need to do a §2-207 analysis to determine the terms of the contract.

We need to determine if any warranties of quality or title were given or were properly disclaimed. If goods were damaged or destroyed during the sales transaction, a question may exist as to whether the buyer or the seller had the risk of loss at the time. We need to also analyze whether any agreements between the parties might be unenforceable on the basis of parol evidence analysis or unconscionability.

Performance

The remedies available to the buyer depend on whether the goods were accepted, rejected, acceptance revoked, or never delivered. It must be determined whether the seller breached the contract at all—if not, the buyer has no remedies available. If the seller did breach and the buyer accepted the goods, then the buyer's remedy is to sue for any damages relating to the nonconforming tender. Courts measure damages in any manner reasonable. If the goods were rejected or acceptance was revoked, the buyer may recover the difference between the price of a reasonable substitute purchase and the contract price or, if no substitute purchase was made, the difference between the market price for the goods and the contract price. If the goods were never delivered, the buyer may in some cases seek specific performance. In all cases, the buyer can recover consequential damages if they can be shown with reasonable certainty and were reasonably foreseeable.

Seller's Remedies

If it turns out that the buyer breached rather than the seller, the seller will have remedies as discussed in the next chapter. For example, the buyer might wrongfully reject goods, wrongfully asserting that the goods were non-conforming to the contract. The seller then would have an action for damages or the price of the goods, as determined in the next chapter.

Third Parties

If damages occurred to goods while the goods were in transit and the risk of loss was on the buyer, the buyer's recourse may be against the shipping company that transported the goods. If a bank properly honored a letter of credit in favor of the seller and the goods prove to be non-conforming, the buyer will have to reimburse the bank but can sue the seller for damages caused by the non-conformity.

Seller's Remedies

8

In this chapter, we will consider the remedies available to the seller in the event of the buyer's breach. If a buyer refuses to take delivery and

OVERVIEW

In this chapter, we will consider the remedies available to the seller in the event of the buyer's breach. If a buyer refuses to take delivery and does not pay for goods, the seller may wish to resell the goods and hold the buyer responsible for the difference between what the buyer agreed to pay and what the goods were sold for. Or, the seller may wish to sue the buyer for the price of the goods. If goods are delivered to the buyer and the buyer doesn't pay, the seller may wish to get the goods back. We will talk about the circumstances in which the seller can obtain these remedies under both the Uniform Commercial Code (UCC) and the United Nations Convention on Contracts for the International Sale of Goods (CISG).

A. SELLER'S REMEDIES UNDER THE UCC

1. Goods Not Delivered Due to Buyer's Breach and Goods Wrongfully Rejected
2. Goods Delivered
3. Liquidated Damages and Breaching Buyer's Right to Restitution

B. SELLER'S REMEDIES UNDER THE CISG

1. Specific Performance
2. Damages
3. Interest on Sums Owed
4. Liquidated Damages

A. Seller's Remedies Under the UCC

Remedies When Goods Wrongfully Rejected or Buyer Breaches Before Delivery	Remedies When Goods Accepted
(1) Complete manufacture — §2-704 (2) Stop delivery — §2-705 (3) Resell, and recover difference between contract price and resale price — §2-706 (4) Recover difference between contract price and market price — §2-708(1) (5) Recover lost profit on sale — §2-708(2) (6) Recover the price — §2-709 (7) Recover incidental damages — §2-710	(1) Right to reclaim — §§2-507, 2-511, 2-702 (2) Recover the price — §2-709

As is the case with buyer's remedies, the policy of the Uniform Commercial Code (UCC) according to §1-305 is to put the injured party in the position that it would have been if the contract had been performed. It is not the goal of the UCC to punish breaching parties beyond what it takes to make the injured party whole. The provisions governing seller's remedies to a great extent mirror those governing buyer's remedies, distinguishing cases in which the goods have not been delivered from those in which the goods have been delivered and accepted.

(1) Goods Not Delivered Due to Buyer's Breach and Goods Wrongfully Rejected

Section 2-703 provides, among other options, that if the buyer fails to make a payment when due or wrongfully rejects or revokes acceptance of goods, the seller may withhold delivery of goods, stop delivery by a *carrier* or other *bailee* pursuant to §2-705, resell the goods and recover the difference between the contract price and the resale price, or recover damages under a contract/market formula similar to the one previously discussed under buyer's remedies. The seller may also refuse delivery except for cash if the seller discovers that the buyer is insolvent.

(a) Right to Refuse Delivery

If a seller discovers the buyer to be *insolvent*, the seller may refuse delivery except for cash, including payment for all goods that have been previously delivered.[1] Insolvency is defined as, among other things, failing to make payments to creditors when due.[2] If the goods have been delivered to a carrier and the buyer repudiates or fails to make a payment when due, the seller may stop delivery of the carload, truckload, planeload, or larger shipments. If goods have been delivered to a carrier

---

[1] UCC §2-702(1).
[2] UCC §1-201(b)(23).

and the seller discovers that the buyer is insolvent, the seller may stop delivery of any shipment.[3]

The right to stop delivery exists until (a) the buyer takes physical possession of the goods, (b) a bailee other than a carrier (e.g., a warehouse operator) acknowledges that the bailee holds the goods for the buyer, (c) the carrier acknowledges the buyer's rights by reshipping the goods on the buyer's direction, or (d) a **negotiable document of title** (e.g., a negotiable bill of lading) is delivered to the buyer.

We will discuss documents of title in more detail on pages 188-191 and 192-195, *infra*, and we discussed them briefly before on pages 78-79, *supra*. Documents of title can be negotiable or non-negotiable, depending on their form. If they are negotiable, they are more easily transferable, and the person obtaining possession of the negotiable document of title can obtain good title in the underlying goods. One can understand, then, that if a negotiable document of title is involved, the carrier should really only follow instructions of someone in possession of such a document.

To demonstrate how the right to stop delivery works, assume that the seller has delivered the goods to a trucking company for transportation across the country. The trucking company, a carrier, issues a bill of lading, which is the contract for shipment of the goods and is a document of title. The bill of lading is not negotiable. The journey will take several days before the goods reach the buyer. On the day after the goods are given to the carrier, the seller learns that the buyer is not paying its debts; this means that the buyer is insolvent. The seller may call the trucking company and stop the shipment of the goods.

(b) Seller's Resale Remedy

If the seller has possession of the goods after the buyer's breach, the seller may resell the goods and hold the buyer responsible for the difference between what the buyer agreed to pay and what the seller is able to obtain for the goods. The seller can also recover any **incidental damages**, such as storage charges incurred until the goods can be resold. Subtracted from this amount would be any expenses saved as a result of the buyer's breach.[4]

SELLER'S RESALE REMEDY — UCC §2-706

Contract Price on Breached Contract – Resale Price + Incidental Damages – Expenses Saved Due to Breach = Seller's Recovery

---

The resale must be in good faith and in a commercially reasonable manner. The seller cannot have a "fire sale," sell the goods for next to nothing, and then hold the buyer responsible for the difference in price.

The resale can be either at a private sale or a public sale (i.e., an auction). Notice of the sale must be given to the breaching buyer within a reasonable period of time

---

[3]UCC §2-705.
[4]UCC §2-706.

before any private sale.[5] Notice of the time and place of a public sale must be given to the breaching party a reasonable time before the sale unless the goods are perishable or threaten to decline speedily in value.[6]

Any public sale must be at a usual place or market for public sale if one is reasonably available.[7] Only identified goods may be sold at a public sale except where there is a recognized market for a public sale of futures in goods of the kind involved.[8] If the goods are not within view at the time of the public sale, the notification of sale must state where the goods may be examined.[9] The seller may purchase the goods at the public sale, but not at a private sale.[10]

Except for public sales as mentioned in the preceding paragraph, it is not necessary that the goods that are being resold be the exact goods that were identified to the contract for sale that was breached. The resale must be reasonably identified as referring to the broken contract.[11] So, if the contract is for fungible goods, for example, oil, the exact oil that was to go to the breaching buyer need not be the oil that is sold in the resale. But, if the seller delays in holding a resale during the time that the market is dropping, the seller will not be permitted after a reasonable period of time to claim that a sale at a lower price is the one that was in replacement of the breached contract.[12]

To demonstrate how the seller's remedy under §2-706 works, assume that the buyer has breached a contract to buy a piece of equipment for $3,000. The seller stores the equipment and notifies the buyer of its intent to sell the equipment by private sale after 20 days. The seller advertises the equipment for sale, and is able ultimately to sell it for $2,500. If the seller's notice of sale to the buyer was reasonable and if the sale was conducted in a commercially reasonable manner, the seller could recover $500 from the breaching buyer ($3,000 − $2,500) plus any reasonable storage charges that were incurred, minus any expenses saved due to breach.

> ## Sidebar
>
> ### THE MITIGATION PRINCIPLE
>
> As we saw with regard to buyer's remedies, the UCC follows the common law requirement that an injured party take reasonable steps to mitigate (reduce) damages. The purpose of requiring notice to the breaching buyer before a resale is to permit that party to supervise the sale to make sure that it brings a fair price. The same is true with regard to the requirement that the sale be commercially reasonable. The breaching party is only responsible for the difference between the contract price and resale price if the seller takes the steps required by §2-706 to reduce the buyer's damages.

If the seller does not hold a sale that conforms with §2-706's requirements, the seller is not without remedy. The seller may still attempt to obtain recovery under the contract/market formula, which we will now discuss.[13]

(c) Seller's Contract/Market Formula

UCC §2-708(1) permits the seller to sue for the difference between the contract price of the breached contract and the market price at the time and place of tender, the

---

[5] UCC §2-706(3).
[6] UCC §2-706(4)(b).
[7] *Id.*
[8] UCC §2-706(4)(a).
[9] UCC §2-706(4)(c).
[10] UCC §2-706(4)(d).
[11] UCC §2-706(2).
[12] See *Apex Oil. Co. v. The Belcher Co.*, 855 F.2d 997 (2d Cir. 1988).
[13] UCC §2-706, comment 2.

contract/market differential. Added to this amount would be any incidental damages, and subtracted would be any expenses saved as a result of breach. This is a hypothetical resale remedy, similar to the hypothetical cover remedy available for buyers.

SELLER'S CONTRACT/MARKET DIFFERENTIAL — UCC §2-708(1)

Contract Price of Breached Contract — Market Price for Substitute Goods + Incidental Damages — Costs Saved Due to Breach = Seller's Recovery

---

Time and Method of Measurement. One difference between the way that seller's damages are measured under the contract/market differential and the way that buyer's damages are measured is that seller's damages are measured "at the time and place for tender" whereas buyer's damages are measured "at the time when the buyer learned of the breach." As we discussed previously, the language "learned of the breach" raises confusion regarding when damages are to be measured when a seller anticipatorily repudiates a contract.[14] Under §2-708, measurement is at the time of tender, that is, the time for performance, unless the case comes to trial before that time, in which case it is at the time the seller learned of the repudiation.[15] Under the 2003 amendments to Article 2, the time for measuring damages for both sellers and buyers will be a commercially reasonable time after the aggrieved party learns of the repudiation.[16]

Market price can sometimes be determined by looking at trade journals or newspapers.[17] It may also be the case that a resale of the goods themselves may be probative of the market price. For example, assume that the seller does not give notice to the breaching buyer of a resale, but goes ahead and sells the goods to several different buyers who all pay roughly the same price. Assuming no evidence of bad faith, the price paid by those buyers is probably the best evidence of the market price for the goods. The seller can then receive the difference between the contract price and the resale price under §2-708(1), even though §2-706 is not available because of the failure to give notice.[18]

Is Remedy Available If Seller Resells? A question exists as to whether a seller has an option to proceed under the contract/market formula if it resells the goods for a greater amount than the market price. For example, assume that the contract price for goods is $10. At the time and place for tender, the market price for the goods is $5. The seller is able to resell the goods for $7. If the seller is allowed to recover under the contract/market formula, the seller will receive $5. If the seller is forced to proceed under the resale formula of §2-706, the seller will receive only $3.

Under buyer's remedies, you may remember that the Code clearly indicates that a buyer who covers is not allowed to proceed under the contract/market differential.

---

[14]See pp. 142-143, *supra.*
[15]UCC §2-723.
[16]Amended UCC §2-708(1)(b) & Amended UCC §2-713(1)(b).
[17]UCC §2-724.
[18]See *B & R Textile Corp. v. Paul Rothman Industries Ltd.,* 101 Misc. 2d 98, 420 N.Y.S.2d 609 (N.Y. Civ. 1979).

The Code is silent on this issue when it comes to seller's remedies. One might assume, then, that the drafters intended to permit the seller to sue for the contract/market differential no matter what, especially because official commentary indicates that the doctrine of election of remedies is rejected.[19] Nevertheless, the overall UCC policy of seeking to put the injured party in the position that it would have occupied if the contract had been performed should be kept in mind. Allowing a greater recovery might unduly penalize a breaching buyer. This discussion may be almost entirely theoretical, as it seems that the seller is generally trying to argue for recovery under the resale formula and the buyer is the one trying to limit the seller to the contract/market differential.

No Consequential Damages for Seller Under Unamended Article 2. You may have noticed in the discussion of the resale remedy and the contract/market differential the conspicuous absence of any recovery of consequential damages by the seller. The UCC permits an injured seller to recover incidental damages, which are defined as "any commercially reasonable charges, expenses or commissions incurred in stopping delivery, in the transportation, care and custody of goods after the buyer's breach, in connection with return or resale of the goods or otherwise resulting from the breach." There is not, however, a provision allowing consequential damages for sellers that is comparable to §2-715(2)(a) for buyers. The view is that a seller can generally resell goods and thus is unlikely to suffer consequential damages. Even if the goods cannot be resold, the seller can sue the buyer for the price of those goods, and the delay in recovering the price is unlikely to harm the seller other than through the loss of interest on the money. The lost interest might be recoverable as incidental damages. The 2003 amendments to Article 2 do permit recovery of consequential damages by sellers in an appropriate case, that is, if they are foreseeable as a probable consequence of breach at the time of contracting. The amendments do not permit recovery of consequential damages from consumers in consumer contracts.

F A Q

Q: When would a seller suffer consequential damages?

A: The commentary to Amended UCC §2-710 notes that "Sellers rarely suffer compensable consequential damages." There might be a case, however, in which the buyer is aware at the time of contracting that the buyer's timely performance under the sales contract is essential to the seller's ability to continue to produce goods. If the buyer stops paying, the seller will have to shut its doors, and may thus lose profits on other transactions in the future. An example of such a case might be *Cherwell-Ralli, Inc. v. Rytman Grain Co.*, 180 Conn. 714, 433 A.2d 984, discussed on pages 121-122, *supra*, in which the buyer's repeated failure to pay for goods delivered ultimately resulted in the seller shutting its doors.

---

[19]UCC §2-703, official comment 1. See also the discussion of the buyer's contract/market differential and the argument that it should be available even if the buyer has not suffered any actual damage, pp. 141-142, *supra*.

(d) Lost Profits

If the resale formula and contract/market formula do not place an injured seller in the position it would have occupied had the contract been performed, the seller is allowed to sue for profits lost on the sale. The *lost-profit rule* of §2-708(2) states that in such a case, the seller is entitled to lost profits, including reasonable overhead, with incidental damages and costs reasonably incurred, subtracting any payments or proceeds from resale.

The lost-profit rule of §2-708(2) is problematic for two reasons. One, it does not tell us exactly when it is to be used. Two, it is vague as to how the lost profits should be calculated.

SELLER'S LOST PROFIT REMEDY — UCC §2-708(2)

Profit Lost on Sale (including reasonable overhead) + Incidental Damages + Costs Reasonably Incurred in Performing Under Contract − Payments or Proceeds of Resale = Seller's Recovery

---

When Should Lost Profits Be Awarded? Perhaps the most common situation in which courts use the lost profits formula is in the situation of the so-called *lost volume seller*. Assume, for example, that a car dealer has ten cars of the same model and color on its lot. The cars are identically equipped. Buyer #1 contracts to purchase one of the cars for the market price of the car. Buyer #1 breaches the contract, and the seller sells the car to Buyer #2 for the same price. Under UCC §§2-706 and 2-708(1), the seller's damages are nominal. The seller argues, however, that it is not made whole by such a recovery because it lost a sale when Buyer #1 breached — if Buyer #1 had not breached, the seller would have made two sales rather than one. To make the seller whole, the seller should be allowed to recover the profit it lost on the contract with Buyer #1.

Contrast this situation to a private party who contracts to sell her car. Buyer #1 breaches the contract, but the seller is able to sell her car to Buyer #2 for the same price that Buyer #1 was supposed to pay. In this situation, there truly are no damages to the seller because she mitigated her loss by selling to Buyer #2. She did not have two cars to sell, and thus did not lose any sales.

Sidebar

THE LAW OF DIMINISHING RETURNS AND THE LOST VOLUME SELLER

In some situations, a seller would choose not to make an extra sale even if the seller could do so. That is because the seller is operating at capacity, and to make another sale would require the seller to hire additional employees or to invest in more equipment or a larger physical plant. For example, assume that a manufacturer can sell a car to a dealer for $20,000. The manufacturer's existing employees cannot make another car, however, within their normal work schedule. To make another car will require the manufacturer to hire two additional employees at a cost of $50,000. Obviously, it does not make sense to make and sell another car at this point. It would make sense to hire the additional employees only if they can manufacture enough cars to justify the additional expense incurred and buyers can be found who are willing to purchase the cars. For more of a discussion on this topic, see Charles J. Goetz & Robert E. Scott, *Measuring Sellers Damages: The Lost-Profits Puzzle*, 31 Stan. L. Rev. 323 (1979).

The seller will have the burden to prove that it could have and would have made two sales rather than one. That will depend on its inventory level and whether it would be profitable for it to make a second sale. At some point, a company operates at capacity and additional sales are not profitable.

Two other situations in which the lost profits formula might be available involve component manufacturers and middlepersons, like brokers. Let's assume that a buyer contracts with a furniture dealer to specially manufacture a sofa for the buyer's living room. Before the seller completes the sofa, the buyer calls the seller and repudiates the contract. We can also assume a situation in which a buyer contracts with a car broker to obtain a certain model car for an agreed price. Before the broker can obtain the car, the buyer repudiates the contract. In both of these cases, the seller (i.e., the manufacturer and the broker) does not have a completed good to resell. Thus, the resale formula and the contract/market formula will not put the seller in the same position it would have occupied if the breaching buyer had performed. To be made whole, the seller would like to sue for the profits lost on the contract with the breaching buyer.

How Are Lost Profits Calculated? Once we determine that the lost profits measure of damages is appropriate, we have to figure out how much profit was lost on the breached contract. The statutory language is a bit unclear. It is helpful to keep in mind the policy of UCC remedies—to put the seller in the position it would have occupied if the contract had been performed. Let's return to our hypothetical involving the car dealer who has an extensive inventory of cars. Buyer #1 breaches. What would have happened if the lost volume seller had sold a car to Buyer #1 and another car to Buyer #2? It would have earned the price on both cars, but it would have lost both of them, which it buys at wholesale. The lost profit then can be determined at least partially as the contract price minus the wholesale cost of the car to the seller. For example, assume that Buyer #1 agreed to pay $20,000 for a car that costs the dealer $15,000. The dealer should receive $5,000 on a lost profits theory, subject to reduction for any expenses that the dealer saved in not making two sales.

Should the rent that the car dealership pays for its showroom and the salaries paid to its salespersons be taken into account in determining the lost profit? The language of §2-708(2) suggests that the lost profit recovery should include reasonable overhead, so it would appear that costs that do not change should not be taken into account. In other words, if it costs the dealership the same in terms of rent and payroll if the dealership makes two sales rather than one, then there are no savings when the buyer breaches and there is nothing to subtract from the profit. It is a question of fact, however, as to how much of a seller's costs are fixed overhead and how much are variable depending on each sale. Figuring this out is a job for accountants and economists rather than lawyers!

Lost profit calculation for the components manufacturer is a little more complicated. First, there is a question as to whether the manufacturer should go ahead and complete the product and try to resell it, or should instead scrap the uncompleted product and sue for lost profits. In making this determination, the UCC requires the seller to exercise reasonable commercial judgment to the end of trying to reduce loss.[20] If the seller makes a commercially unreasonable choice, the court will limit the seller's damages to damages the seller would have suffered had the

---

[20]UCC §2-704.

seller acted reasonably.[21] If the good is almost complete, it probably makes sense to complete it in most cases. This will reduce the damages that the buyer will incur, even if the buyer winds up paying the price for a good the buyer does not want. In all likelihood, the good will have some value to somebody else, so the buyer could get back at least some of the price by reselling it. If the good is not very far along, it may not make sense to complete it, especially if it is a specialty item that is unlikely to be saleable on the open market. The buyer will wind up paying the lost profits that the seller would have made on the deal, but that will be less than the purchase price for a good the buyer does not want.

Assuming the seller makes a commercially reasonable decision to scrap goods, we should again try to figure out how much money will put the seller in the position that it would have occupied if the goods had been completed and the buyer had paid for them. Let's assume a contract price of $100 and an estimate that it will cost another $50 to complete manufacture of the goods. The scrap value of the goods is $20. If the contract would have been performed, the seller would have made $100, but it would have had to pay another $50 to complete the goods. Because of the breach, the seller also has $20 worth of scrap that it would not have had if the contract had been performed. So, to put the seller in the position it would have occupied if the buyer had performed, we should award the seller $100 minus $50 (cost saved by breach) minus $20 (the scrap that can be sold), for a total recovery of $30. The "due credit for payments or proceeds of resale" language in §2-708(2) supports crediting the breaching buyer for the scrap value.

(e) Action for the Price

In cases in which the buyer has not accepted the goods, the seller may sue for the price of the goods in two situations: (1) where the risk of loss has passed to the buyer but the goods have not yet been accepted, and (2) where the goods have been identified to the contract and the seller is unable to resell the goods at a reasonable price or circumstances reasonably indicate that the seller will be unable to do so.[22] In the first situation, the seller's right to sue for the price exists for only a commercially reasonable time after the risk of loss passes to the buyer; the Code places a burden on the seller to reclaim the goods or make certain that there is insurance in place if the buyer wrongfully rejects goods after the risk of loss has passed to the buyer.

To give an example of the first situation in which the price is available, assume a contract for the sale of a car that the buyer has driven home. Immediately and within the reasonable period of time permitted for inspection, the buyer contacts the seller and wrongfully rejects the car; the buyer just had a change of heart. The buyer puts a stop payment on the check that had been given to the seller to pay the price of the car. Assume that the next day, the car is stolen from the buyer's driveway, even though the car was locked. The risk of loss passed to the buyer when the buyer drove the car off the seller's lot. The seller would be allowed to sue the buyer for the price. Now, if the seller allowed the car to remain in the buyer's possession for a significant period of time while the parties haggled over whether the buyer had a right to reject, at some point a commercially reasonable time would have lapsed, so that if the car were stolen after that time, the seller would no longer have a right to sue for the price.

.

---

[21] See *Detroit Power Screwdriver Co. v. Ladney*, 25 Mich. App. 478, 181 N.W.2d 828 (1970).
[22] UCC §2-709.

The second situation in which the action for the price is available is really the seller's right to specific performance. Because the goods are difficult to resell, monetary damages are inadequate. So, the Code permits the seller to get the price for the goods and the buyer gets the goods, like it or not. This remedy will probably be available in situations involving specialty goods that have been specially ordered by the breaching buyer—there may not be a ready market for resale of such goods.

The Code provides that if the seller is subsequently able to resell the goods, any proceeds obtained from the sale are for the buyer's account.[23] Assume, for example, that the seller is unable to sell specially manufactured goods for a considerable period of time after the buyer's breach and that there really is no market for the goods. The seller tells the buyer that it will hold the buyer responsible for the price, which is $100. The buyer continues to refuse to pay. Finally, someone comes along who is willing to buy the goods for $80. The covenant of good faith and fair dealing should prevent a seller from selling the goods at a fire sale price and then holding the buyer responsible for the difference between the price and the low proceeds of resale.[24] Assuming that it would be good faith for the seller to sell the goods at the discount rather than going to court and suing the buyer for the full price, the seller could recover the difference between the price and the proceeds ultimately obtained, or $100 - $80 = $20.

(2) Goods Delivered

In situations in which the goods have been delivered and the buyer does not pay, the seller might like to either recover the goods themselves or sue the buyer for the price. With respect to reclaiming the goods themselves, the seller has limited rights to do so, unless the seller has reserved a security interest in the goods.

(a) Reclamation of Goods

Under Article 2, the seller may reclaim goods if either the buyer has paid with a check that has been dishonored by the bank ("bounced") or if the seller discovers that the buyer received the goods on credit while insolvent.[25] In both cases, the right to reclaim goods is cut off if the goods are subsequently transferred to a good faith purchaser for value. In the case of goods sold to an insolvent buyer, the demand for reclamation must be made within ten days after the goods are received, unless misrepresentation of solvency was made by the buyer to the seller in writing within three months before delivery.[26] Under the 2003 amendments to Article 2, the time within which the seller must reclaim goods received on credit while the buyer is insolvent is changed to a reasonable time in all cases, whether written representation of solvency is given or not. Also in the case of insolvency, if the seller reclaims the goods, the seller has no further remedy against the breaching buyer.[27]

A seller who is interested in reclaiming goods after the buyer fails to pay is better off taking a security interest in the goods. A security interest is a consensual lien on goods given to secure the obligation to pay for them. Security interests are governed

---

[23] UCC §2-709(2).
[24] UCC §1-304.
[25] UCC §§2-507, 2-511 & 2-702.
[26] UCC §2-702(2).
[27] UCC §2-702(3).

by Article 9 of the UCC and are covered in other commercial law courses. They are beyond the scope of this book.

Q: Why can't a seller always take the goods back if the buyer doesn't pay?

A: The law disfavors secret property interests in either real property or in goods. Once goods are in the hands of a buyer, the world believes that the buyer has title to the goods and is free to transfer them to others. If a buyer doesn't pay for goods the buyer has received, the seller can sue for monetary damages. The Code permits reclamation of goods in situations in which the buyer's ability to pay those damages is in question, such as when the buyer is insolvent or has bounced a check. If a seller wants more rights to reclaim goods when a buyer doesn't pay, the seller can take a security interest as noted previously. Generally, a seller doing this will be required to file a public notice, known as a "financing statement," telling the world of its interest in the goods. This is like recording a mortgage on real property. As noted, security interests are typically covered in other UCC courses.

(b) Action for Price

If goods have been accepted, the seller is allowed to sue the buyer for the price of the goods.[28] As previously noted, acceptance of goods triggers the buyer's obligation to pay for them. What happens if a buyer wrongfully revokes acceptance of goods before having paid the price? If the goods are still in the possession of the buyer, courts have held that the seller still has a right to sue for the price—the wrongful revocation does not undo the acceptance.[29] The UCC suggests, however, that there may be situations where a wrongful revocation will occur and the seller will not have a right to sue for the price—it suggests that in such situations the seller may sue under §2-708.[30] The UCC does not tell us under what circumstances the seller would be precluded from suing on the price, but it might make sense to say that if the goods have been returned to the seller, the seller should take some action, if possible, to resell them to reduce loss. The seller will generally be in a better position to sell the goods than the buyer.

(3) Liquidated Damages and Breaching Buyer's Right to Restitution

(a) Liquidated Damages

The parties may contractually agree to liquidate damages, but may not set an amount that would constitute a penalty. "**Liquidated damages**" simply means that the parties agree how much money will be paid if one or both of the parties are in

---

[28]UCC §2-709(1)(a).
[29]*F & P Builders v. Lowe's of Texas, Inc.*, 786 S.W.2d 502 (1990).
[30]UCC §2-709(3).

UNENFORCEABILITY OF PENALTY CLAUSES—THE EFFICIENT BREACH THEORY REVISITED

In the previous chapter, we discussed why courts generally do not award punitive damages in contract cases. Arguably, we do not want to deter so-called efficient breaches in which goods are moved to someone who values them more highly. As long as the injured party is given the benefit of the bargain, we should not care what the breaching party does. That theory may also explain why penalty clauses are unenforceable—we don't even want parties to consent to being penalized for breaching a contract. There is also a concern that a penalty clause might indicate unfair bargaining—a stronger party taking advantage of a weaker one. It seems that nowadays there may be more of a concern with unfair bargaining, and for that reason the amendments to Article 2 are more likely to uphold liquidated damage provisions in commercial contracts as compared to consumer contracts.

breach of contract. Under the law, any amount of liquidated damages must be "reasonable in light of the anticipated or actual harm caused by the breach, the difficulties of proof of loss, and the inconvenience or nonfeasibility of otherwise obtaining an adequate remedy."[31] This rule is essentially the same as the rule in *Restatement (Second) of Contracts* §356.

Let's assume that in a contract for the sale of goods the parties set $5,000 as liquidated damages in the event that the buyer breaches the contract. They set this amount because it is unclear whether the seller will be able to resell the goods. If it turns out that the seller can resell the goods for the same price that the buyer had agreed to pay, then the $5,000 would be an unlawful penalty and the court would refuse to require the buyer to pay it. Under the 2003 amendments to Article 2, the analysis would be different because, except in consumer contracts, the difficulty of proof of loss is not to be considered. If the $5,000 was reasonable in light of anticipated harm caused by the breach, it would be upheld under the amended version of §2-718. The commentary to the amendments also suggests that an unreasonably low liquidated damage amount should also be unenforceable.

(b) The Breaching Buyer's Right to Restitution

Sometimes a buyer may have made a deposit or down payment on the price of goods and the seller justifiably withholds delivery because of the buyer's breach. Perhaps the buyer has repudiated its obligation to take delivery and pay the balance of the purchase price for the goods. The deposit or down payment exceeds damages suffered by the seller. In such a case, the buyer may be entitled to restitution under rules set forth in UCC §2-718(2)-(4).

The Parties Have an Enforceable Liquidated Damages Provision. If the buyer has paid part of the purchase price and the seller has justifiably withheld delivery because of the buyer's subsequent breach, §2-718(2) allows the seller to keep an enforceable liquidated damages amount. The breaching buyer is entitled to restitution of any amount exceeding the liquidated damages amount. So, let's assume that the parties' contract calls for $1,000 in liquidated damages if the buyer breaches. Let's assume that the provision is reasonable and is therefore enforceable. If the buyer has made a deposit in the amount of liquidated damages ($1,000 in this case) or less, the seller may keep all of it. If the buyer has made a deposit in excess of the liquidated damages amount, for example $1,500, the buyer is entitled to restitution of any amount exceeding the liquidated damages, in this example, $500.

---

[31]UCC §2-718(1).

The Parties Do Not Have an Enforceable Liquidated Damages Provision. In the absence of liquidated damages, the seller is allowed to keep the lesser of 20% of the contract price or $500 of any deposit or down payment that the buyer has made, no matter how much actual damage has been caused by breach. If the seller has actual damages of more than this amount, it can keep up to the amount of actual damages. Let's assume that a buyer has paid $1,000 of the purchase price on a contract with a total price of $2,000. The buyer breaches, and the seller's actual damages are only $50. There is no liquidated damages amount in the contract. Twenty percent of the contract price is $400, which is less than $500. What this means is that the seller gets to keep $400 of the amount that the buyer has paid, and the buyer has a right to restitution of $600. If the seller had suffered actual damages of $700, however, the buyer would have been entitled to restitution of only $300.

Under the approved amendments to §2-718, the buyer will be entitled to restitution of any amount paid exceeding actual damages or an enforceable liquidated damages provision. The seller does not have an automatic right to the lesser of 20% of the contract price or $500.

F   A   Q

Q: Should the seller be entitled to retain actual damages and the lesser of 20% of the contract price or $500?

A: No. Section 2-718(3) does indicate that the buyer's right of restitution under subsection (2) "is subject to offset" by "a right to recover damages under provisions of this Article other than subsection (1) [permitting reasonable liquidated damages]." In the previous hypothetical in which the contract price was $2,000 and actual damages for the seller were only $50, maybe you could argue that the seller is entitled to keep $400 (20% of the contract price which is less than $500) and $50, so that the buyer only gets restitution of $550 of the $1000 deposit (compared to $600). This seems to be an unduly punitive interpretation of §2-718(2) & (3). The statute should be interpreted to permit the seller to retain actual damages if they exceed the statutory floor of the lesser of 20% of the contract price or $500, but not on top of that amount. As noted in the text, the approved amendments do away with any statutory floor on seller's damages.

B. Seller's Remedies Under the CISG

(1) Specific Performance

As is the case with buyer's remedies under the United Nations Convention on Contracts for the International Sale of Goods (CISG), the seller has a right to demand specific performance by the buyer.[32] That right is limited, however, if the case is

---

[32]CISG Art. 62.

being litigated in a country in which domestic law would not grant specific performance, such as in any jurisdiction that has adopted the UCC.[33]

(2) Damages

Seller's Remedies If Contract Avoided	Seller's Remedies If Contract Not Avoided
If goods resold, difference between contract price and resale price — Art. 75	Specific performance — Art. 62
If goods not resold, difference between market price and contract price — Art. 76	Damages, including consequential damages — Art. 74
Consequential damages, including lost profits — Art. 74	Interest — Art. 78
Interest — Art. 78	

Similar to the UCC, the CISG permits a seller who avoids the contract to resell the goods involved and recover the difference between the contract price and the resale price.[34] Unlike the UCC, the provisions regarding resale do not require the seller to give notification of resale to the breaching buyer. The rule does require, however, that the seller act reasonably and there is a general obligation under the CISG that injured parties take reasonable steps to mitigate damages.[35]

If the seller does not resell the goods, the seller may recover the difference between the contract price and the market price for the goods at the time of avoidance.[36] Generally, the relevant market price is considered to be at the place that the delivery was to be made.[37]

Unlike the UCC, the CISG permits the seller to recover consequential damages if they were reasonably foreseeable as a possible result of the breach at the time of contracting. As noted previously, the seller must take reasonable steps, however, to mitigate any such damages which will occur generally by reselling the goods.

(3) Interest on Sums Owed

The CISG also allows for a party to receive interest on any sums in arrears.[38] The method of calculation of such an amount is not provided by the CISG, but the policy of trying to put the injured party in the position that it would have occupied but for breach is something to be kept in mind. If the breaching party had performed, how much interest would the injured party have either earned on money that would have been paid or avoided in not having to obtain credit to make up the shortfall? The UNIDROIT Principles of International Commercial Contracts, sort of an

---

[33]CISG Art. 28.
[34]CISG Art. 75.
[35]CISG Art. 78.
[36]CISG Art. 76(1).
[37]CISG Art. 76(2).
[38]CISG Arts. 74 & 78.

international *Restatement of Contracts*, suggests that the rate of interest should be the prime lending rate in the currency used in the contract in the place where payment is to be made.[39] Courts or arbitral tribunals might be tempted to use this calculation as it represents international contract principles. Other possibilities would be the legal rate of interest in the nation in which the price is to be paid or the interest rate generally paid in the buyer's country on liquid bank accounts.

(4) Liquidated Damages

Finally, the CISG says nothing about liquidated damages. Because parties have broad leeway in drafting contractual provisions under the CISG, arguably penalty provisions are permitted. It should be kept in mind, however, that the CISG is generally silent on questions of contract validity.[40] If governing law filling gaps left by the CISG forbids penalty provisions, a court might find a liquidated damages provision invalid if it is unreasonably high. Civil law legal systems tend not to look as unfavorably on penalty provisions as do U.S. courts.[41]

SUMMARY

Sellers' Remedies Under the UCC

- ■ If a seller discovers the buyer to be insolvent, the seller may refuse delivery except for cash, including payment for all goods that have been previously delivered.

- ■ If the goods have been delivered to a carrier and the buyer repudiates or fails to make a payment when due, the seller may stop delivery of a carload, truckload, planeload, or larger shipments. If goods have been delivered to a carrier and the seller discovers that the buyer is insolvent, the seller may stop delivery of any shipment.

- ■ If the seller has possession of the goods after the buyer's breach, the seller may resell the goods and hold the buyer responsible for the difference between what the buyer agreed to pay and what the seller is able to obtain for the goods. The resale must be commercially reasonable and normally the seller must give notice to the breaching buyer before the sale takes place.

- ■ If the seller does not follow the rules for resale, the seller may sue for the difference between the contract price and market price for the goods at the time and place for tender.

- ■ Although the seller is allowed incidental damages resulting from breach, the seller is not allowed to recover consequential damages under the unamended version of Article 2. Costs saved as a result of breach are to be subtracted from damages. The 2003 amendments permit consequential damages for sellers in appropriate circumstances.

---

[39]Unidroit Principles of International Commercial Contracts Art. 7.4.9.
[40]CISG Art. 4.
[41]See Mattei, *The Comparative Law and Economics of Penalty Clauses in Contracts*, 43 Am. J. Comp. Law. 427 (1995).

- If the resale or contract/market measure of damages do not put the seller in the position it would have been in if the contract had been performed, the seller may sue for lost profits. One type of seller that would be entitled to recovery of lost profits is a seller who lost a sale, that is, a lost volume seller.

- In calculating damages for lost profits, the focus should be on the revenue that the seller would have earned if the buyer had performed. Any costs saved because of breach should be subtracted from those revenues in determining damages.

- The seller may sue for the price of goods if they cannot reasonably be resold, if they are accepted by the buyer, or if they are lost or destroyed within a commercially reasonable time after the risk of loss has passed to the buyer.

- The seller may reclaim goods within a reasonable time if they were purchased with a check that was subsequently dishonored. The right to reclaim is lost if the goods are resold to a bona fide purchaser.

- The seller may reclaim goods from a buyer if the buyer was insolvent when receiving the goods. The demand must be made within ten days of receipt unless the buyer made a written misrepresentation of solvency to the seller, in which case it must be within three months. Again, the right to reclaim is lost if the goods are resold to a bona fide purchaser.

- The parties may liquidate damages in a reasonable amount. Parties may not stipulate an amount intended as a penalty.

- The breaching buyer may obtain restitution for any amount paid that exceeds damages suffered by the seller or a reasonable liquidated damages amount set by the parties. In the absence of a liquidated damages provision, the law gives the seller statutory liquidated damages of the lesser of 20% of the contract price or $500.

Seller's Remedies Under the CISG

- As is the case with buyer's remedies, the seller is entitled to specific performance under the CISG. Courts are permitted to refuse to award specific performance, however, if they would not do so under their domestic law.

- The seller is entitled to recover damages based on the difference between the contract price and the price obtained on a reasonable resale of the goods.

- If the seller does not resell the goods, the seller is entitled to the difference between the contract price and the market price of the goods at the place of delivery at the time of avoidance.

- The seller is entitled to consequential damages under the CISG if such damages were reasonably foreseeable as a possible consequence of breach at the time of contracting and if such damages were not reasonably avoidable.

- Injured parties under the CISG are entitled to prejudgment interest on amounts in arrears.

- The CISG does not address the enforceability of liquidated damage provisions. The validity of such a provision will be determined under applicable domestic law under choice of law principles.

Choice of Law

The remedies available to the seller depend to some extent on the law that governs the transaction. The general policy of the common law, UCC, and CISG is essentially the same, namely, to put the injured party in the position that the party would have occupied if the contract had been performed. The unamended version of UCC Article 2 denies consequential damage recovery to sellers, whereas under common law and the CISG such damages would be recoverable if reasonably foreseeable as a consequence of breach.

The CISG is more liberal than the UCC or common law in permitting specific performance, although the difference is not significant if the case is litigated in the United States as the CISG in such situations yields to domestic law. On the question of liquidated damages, the CISG does not address the enforceability of such provisions. Whether a liquidated damages provision is enforceable is a question of validity to be determined based on domestic law, and the law of civil law countries is likely to look more favorably on such provisions than the common law.

Contract Formation and Terms

The seller is only entitled to a remedy if the buyer breaches, so it is important to determine the terms of the contract to determine if the buyer breached as compared to the seller. That, in turn, may depend on how the contract was formed. If the parties formed the contract through an exchange of forms containing varying terms, analysis will need to be done under UCC §2-2-207 or under the CISG, if applicable.

Whether the seller breached or the buyer breached may depend on whether the seller gave any warranties of quality or title and whether such warranties were properly disclaimed. If the goods were damaged or destroyed at some point during the transaction, it will be important to determine which party had the risk of loss. The parol evidence rule and the doctrine of unconscionability may also play important roles in determining the enforceable terms of the contract.

Performance

The remedies available to the seller depend on whether the buyer accepted, wrongfully rejected or wrongfully revoked acceptance of goods or repudiated its contractual obligations. If the buyer accepts the goods (including cases of wrongful revocation of acceptance, at least if the buyer retains possession), the seller is generally entitled to the price. If the buyer wrongfully rejects or repudiates, the seller is normally entitled to damages based on the difference between the contract price and resale price, contract price and market price, or lost profits.

Buyer's Remedies

If it is determined that the seller breached rather than the buyer, it is the buyer who has remedies, and those remedies are discussed in the previous chapter.

Third Parties

If goods are damaged or destroyed while in transit while the risk of loss is on the seller, the seller's remedies will be against the carrier, as will be discussed in the next chapter. The seller may also have recourse against a bank issuing a letter of credit if the bank wrongfully dishonors a presentation made under it.

Third Parties Involved in the Sales Transaction

9

In a sale of goods transaction, third parties will sometimes be involved. This is particularly the case if the buyer and seller live at some distance

from each other. In such cases, it will be necessary to hire a shipping company (called a *carrier*) to transport the goods from the seller to the buyer. In addition, the seller may want assurances of payment on shipment of the goods. Such an assurance may be provided by a bank issuing a document called a *letter of credit* that assures payment to the seller on the seller's presentation of documents showing that the goods have been shipped. A letter of credit is a contract pursuant to which a bank agrees to pay a designated person on presentation of certain specified documents. In a sale of goods transaction, these documents show that the goods required under the sales contract have been shipped. The duties of carriers and banks involved in these transactions are discussed in this chapter.

A. THE LETTER OF CREDIT TRANSACTION

B. BANK OBLIGATIONS UNDER LETTERS OF CREDIT

1. Has a Letter of Credit Been Issued?
2. Has the Documentary Presentation Complied with the Terms of the Letter of Credit?
3. Fraud

C. BANK COLLECTION OF DOCUMENTARY DRAFTS

D. OBLIGATIONS OF CARRIERS

　　1.　Misdelivery
　　2.　Damage to Goods and Delays in Delivery

E. OBLIGATIONS OF WAREHOUSE OPERATORS

　　1.　Warehouse Receipts
　　2.　To Whom Should the Warehouse Operator Deliver the Goods?
　　3.　Warehouse Operator Liability for Misdescription of Goods on Warehouse Receipt

A. The Letter of Credit Transaction

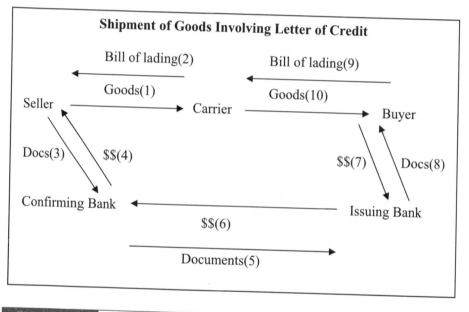

FIGURE 9.1

The sale of goods transaction may involve third parties, such as carriers who transport the goods and banks that help in the financing of the transaction. When goods are being shipped at a distance, the seller may wish to take special steps to make sure that it gets paid. It may not have had many dealings in the past with the buyer and is concerned that it may have to litigate in a foreign jurisdiction if it does not get paid. The seller may insist that the buyer obtain an irrevocable letter of credit issued by a bank of good repute naming the seller as **beneficiary**.[1] Under the letter of credit, once the bank sees documents showing that the goods have been shipped, the bank is obligated to pay the beneficiary.

---

[1]UCC §§5-102(a)(10) ("letter of credit") & 5-102(a)(3).

Figure 9.1 shows a sale of goods involving a carrier (e.g., a trucking company or air freight company) independent of the seller, and two banks that are involved in a letter of credit transaction — the numbers indicate the chain of events after the letter of credit has been issued and confirmed. The buyer may use its normal local bank to issue the letter of credit, and that bank might be happy to do so for its good customer, the buyer. The buyer will apply to its bank for a letter of credit, and the buyer is thus called the **applicant** in a letter of credit transaction.[2] The bank issuing a letter of credit is called the **issuing bank** or **issuer**. The seller, however, will not necessarily want to deal with the buyer's bank. The seller may then ask that the letter of credit be confirmed by a local bank near the seller. A bank that agrees to honor a letter of credit issued by another bank is called a **confirming bank** or **confirmer**.[3] Sometimes a bank will not agree to honor the letter of credit but will agree to advise the beneficiary regarding the letter of credit's terms and its authenticity. That bank is called the **advising bank** or **advisor**.[4] The figure shows both an issuing bank and a confirming bank.

The first event is the delivery of the goods to the carrier (1). The carrier will then issue a **bill of lading**, which indicates that the carrier has received the goods and promises to deliver them pursuant to the terms of the bill of lading, which is a contract between the seller and the carrier (2). The bill of lading is also called a **document of title**, and may be **negotiable** (i.e., transferable to someone who will then have title to the underlying goods) or non-negotiable. The buyer may also have required under the contract of sale that the goods be inspected by an independent inspector before the goods are loaded onto the carrier. The inspection certificate may be required as a prerequisite to payment under the letter of credit.

Any documents required by the letter of credit (e.g., a bill of lading and inspection certificate) are then presented to the confirming bank (3). If the documents comply with the letter of credit on their face (e.g., they show that the proper goods were shipped and passed inspection), the confirming bank is required to pay the seller the amount of the letter of credit (4). The confirming bank will then forward the documents to the issuing bank (5), and if they comply on their face, the issuing bank will pay the confirming bank (6). The issuing bank will then contact the buyer, who will be presented with the documents. If the issuing bank properly honored the documents, the issuing bank has a right to be reimbursed by its customer, although the bank may be willing to extend credit to the buyer (7).[5] Assuming the buyer either pays the bank or obtains credit, the documents will be given to the buyer (8), who will then present the bill of lading to the carrier to receive the goods (9, 10).

In this chapter, we will explore in more detail the duties of the banks and carriers in these transactions. We will also explore the duties of carriers and warehouse operators who may be involved in the sales transaction.

B. Bank Obligations Under Letters of Credit

A bank's obligation to pay under a letter of credit is conditioned on the beneficiary's presentation of documents that comply with the letter of credit on their face.

---

[2]UCC §5-102(a)(2).
[3]UCC §5-102(a)(4).
[4]UCC §5-102(a)(1).
[5]UCC §5-108(i)(1).

This should be contrasted with the obligation of someone who is guaranteeing the obligation of someone else. The obligation of a guarantor is conditioned on the primary obligor not having performed. We must thus determine whether a bank's obligation is pursuant to a letter of credit or is instead a guarantee.

(1) Has a Letter of Credit Been Issued?

A letter of credit is a contract pursuant to which the issuer of the letter of credit obligates itself to pay the beneficiary on presentation of documents that meet the requirements of the letter of credit.[6] The documents will purport to show that some event has happened, such as the shipping of goods, but the obligation of the issuer to pay is independent of whether the event has happened or not. As long as the documents comply on their face with the terms of the letter of credit, the issuer is required to pay.[7]

A letter of credit should be distinguished from a guarantee or other obligation that depends on whether an event actually happened. For example, an agreement to pay if goods are shipped and the buyer does not pay for them is not a letter of credit, because the obligation to pay is dependent on (1) the shipping of the goods and (2) the failure of the buyer to pay for them. This type of agreement would be a guarantee. If, on the other hand, somebody promises to pay upon presentation of documents showing that goods have been shipped, that is a letter of credit. The obligation to pay is dependent on the presentation of conforming documents, not on whether the goods have actually been shipped.

Not a Letter of Credit
"The undersigned promises to pay the seller if 100 bushels of wheat have been shipped from seller to buyer."

A Letter of Credit
"The undersigned promises to pay the seller if the seller presents a bill of lading to the undersigned showing that 100 bushels of wheat have been shipped from seller to buyer."

If an obligation qualifies as a letter of credit, Article 5 of the Uniform Commercial Code (UCC) governs the transaction, assuming the law of a state enacting the UCC applies. Article 5 of the UCC was revised in 1995, and the citations in this book are to the revised version. In addition, parties to a letter of credit frequently agree that the Uniform Customs and Practice for Documentary Credits (UCP) will govern performance under the letter of credit. The UCP is a compendium of bank practices (trade usages) in dealing with letters of credit. The UCP is promulgated by the International Chamber of Commerce, and its current edition is referred to as UCP 600 (effective July 1, 2007). The UCP contains rules regarding how banks will determine if documents presented comply with the terms of the letter of credit.[8] The UCP and Article 5 are largely complementary, but to the extent that they conflict the UCC generally yields to the UCP.[9]

---

[6]UCC §5-102(a)(10).
[7]UCC §5-108(a).
[8]UCP 600 Art. 14.
[9]UCC §5-116(c).

Article 5 does permit a letter of credit to have minor non-documentary conditions. The commentary to Article 5 indicates that a condition such as "shipment on vessels more than 15 years old is prohibited," as long as it is not fundamental, is a minor condition that is to be ignored by the issuer of the letter of credit.[10] As long as the fundamental nature of the obligation is that the issuer will pay against presentation of documents, the obligation is a letter of credit.

If an obligation does not qualify as a letter of credit, it will be governed by other contract law. It may be a guarantee, in which case suretyship law will apply. Discussion of this topic is beyond the scope of this book.

Form of a Simple Irrevocable Letter of Credit

[Name and Address of Issuing Bank]

Date: _____

Irrevocable Letter of Credit No._____

Expiry date:_____

[Name and address of beneficiary]

Dear Sir or Madam:

We hereby authorize you to draw on [Issuing Bank] for the account of [Applicant] in the amount of $[dollar amount]. This letter of credit is available by your draft at sight for the aforestated amount if drawn and presented with the following documents:

    (1) Commercial invoice indicating shipment of [goods being sold]
    (2) Certificate of inspection from [inspection company]
    (3) Clean bills of lading consigned to [name of issuing bank], showing freight collect/prepaid, marked: [description of goods]

Each draft drawn hereunder must be marked "Drawn under [Issuing Bank] L/C No. _____," referencing the number of this credit.

We hereby engage with bona fide holders that drafts drawn strictly in compliance with the terms of this credit and amendments thereto, shall meet with due honor upon presentation.

This credit is subject to the "Uniform Customs & Practice for Documentary Credits (2007 Revision), International Chamber of Commerce, Publication No. 600."

[Issuing Bank]

By [Authorized Agent]

---

[10]UCC §5-108, comment 9.

(2) Has the Documentary Presentation Complied with the Terms of the Letter of Credit?

Assuming that a letter of credit has been issued, the beneficiary will present whatever documents are required by the letter of credit to a confirming bank or to the issuing bank. The bank will then examine the documents to make sure that they comply. Under the UCC, the bank has a reasonable time after presentation, not beyond seven business days of the issuer after the day of receipt of the documents, to either honor the presentation or to give its reasons for dishonor.[11] UCP 600, if it applies to the letter of credit, changes this rule to a maximum of five banking days.[12] A bank that does not give notice of dishonor specifying the reason for dishonor is precluded from relying on that reason, unless the reason is a fraud which is subsequently discovered.[13]

(a) The "Strict Compliance" Rule

The standard for determining compliance with the letter of credit is **strict compliance**.[14] To demonstrate what is meant by strict compliance, the drafters of revised Article 5 cite with approval the case of *Courtaulds North America, Inc. v. North Carolina Nat'l Bank*.[15] In that case, the letter of credit called for presentation of an invoice indicating that the goods shipped were "100% acrylic yarn." The beneficiary presented instead an invoice indicating that the goods were "imported acrylic yarn." The packing lists accompanying the invoice did state, "cartons marked 100% acrylic." Ultimately, the issuing bank refused to honor the letter of credit, and by the time the beneficiary presented a corrected invoice, the letter of credit had expired. Because the buyer had filed for bankruptcy, that meant that the seller would probably not be paid unless the bank erred in dishonoring the original presentation of documents.

The appellate court ultimately held that the bank properly dishonored the presentation. The doctrine of strict compliance required that the documents exactly correspond to the letter of credit. The letter of credit was governed also by the UCP in effect at that time, which required that descriptions of goods in an invoice strictly correspond to the terms of the letter of credit, while descriptions of the goods in other documents could be more general. The presentation by the beneficiary in this case was backward; the description in the accompanying documents was more specific than the description in the invoice.

Strict compliance does not necessarily mean slavish compliance. The commentary to the UCC indicates that obvious typographical errors can be ignored.[16] When in doubt, the bank should probably ask the applicant whether it is willing to waive any apparent non-compliance. If an applicant waives non-compliance, then the bank must honor the presentation.[17]

---

[11]UCC §5-108(b).
[12]UCP 600 Art. 14.
[13]UCC §5-108(c) & (d).
[14]UCC §5-108(a).
[15]528 F.2d 802 (4th Cir. 1975).
[16]UCC §5-108, comment 1.
[17]See *Marsala International Trading Co. v. Comerica Bank*, 976 P.2d 275, 39 UCC Rep. Serv. 2d 217 (Colo. App. 1998).

(b) The Statutory Right of Reimbursement and Liability for Wrongful Honor or Dishonor

If the bank properly honors a presentation under a letter of credit, the bank has a right to be reimbursed by its customer.[18] If a confirming bank properly honors a letter of credit, it has a right to be reimbursed by the issuer of the letter of credit.[19]

If a bank improperly honors a presentation under a letter of credit, it does not have a statutory right of reimbursement. It is, however, subrogated to the position of the beneficiary and also of the applicant.[20] That means that it may be able to sue one of the parties to get its money back. For example, if conforming goods were shipped and accepted by the buyer but the documents for some reason did not conform to the requirements of the letter of credit, the issuing bank would not have a statutory right of reimbursement. It could, however, step into the shoes of the seller and sue the buyer for the price of the goods, because they had been accepted. If the goods were non-conforming and were rejected by the applicant (buyer), the bank could sue the seller to recover its money.

If a bank improperly dishonors a letter of credit, it is liable to the beneficiary for the amount that is the subject of the dishonor, minus any amount of damages avoided by mitigation.[21] It is also liable for incidental damages and reasonable attorney's fees incurred by the beneficiary in obtaining payment.[22] Although the amount is subject to offset by any mitigation, for example if the beneficiary (seller) were to resell the goods involved, there is no requirement that the beneficiary actually take affirmative steps to mitigate loss.[23] Under no circumstances is the issuing bank liable for consequential damages caused by dishonor.[24]

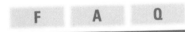

Q: Why not require that a beneficiary mitigate its loss if an issuer wrongfully refuses to pay under a letter of credit?

A: To further the utility of letters of credit, the UCC encourages issuers to honor proper presentations by holding the issuer liable up to the face amount of the letter of credit. The issuer is given the burden of showing that the beneficiary actually mitigated if the issuer wishes to reduce its liability below the amount of the letter of credit, but is not allowed to argue that the beneficiary should have mitigated. UCC §5-111, comment 1.

A wrongful dishonor of a presentation under a letter of credit may also cause damage to the applicant, the buyer. It might prevent the buyer from obtaining possession of needed goods, as the buyer will not be able to obtain possession of the bill of lading. Likewise, the wrongful honor of a presentation may cause damage to the

---

[18]UCC §5-108(i).
[19]UCC §5-107(a).
[20]UCC §5-117.
[21]UCC §5-111(a).
[22]Id.
[23]Id.
[24]Id.

buyer if the buyer winds up with non-conforming goods. The UCC permits the applicant to recover damages, including incidental damages, resulting from the issuer's breach of its obligations under the letter of credit. Consequential damages may not be recovered, however. There is a concern that imposing liability for consequential damages on an issuer would increase the cost of letters of credit and make them less useful in commercial transactions.[25] The applicant's recoverable damages against the issuer may not be that great, because the applicant can refuse to reimburse the issuer if the issuer wrongfully honored the presentation of documents and does not have to pay the issuer if the issuer wrongfully refuses to honor. The applicant could not sue the issuer for any lost profits arising from not having the goods under the rule preventing recovery of consequential damages.

(c) The Independence Principle of Letters of Credit

It is important to note the *independence principle* of letters of credit. The obligation on the part of the issuing bank to pay is independent of the underlying sales contract. That means that as long as the documents conform on their face to the terms of the letter of credit, the issuing bank is required to make payment, with the exception of fraud cases discussed later. If it turns out that the goods do not conform to the sales contract, the buyer's recourse is against the seller, not against the issuing bank. The buyer is required to pay the bank if it paid on conforming documents. The buyer then will have to seek reimbursement from the breaching seller under UCC Article 2. Letter of credit transactions obviously pose a risk to buyers in that the seller will be paid even though the goods prove to be defective. That is why buyers may insist that the letter of credit require an inspection certificate be presented to the issuer as a condition to payment.

(3) Fraud

Forged documents or material fraud in the transaction are exceptions to the independence principle of letters of credit. If a beneficiary forges the documents so as to make them conform to the letter of credit or commits a material fraud by shipping rubbish instead of the goods called for under the contract, the bank may, unless an innocent third party is requesting payment, dishonor the presentation, even though the documents comply with the letter of credit on their face.[26] In cases of forgery or other material fraud, the applicant for the letter of credit may obtain an injunction forbidding the issuer from paying unless an innocent third party is involved.[27]

(a) "Material Fraud" Requirement

The official commentary to UCC §5-109 explains what the drafters had in mind when they require "material fraud" as a requirement for an injunction against payment. As to materiality, comment 1 notes that if a contract calls for 1,000 barrels of salad oil but the seller knowingly ships only 998 barrels, the fraud may nonetheless be immaterial and the letter of credit should be honored if the documents comply on their face. The comment goes on to state: "Material fraud by the beneficiary occurs

---

[25]See UCC §5-111, comment 4.
[26]UCC §5-109(a).
[27]UCC §5-109(b).

only when the beneficiary has no colorable right to expect honor and where there is no basis in fact to support such a right to honor."

F   A   Q

Q: Why is fraud an exception to the independence principle of letters of credit?

A: If a seller ships non-conforming goods but the documents conform to the letter of credit, the issuing bank must normally pay anyway. The buyer's recourse is against the seller. In cases involving material fraud or forgery, however, it would be unjust to permit the seller to be paid. It is very unlikely that the buyer would be able to successfully obtain recourse against a fraudulent seller, who would probably hide the proceeds of the letter of credit. Because of the concern that frequent injunctions against payment would erode the utility of letters of credit, the drafters of Article 5 impose a high standard of proof for applicants seeking such injunctions. The independence principle is still very important.

Unless an injunction is obtained, an issuer in good faith may honor a presentation of documents if they conform on their face to the letter of credit.[28] This would be true even if the issuer hears of fraud. Just because the applicant for the letter of credit cries "fraud" does not mean that a fraud was committed. The issuer must keep in mind that if there was in fact no fraud and the documents conform to the letter of credit, the issuer would be liable to the beneficiary if it did not pay when it should have. Thus, when the applicant cries "fraud," it might make sense for the issuer to tell the applicant to get an injunction.

(b) Protection of Parties that Accept or Pay Drafts Drawn Under Letters of Credit in Good Faith

The issuing bank must pay and no injunction can be ordered if an innocent third party is demanding payment.[29] For example, if conforming documents are presented to a confirming bank and the confirming bank pays, it would be unfair if an injunction could be obtained ordering the issuing bank not to pay the confirming bank, assuming the confirming bank acted in good faith in paying. Also, sometimes a bank will honor a letter of credit by agreeing to accept a time *draft* entitling the holder to payment. By accepting the draft, the bank is agreeing that it will pay the holder at the time indicated on the draft. If after this agreement (called an *acceptance*) a bona fide purchaser buys the draft, it would be unfair to enjoin the bank from paying it later.

The preceding discussion may have confused you if you do not know what a draft is in this context. It isn't a beer that comes out of the tap! A draft is a type of *negotiable instrument*, like a check. When a beneficiary seeks payment under a letter of credit, the beneficiary will draw up a draft ordering the issuing bank to pay the beneficiary (seller) or somebody to whom the beneficiary may transfer the draft. Just like a check, it will say "pay to the order of" the seller. The sales contract and letter of credit may

---

[28]UCC §5-109(a)(2).
[29]UCC §5-109(a)(1).

require that the draft call for payment after some period of time. Essentially, this extends credit to the buyer until the draft is paid. A draft calling for payment in 90 days might look like the following:

Example of a Draft Drawn by a Seller Under a Letter of Credit

[Date]

At 90 days deferred from acceptance, pay to the order of [Seller] $[amount] and charge to account of [Buyer].

To: First National Bank

[Address]

/s/ Seller

Accepted [date]:

If the documents comply with the terms of the letter of credit, the bank will sign and date the draft where it says "accepted." The draft is now more valuable because a bank, presumably a creditworthy party, has agreed to pay it when it is due. If the seller doesn't want to wait until the time the draft is due, the seller may sell it at a discount to somebody else, frequently another financial institution. The discount will take into account the time value of money, a dollar today being worth more than a dollar tomorrow. If the entity buying the instrument is unaware of any problems arising out of the transaction that gave rise to the draft, that entity will be a bona fide purchaser of the draft who is called a ***holder in due course***.[30] If the entity buying the instrument is aware of problems arising out of the transaction, the entity may still be a holder of the instrument and can enforce it but will be subject to any claims or defenses that the obligor on the instrument may have in the underlying transaction. Further discussion of negotiable instruments and holders in due course is beyond the scope of this book and would be considered in a course on commercial law or payments law.[31]

In any event, once a holder in due course comes into the picture holding an accepted draft, it is too late for the applicant to enjoin the issuing bank from paying under the letter of credit.[32] The bank that accepted the draft must pay the draft, and the buyer's only recourse is against the seller. The buyer could reject the non-conforming goods that are delivered (assuming any are delivered at all) and could sue for damages for the seller's failure to deliver conforming goods.

---

[30]See UCC §3-302.
[31]For more discussion, see James J. White & Robert S. Summers, *Uniform Commercial Code* Ch. 14 (5th ed.).
[32]UCC §5-109(b)(1).

C. Bank Collection of Documentary Drafts

In some situations, the parties may decide to forgo a letter of credit and instead condition delivery of the document of title to the buyer on the buyer's payment for the goods. The banking system may be used in these cases to transmit the documents from the seller's place of business to the buyer's place of business. At that location, the buyer will inspect the documents and if they are in order, make payment. The presenting bank will then give the documents to the buyer, enabling the buyer to take delivery of the goods. If the buyer doesn't pay, the buyer doesn't get the goods and the seller can then sell them to somebody else.

In this transaction, the seller of goods will draw up a document ordering the buyer to pay for the goods. We just talked about drafts in the preceding section of the book. The draft used in a documentary draft collection would look similar to one on page 186, *supra*, except that it would be addressed to the buyer to pay rather than to a bank.

The draft, the bill of lading, and any other documents required by the sales contract, such as inspection certificates, will then be forwarded by the seller through the banking system to a bank located near the buyer. The buyer will be notified that the documents have arrived, and will go to the bank to inspect them. If the documents are in order, the buyer will pay the draft and receive possession of the documents if the draft is immediately payable. If the parties have decided to do business on credit, meaning that the buyer has more than three days to make payment after presentment of the draft, the buyer is required to "accept" the draft, meaning that the buyer acknowledges liability.[33] "Acceptance" occurs by the buyer simply signing the draft.[34] If the buyer refuses to accept or pay, the presenting bank is required to give notification to the seller of dishonor, and await instructions regarding disposition of the goods.[35] The duty of a bank handling an item for collection is to use due care.[36]

An example of how a collecting bank can violate its obligation to use due care is presented in *Rheinberg Kellerei Gmbh v. Brooksfield National Bank of Commerce*.[37] In that case, the documents arrived before the goods arrived. The letter of collection sent along with the draft and other documents indicated that payment was due once the goods arrived in Houston. It also indicated that the seller should be notified in the event of difficulty in obtaining payment. When the documents were presented to the buyer before the goods arrived, the buyer indicated that it would have to raise money to make the payment. The bank did not notify the seller or the seller's bank, and the goods (wine) sat in the Houston harbor for a couple of months and spoiled. The court held that under the UCC and the International Chamber of Commerce Uniform Rules for Collections governing international collection of documentary drafts, the bank presenting the documents had a duty to notify the seller's bank upon the buyer's refusal to pay. Under UCC §4-502, when a draft is to be paid on arrival of goods, the bank is required to notify its transferor if a draft is presented before the goods arrive and is not paid. The bank was liable for the loss

---

[33]UCC §4-503(1).
[34]UCC §3-409.
[35]UCC §§4-501 & 4-503.
[36]UCC §4-202.
[37]901 F.2d 481 (1990).

that was caused to the seller as a result of its breach of duty of care in handling the documents.

As is the case with the letter of credit transaction, when the buyer agrees to pay against presentation of documents, the buyer is generally forfeiting the right to inspect the goods before payment.[38] The buyer still has a right to inspect the goods before accepting them, but if the buyer decides to reject, the buyer will be forced to sue the seller to obtain a refund of the price.

In payment against documents situations, the buyer must rely on the descriptions of the goods found in the bills of lading and other documents that are tendered. The carrier issuing a bill of lading generally owes a duty to the person who must pay against the documents that the description of the goods and the date of the bill of lading are accurate.[39] The carrier can generally avoid liability for misdescription of goods that were packaged by the shipper by providing a disclaimer such as "shipper's weight, load, and count," provided that the carrier is not aware of the misdescription. A carrier is required, however, to count the number of packages and determine the kind and quantity of bulk freight. This obligation cannot be disclaimed. The bank presenting the documents only warrants that it is acting in good faith and with proper authority.[40]

D. Obligations of Carriers

The carrier is obligated to deliver goods to the holder of a negotiable bill of lading or the consignee of a non-negotiable (straight) bill of lading.[41] This section deals with the liability of carriers if (a) goods are delivered to the wrong person or (b) goods are lost or destroyed in transit.

The obligations of carriers are covered by UCC Article 7, which was most recently revised in 2003,[42] and the Federal Bill of Lading Act, 49 U.S.C. 80101, et seq., for shipments in interstate commerce. The differences between the Federal Bill of Lading Act and UCC Article 7 are not great.

(1) Misdelivery

In determining the obligation of a carrier to deliver, one must ascertain whether the bill of lading is negotiable or non-negotiable. A document of title that states that the goods are to be delivered to the bearer of the document or to the order of the named person is negotiable, unless it states that it is "non-negotiable."[43] Other documents of title are non-negotiable — they simply state to whom the goods are to be delivered, the consignee. A non-negotiable bill of lading is often referred to as a "straight" bill of lading because delivery is to be straight to the consignee (without intervening holders of the bill). Following is an example of a "straight" (non-negotiable) bill of lading:

---

[38]UCC §2-513(3)(b).
[39]UCC §7-301 & 49 U.S.C. §80113.
[40]UCC §7-508.
[41]UCC §7-403 & 49 U.S.C. §80110.
[42]The revisions mostly accommodate the creation of electronic documents of title and modernize the terminology of Article 7.
[43]UCC §7-104, 49 U.S.C. §80103.

UNIFORM STRAIGHT BILL OF LADING
Original – Not Negotiable

I W L A

Name of Carrier _____

RECEIVED, subject to individually determined rates or contracts that have been agreed upon in writing between the carrier and shipper, if applicable, otherwise to the rates, classifications and rules that have been established by the carrier and are available to the shipper, on request;

From _____ **(Warehouse),**

as Agent for the Shipper/Consignor Whose Name and Address is Shown Below Date _____

Carrier's Pro No. _____

Shipper's Bill of Lading No. _____

Consignee's Reference/PO No. _____

Carrier's Code (SCAC) _____

Street _____

City _____ County _____ State _____ Zip/Postal Code _____

the property described below, in apparent good order, except as noted (contents and condition of contents of packages unknown) marked, consigned, and destined as shown below, which said carrier agrees to carry to destination, if on its route, or otherwise to deliver to another carrier on the route to destination. Every service to be performed hereunder shall be subject to all the conditions not prohibited by law, whether printed or written, herein contained, including the conditions on the back hereof, which are hereby agreed to by the shipper and accepted for himself and his assigns. Carrier acknowledges that _____ **(Warehouse), as agent for the disclosed shipper/consignor, has no liability for payment of freight or any other charges, and the transportation contract** evidenced by this bill of lading is between the carrier and the designated shipper/consignor.

Consigned to _____

On Collection Delivery Shipments, the letters 'COD' must appear before consignee's name

Destination Street _____

City _____ County _____ State _____ Zip/Postal Code _____

Delivering Carrier _____ Trailer No. _____

Additional Shipment Information _____

_____

Collect on Delivery $ _____ and remit to: _____

Street _____ City _____ State _____

C.O.D. charge   Shipper ○

To be paid by   Consignee ○

Hdlg. Units No. Type	Packages No. Type	HM (*)	Kind of Package, Desription of Articles, Special Marks and Exceptions (Subject to Corrections)	Weight (Subject to Correction)	Cass or Rate Ref. (For info. only)	Cube (optional)

* Mark 'X' to designate Hazardous Materials as defined in DOT Regulations.

NOTE (1) Where the rate is dependent on value, shippers are required to state specifically in writing the agreed or declared value of the property as follows:

"The agreed or declared value for the property is specifically stated by the shipper to be not exceeding _____ per _____."

NOTE (2) Liability Limitation of or loss or damage on this shipment may be applicable. See 49 U.S.C. 14706(c)(1)(A) and (B)

NOTE (3) Commodities requiring special or additional care or attention in handling or stowing must be so marked and packages as to ensure safe transportation with ordinary care. See Sec. 2(e) of NMFC Item 360. Notify if problem enroute or at delivery:

Freight charges are PREPAID unless market collect

CHECK BOX IF COLLECT [ ]

FOR FREIGHT COLLECT SHIPMENTS:
If this shipment is to be delivered to the consignee, without recourse on the consignor, the consignor shall sign the following statement: The carrier may decline to make delivery of this shipment without payment of freight and all other lawful charges.

(Signature of Consignor)

Name _____ Fax No. _____ Tel. No. _____ *(for informational purposes only)*

Send freight bill to _____

Company Name _____ City _____ State _____ Zip/Postal Code _____

Shipper/Consignor _____ Carrier _____

Per _____ , Agent   Per _____ Date _____

Shipper/Consignor's Address _____

Shipper Certification
This is to certify that the above named materials are properly classified, packaged, marked and labeled, and are in proper condition for transportation according to the applicable requirements of the DOT.
Per_____ Date _____

Carrier Certification
Carrier acknowledges receipt of packages and required placards. Carrier certifies emergency response information was made available and /or carrier has the DOT emergency response guidebook or equivalent document in the vehicle.
Per _____ Package Nos. _____
Date _____

At the time of this writing (May 1, 2008), this form is in the revision process by the IWLA and is being reproduced here for illustrative purposes only.

Uniform Straight Bill of Lading Terms and Conditions

(Reverse side of form)

Sec. 1. (a) The carrier or the party in possession of any of the property described in this bill of lading shall be liable as at common law for any loss thereof or damage thereto, except as hereinafter provided.

(b) No carrier shall be liable for any loss or damage to a shipment or for any delay caused by an Act of God, the public enemy, the authority of law, or the act or default of shipper. Except in the case of negligence of the carrier or party in possession, the carrier or party in possession shall not be liable for loss, damage or delay which results: when the property is stopped and held in transit upon request of the shipper, owner or party entitled to make such request; or from fault or impassible highway, or by lack of capacity of a highway bridge or ferry; or from a defect or vice in the property; or from riots or strikes. The burden to prove freedom from negligence is on the carrier or the party in possession.

Sec 2. Unless arranged or agreed upon, in writing, prior to shipment, carrier is not bound to transport a shipment by a particular schedule or in time for a particular market, but is responsible to transport with reasonable dispatch. In case of physical necessity, carrier may forward a shipment via another carrier.

Sec. 3. (a) As a condition precedent to recovery, claims must be filed in writing with: any participating carrier having sufficient information to identify the shipment.

(b) Claims for loss or damage must be filed within nine months after the delivery of the property (or, in the case of export traffic, within nine months after delivery at the port of export), except that claims for failure to make delivery must be filed within nine months after a reasonable time for delivery has elapsed.

(c) Suits for loss, damage, inquiry or delay shall be instituted against any carrier no later than two years and one day from the day when written notice is given by the carrier to the claimant that the carrier has disallowed the claim or any part or parts of the claim specified in the notice. Where claims are not filed or suits are not instituted thereon in accordance with the foregoing provisions, no carrier shall be liable, and such claims will not be paid.

(d) Any carrier or party liable for loss of or damage to any of said property shall have the full benefit of any insurance that may have been effected upon or on account of said property, so far as this shall not avoid the policies or contracts of insurance, PROVIDED, that the carrier receiving the benefit of such insurance will reimburse the claimant for the premium paid on the insurance policy or contract.

Sec. 4. (a) If the consignee refuses the shipment tendered for delivery by carrier or if carrier is unable to deliver the shipment, because of fault or mistake of the consignor or consignee, the carrier's liability shall then become that of a warehouseman. Carrier shall promptly attempt to provide notice, by telephonic or electronic communication as provided on the face of the bill of lading, if so indicated, to the shipper or the party, if any, designated to receive notice on this bill of lading. Storage charges, based on carrier's tariff, shall start no sooner then the next business day following the attempted notification. Storage may be, at the carrier's option, in any location that provides reasonable protection against loss or damage. The carrier may place the shipment in public storage at the owner's expense and without liability to the carrier.

(b) If the carrier does not receive disposition instructions within 48 hours of the time of carrier's attempted first notification, carrier will attempt to issue a second and final confirmed notification. Such notice shall advise that if carrier does not receive disposition instructions within 10 days of that notification, carrier may offer the shipment for sale at a public auction and the carrier has the right to offer the shipment for sale. The amount of sale will be applied to the carrier's invoice for transportation, storage and other lawful charges. The owner will be responsible for the balance of charges not covered by the sale of the goods. If there is a balance remaining after all charges and expenses are paid, such balance will be paid to the owner of the property sold hereunder, upon claim and proof of ownership.

(c) Where carrier has attempted to follow the procedure set forth in subsections 4(a) and

(b) above and the procedure provided in this section is not possible, nothing in this section shall be construed to abridge the right of the carrier at its option to sell the property under such circumstances and in such manner as may be authorized by law. When perishable goods cannot be delivered and disposition is not given within a reasonable time, the carrier may dispose of property to the best advantage.

(d) Where a carrier is directed by consignee or consignor to unload or deliver property at a particular location where consignor, consignee, or the agent of either, is not regularly located, the risk after unloading or delivery shall not be that of the carrier.

Sec. 5. (a) In all cases not prohibited by law, where a lower value than the actual value of the said property has been stated in writing by the shipper or has been agreed upon in writing as the released value of the property as determined by the classification or tariffs upon which the rate is based, such lower value plus freight charges if paid shall be the maximum recoverable amount for loss or damage, whether or not such loss or damage occurs from negligence.

(b) No carrier hereunder will carry or be liable in any way for any documents, coin money, or for any articles of extraordinary value not specifically rated in the published classification or tariffs unless a special agreement to do so and a stipulated value of the articles are endorsed on this bill of lading.

Sec. 6. Ever party, whether principal or agent, who ships explosives or dangerous goods, without previous full written disclosure to the carrier of their nature, shall be liable for and indemnify the carrier against all loss or damage caused by such goods. Such goods may be warehoused at owner's risk and expense or destroyed without compensation.

Sec. 7. (a) The consignor or consignee shall be liable for the freight and other lawful charges accruing on the shipment, as billed or corrected, except that collect shipments may move without recourse to the consignor when the consignor so stipulates by signature or endorsement in the space provided on the face of the bill of lading. Nevertheless, the consignor shall remain liable for transportation charges where there has been an erroneous determination of the freight charges assessed, based upon incomplete or incorrect information provided by the consignor.

(b) Notwithstanding the provisions of subsection (a) above, the consignee's liability for payment of additional charges that may be found to be due after delivery shall be as specified by 49 U.S.C. Section 13706, except that the consignee need not provide the specified written notice to the delivering carrier if the consignee is a for-hire carrier.

(c) Nothing in this bill of lading shall limit the right of the carrier to require the prepayment or guarantee of the charges at the time of shipment or prior to delivery. If the description of articles or other information on this bill of lading is found to be incorrect or incomplete the freight charges must be paid based upon the articles actually shipped.

Sec. 8. If this bill of lading is issued on the order of the shipper, or his agent, in exchange or in substitution for another bill of lading, the shipper's signature on the prior bill of lading as to the statement of value or otherwise, or as to the election of common law or bill of lading liability shall be considered a part of this bill of lading as fully as if the same were written on or made in connection with this bill of lading.

Sec. 9. If all or any part of said property is carried by water over any party of said route, such water carriage shall be performed subject to the terms and provisions and limitations of liability specified by the "Carriage of Goods By Sea Act" and any other pertinent laws applicable to water carriers.

The carrier is contractually obligated to deliver goods to the consignee if the bill of lading is non-negotiable and to the holder of the bill if it is negotiable. The carrier may divert delivery on the instructions of the consignor if the bill of lading is non-negotiable and may obey instructions of the holder of a negotiable bill of lading to deliver goods elsewhere than originally indicated.[44] Failure to properly deliver goods will result in liability of the carrier to the consignor or consignee of a non-negotiable bill or to the holder of a negotiable bill of lading.

As an example of misdelivery, in one case a carrier was required by the terms of the bill of lading to obtain the bill of lading from the buyer before handing over the goods. The buyer was supposed to obtain the bill by first paying a bank presenting the bill pursuant to a documentary collection. The buyer did not pay for the goods and persuaded the carrier to hand over the goods on its guarantee of payment; the buyer then filed for bankruptcy. In the suit between the seller who shipped the goods and the carrier, the court held that the carrier was liable for the loss as it had violated the terms of the bill of lading, which was its contract with the shipper, the seller.[45]

(2) Damage to Goods and Delays in Delivery

The general common law rule regarding damage to goods during shipment is that the carrier is absolutely liable, subject to exceptions for acts of God, acts of public enemy, acts of shipper, acts of public authority, or loss due to the inherent vice or nature of the goods. This rule is recognized in statutes regulating carriers.[46] Carriers are thus placed in the position of being insurers of the goods. Carriers are able to limit their liability by requiring that the shipper state a value of the goods being transported.[47] Different rates may be charged depending on the value of the goods. In addition, for international shipments by air and sea, the Warsaw Convention and the Carriage of Goods by Sea Act limit the liability of carriers.[48]

On the question of damages caused by delay in delivery, the case law holds that the carrier is only responsible to use due diligence in making delivery. A duty is imposed on the carrier to notify the shipper of any known reasons why delivery might be delayed, if such information is not known by the shipper.[49]

---

[44]UCC §7-303 & 49 U.S.C. §80111.
[45]*C-Art, Ltd. v. Hong Kong Island Lines America*, 940 F.3d 530 (9th Cir. 1991).
[46]See 49 U.S.C §§11706, 14706; UCC §7-309; White & Summers, *Uniform Commercial Code* §21-1 (2d ed.); 8A Am. Jur. 2d Aviation §75.
[47]See, e.g., UCC §7-309(2).
[48]See 46 App. U.S.C. §1300 *et seq.*; 49 U.S.C. §40105 (note following statute reprints Warsaw Convention). The Carriage of Goods by Sea Act largely follows the 1924 Brussels Convention, which has been ratified by most of the significant commercial countries. The United Nations Convention on the Carriage of Goods by Sea was finalized in Hamburg in 1978, and is in force in 29 countries at the time of this writing (Fall, 2004). For a list of countries adopting the "Hamburg Rules," visit http://www.uncitral.org.
[49]See *Gold Star Meat Co. v. Union Pac. R.R. Co.*, 438 F.2d 1270 (10th Cir. 1971).

E. Obligations of Warehouse Operators

Sometimes the goods that are being sold will be located in a warehouse operated by someone who is neither controlled by the seller or the buyer. The goods will not be moved after the sale — the warehouse operator will now be holding the goods for the benefit of the buyer rather than the seller. This section discusses the obligations of such a warehouse operator, which are covered by UCC Article 7.

(1) Warehouse Receipts

When goods are delivered to a warehouse operator, the owner of the goods is a bailor and the warehouse operator is a bailee.[50] The warehouse operator will sometimes deliver a **warehouse receipt** to the bailor, which is a document of title. As is the case with bills of lading, the warehouse receipt can be either negotiable or non-negotiable. A warehouse receipt is negotiable if it states that the goods covered by it are to be delivered to bearer or to order of a named person.[51] Negotiable warehouse receipts will normally be marked "NEGOTIABLE" while non-negotiable warehouse receipts will be marked "NON-NEGOTIABLE."

The warehouse receipt constitutes a contract between the bailor and the bailee in addition to indicating who might have title to the goods represented by the receipt. Section 7-202, while not requiring that a warehouse receipt take any particular form, mandates that certain terms be in the warehouse receipt. Those terms are as follows:

(1) the location of the warehouse where the goods are being stored;
(2) the date of issue of the warehouse receipt;
(3) the unique identification code of the receipt;
(4) a statement indicating whether the goods will be delivered to the bearer, to a named person, or to a named person or its order (i.e., whether the receipt is negotiable or non-negotiable);
(5) the rate of storage or handling charges, or a statement that the goods are being held under a field warehouse arrangement;
(6) a description of the goods or the packages containing them;
(7) the signature of the warehouse or its agent;
(8) a statement indicating that the warehouse owns the goods if that is the case; and
(9) a statement of advances made and of liabilities incurred for which the warehouse claims a lien, unless the precise amount at the time of issuance of the receipt is unknown, in which case a statement of the fact that advances have been made or liabilities incurred and the purpose of the advances or liabilities is sufficient.

A form non-negotiable warehouse receipt is reproduced here:

---

[50]UCC §7-102(a)(1).
[51]UCC §7-104.

_____ Warehouse Company

A Public Warehouse Company
123 Main Street, Anytown, USA
Telephone
Fax

Non-Negotiable Warehouse Receipt

_____ **(Warehouse)** claims a lien for all lawful charges for storage and preservation of the goods; also for all lawful claims for money advanced, interest, insurance, transportation, labor, weighing, coopering, and other charges and expenses in relation to such goods, and for the balance on any other accounts that may be due. The property covered by this receipt has NOT been insured by this Company for the benefit of the depositor against fire or any other casualty.

THIS IS TO CERTIFY THAT WE HAVE RECEIVED the goods listed herein in apparent good order, except as noted herein (contents, condition, and quality unknown). SUBJECT TO ALL TERMS AND CONDITIONS INCLUDING LIMITATION OF LIABILITY HEREIN AND ON THE REVERSE HEREOF. Such property to be delivered to THE DEPOSITOR upon the payment of all storage, handling, and other charges. Advances have been made and liability incurred on these goods as follows:

RECEIVED FROM

FOR ACCOUNT OF

| DOCUMENT NUMBER |
| DATE |
| CUSTOMER NUMBER |
| CUSTOMER ORDER NO. |
| WAREHOUSE NO. |

| DELIVERING CARRIER | CARRIER NUMBER | PREPAID/COLLECT | SHIPPERS NUMBER |

QUANTITY	SAID TO BE OR CONTAIN (CUSTOMER ITEM NO., WAREHOUSE ITEM NO., LOT NO., DESCRIPTION, ETC.)	WEIGHT	RATE CODE	STORAGE RATE / HANDLING RATE	DAMAGE & EXCEPTIONS
TOTALS					

NO DELIVERY WILL BE MADE ON THIS RECEIPT EXCEPT ON WRITTEN ORDER

BY _____
AUTHORIZED SIGNATURE

At the time of this writing (May 1, 2008), this form is in the revision process by the IWLA and is being reproduced here for illustrative purposes only.

Standard Contract Terms and Conditions for Merchandise Warehousemen

(Approved and promulgated by American Warehouse Association, October 1968; revised and promulgated by International Warehouse Logistics Association, January 1998)

ACCEPTANCE – Sec. 1

(a) This contract and rate quotation including accessorial charges endorsed on or attached hereto must be accepted within 30 days from the proposal date by signature of depositor on the reverse side of the contract. In the absence of written acceptance, the act of tendering goods described herein for storage or other services by warehouseman within 30 days from the proposal date shall constitute such acceptance by depositor.

(b) In the event that goods tendered for storage or other services do not conform to the description contained herein, or conforming goods are tendered after 30 days from the proposal date without prior written acceptance by depositor as provided in paragraph (a) of this section, warehouseman may refuse to accept such goods. If warehouseman accepts such goods, depositor agrees to rates and charges as may be assigned and invoiced by warehouseman and to all terms of this contract.

(c) This contract may be canceled by either party upon 30 days written notice and is canceled if no storage or other services are performed under this contract for a period of 180 days.

SHIPPING – Sec. 2

Depositor agrees not to ship goods to warehouseman as the named consignee. If, in violation of this agreement, goods are shipped to warehouseman as named consignee, depositor agrees to notify carrier in writing prior to such shipment, with copy of such notice to the warehouseman, that warehouseman named as consignee is a warehouseman and has no beneficial title or interest in such property and depositor further agrees to indemnify and hold harmless warehouseman from any and all claims for unpaid transportation charges, including undercharges, demurrage, detention or charges of any nature, in connection with goods so shipped. Depositor further agrees that, if it fails to notify carrier as required by the preceding sentence, warehouseman shall have the right to refuse such goods and shall not be liable or responsible for any loss, injury or damage of any nature to, or related to, such goods.

TENDER FOR STORAGE – Sec. 3

All goods for storage shall be delivered at the warehouse properly marked and packaged for handling. The depositor shall furnish at or prior to such delivery, a manifest showing marks, brands, or sizes to be kept and accounted for separately, and the class of storage and other services desired.

STORAGE PERIOD AND CHARGES – Sec. 4

(a) All charges for storage are per package or other agreed unit per month.

(b) Storage charges become applicable upon the date that warehouseman accepts care, custody and control of the goods, regardless of unloading date or date of issue of warehouse receipt.

(c) Except as provided in paragraph (d) of this section, a full month's storage charge will apply on all goods received between the first and the 15th, inclusive, of a calendar month; one-half month's storage charge will apply on all goods received between the 16th and the last day, inclusive, of a calendar month, and a full month's storage charge will apply to all goods in storage on the first day of the next and succeeding calendar months. All storage charges are due and payable on the first day of storage for the initial month and thereafter on the first day of the calendar month.

(d) When mutually agreed by the warehouseman and the depositor, a storage month shall extend from a date in one calendar month to, but not including, the same date of the next and all succeeding months. All storage charges are due and payable on the first day of the storage month.

TRANSFER, TERMINATION OF STORAGE, REMOVAL OF GOODS – Sec. 5

(a) Instructions to transfer goods on the books of the warehouseman are not effective until delivered to and accepted by warehouseman, and all charges up to the time transfer is made are chargeable to the depositor of record. If a transfer involves rehandling the goods, such will be subject to a charge. When goods in storage are transferred from one party to another through issuance of a new warehouse receipt, a new storage date is established on the date of transfer.

(b) The warehouseman reserves the right to move, at his expense, 14 days after notice is sent by certified or registered mail to the depositor of record or to the last known holder of the negotiable warehouse receipt, any goods in storage from the warehouse in which they may be stored to any other of his warehouses; but if such depositor or holder takes delivery of his goods in lieu of transfer, no storage charge shall be made for the current storage month. Warehouseman will store the goods at, and may without notice move the goods within and between, any one or more of the warehouse buildings which comprise the warehouse complex identified on the front of this warehouse receipt.

(c) The warehouseman may, upon written notice to the depositor of record and any other person known by the warehouseman to claim an interest in the goods, require the removal of any goods by the end of the next succeeding storage month. Such notice shall be given to the last known place of business or abode of the person to be notified. If goods are not removed before the end of the next succeeding storage month, the warehouseman may sell them in accordance with applicable law.

(d) If warehouseman in good faith believes that the goods are about to deteriorate or decline in value to less than the amount of warehouseman's lien before the end of the next succeeding storage month, the warehouseman may specify in the notification any reasonable shorter time for removal of the goods and in case the goods are not removed, may sell them at public sale held one week after a single advertisement or posting as provided by law.

(e) If as a result of a quality or condition of the goods of which the warehouseman had no notice at the time of deposit the goods are a hazard to other property or to the warehouse or to persons, the warehouseman may sell the goods at public or private sale without advertisement on reasonable notification to all persons known to claim an interest in the goods. If the warehouseman after a reasonable effort is unable to sell the goods he may dispose of them in any lawful manner and shall incur no liability by reason of such disposition. Pending such disposition, sale or return of the goods, the warehouseman may remove the goods from the warehouse and shall incur no liability by reason of such removal.

HANDLING – Sec. 6

(a) The handling charge covers the ordinary labor involved in receiving goods at warehouse door, placing goods in storage, and returning goods to warehouse door. Handling charges are due and payable on receipt of goods.

(b) Unless otherwise agreed, labor for unloading and loading goods will be subject to a charge. Additional expenses incurred by the warehouseman in receiving and handling damaged goods, and additional expense in unloading from or loading into cars or other vehicles not at warehouse door will be charged to the depositor.

(c) Labor and materials used in loading rail cars or other vehicles are chargeable to the depositor.

(d) When goods are ordered out in quantities less than in which received, the warehouseman may make an additional charge for each order or each item of an order.

(e) The warehouseman shall not be liable for demurrage or detention, delays in unloading inbound cars, trailers or other containers, or delays in obtaining and loading cars, trailers or other containers for outbound shipment unless warehouseman has failed to exercise reasonable care.

DELIVERY REQUIREMENTS – Sec. 7

(a) No goods shall be delivered or transferred except upon receipt by the warehouseman of complete written instructions. Written instructions shall include, but are not limited to, FAX, EDI, TWX or similar communication, provided warehouseman has no liability when relying on the information contained in the communication as received. However, when no negotiable receipt is outstanding, goods may be delivered upon instruction by telephone in accordance with a prior written authorization, but the warehouseman shall not be responsible for loss or error occasioned thereby.

(b) When a negotiable receipt has been issued no goods covered by that receipt shall be delivered, or transferred on the books of the warehouseman, unless the receipt, properly endorsed, is surrendered for cancellation, or for endorsement of partial delivery thereon. If a negotiable receipt is lost or destroyed, delivery of goods may be made only upon order of a court of competent jurisdiction and the posting of security approved by the court as provided by law.

(c) When goods are ordered out a reasonable time shall be given the warehouseman to carry out instructions, and if he is unable because of acts of God, war, public enemies, seizure under legal process, strikes, lockouts, riots and civil commotions, or any reason beyond the warehouseman's control, or because of loss or destruction of goods for which warehouseman is not liable, or because of any other excuse provided by law, the warehouseman shall not be liable for failure to carry out such instructions and goods remaining in storage will continue to be subject to regular storage charges.

EXTRA SERVICES (SPECIAL SERVICES) – Sec. 8

(a) Warehouse labor required for services other than ordinary handling and storage will be charged to the depositor.

(b) Special services requested by depositor including but not limited to compiling of special stock statements; reporting marked weights, serial numbers or other data from packages; physical check of goods; and handling transit billing will be subject to a charge.

(c) Dunnage, bracing, packing materials or other special supplies, may be provided for the depositor at a charge in addition to the warehouseman's cost.

(d) By prior arrangement, goods may be received or delivered during other than usual business hours, subject to a charge.

(e) Communication expense including postage, teletype, telegram, or telephone will be charged to the depositor if such concern more than normal inventory reporting or if, at the request of the depositor, communications are made by other than regular United States Mail.

BONDED STORAGE – Sec. 9

(a) A charge in addition to regular rates will be made for merchandise in bond.

(b) Where a warehouse receipt covers goods in U.S. Customs bond, such receipt shall be void upon the termination of the storage period fixed by law.

MINIMUM CHARGES – Sec. 10

(a) A minimum handling charge per lot and a minimum storage charge per lot per month will be made. When a warehouse receipt covers more than one lot or when a lot is in assortment, a minimum charge per mark, brand, or variety will be made.

(b) A minimum monthly charge to one account for storage and/or handling will be made. This charge will apply also to each account when one customer has several accounts, each requiring separate records and billing.

LIABILITY AND LIMITATION OF DAMAGES – Sec. 11

(a) THE WAREHOUSEMAN SHALL NOT BE LIABLE FOR ANY LOSS OR INJURY TO GOODS STORED HOWEVER CAUSED UNLESS SUCH LOSS OR INJURY RESULTED FROM THE FAILURE BY THE WAREHOUSEMAN TO EXERCISE SUCH CARE IN REGARD TO THEM AS A REASONABLY CAREFUL MAN WOULD EXERCISE UNDER LIKE CIRCUMSTANCES AND WAREHOUSEMAN IS NOT LIABLE FOR DAMAGES WHICH COULD NOT HAVE BEEN AVOIDED BY THE EXERCISE OF SUCH CARE.

(b) GOODS ARE NOT INSURED BY THE WAREHOUSEMAN AGAINST LOSS OR INJURY HOWEVER CAUSED.

(c) THE DEPOSITOR DECLARES THAT DAMAGES ARE LIMITED TO ______________, PROVIDED, HOWEVER, THAT SUCH LIABILITY MAY AT THE TIME OF ACCEPTANCE OF THIS CONTRACT AS PROVIDED IN SECTION 1 BE INCREASED UPON DEPOSITOR'S WRITTEN REQUEST ON PART OR ALL OF THE GOODS HEREUNDER IN WHICH EVENT AN ADDITIONAL MONTHLY CHARGE WILL BE MADE BASED UPON SUCH INCREASED VALUATION.

(d) WHERE LOSS OR INJURY OCCURS TO STORED GOODS, FOR WHICH THE WAREHOUSEMAN IS NOT LIABLE, THE DEPOSITOR SHALL BE RESPONSIBLE FOR THE COST OF REMOVING AND DISPOSING OF SUCH GOODS AND THE COST OF ANY ENVIRONMENTAL CLEAN UP AND SITE REMEDIATION RESULTING FROM THE LOSS OR INJURY TO THE GOODS.

NOTICE OF CLAIM AND FILING OF SUIT – Sec. 12

(a) Claims by the depositor and all other persons must be presented in writing to the warehouseman within a reasonable time, and in no event longer than either 60 days after delivery of the goods by the warehouseman or 60 days after depositor of record or the last known holder of a negotiable warehouse receipt is notified by the warehouseman that loss or injury to part or all of the goods has occurred, whichever time is shorter.

(b) No action may be maintained by the depositor or others against the warehouseman for loss or injury to the goods stored unless timely written claim has been given as provided in paragraph (a) of this section and unless such action is commenced either within nine months after date of delivery by warehouseman or within nine months after depositor of record or the last known holder of a negotiable warehouse receipt is notified that loss or injury to part or all of the goods has occurred, whichever time is shorter.

(c) When goods have not been delivered, notice may be given of known loss or injury to the goods by mailing of a registered or certified letter to the depositor of record or to the last known holder of a negotiable warehouse receipt. Time limitations for presentation of claim in writing and maintaining of action after notice begin on the date of mailing of such notice by warehouseman.

LIABILITY FOR CONSEQUENTIAL DAMAGES – Sec. 13

Warehouseman shall not be liable for any loss of profit or special, indirect, or consequential damages of any kind.

LIABILITY FOR MISSHIPMENT – Sec. 14

If warehouseman negligently misships goods, the warehouseman shall pay the reasonable transportation charges incurred to return the misshipped goods to the warehouse. If the consignee fails to return the goods, warehouseman's maximum liability shall be for the lost or damaged goods as specified in Section 11 above, and warehouseman shall have no liability for damages due to the consignee's acceptance or use of the goods whether such goods be those of the depositor or another.

MYSTERIOUS DISAPPEARANCE – Sec. 15

Warehouseman shall not be liable for loss of goods due to inventory shortage or unexplained or mysterious disappearance of goods unless depositor establishes such loss occurred because of warehouseman's failure to exercise the care required of warehouseman under Section 11 above. Any presumption of conversion imposed by law shall not apply to such loss and a claim by depositor of conversion must be established by affirmative evidence that the warehouseman converted the goods to the warehouseman's own use.

RIGHT TO STORE GOODS – Sec. 16

Depositor represents and warrants that depositor is lawfully possessed of the goods and has the right and authority to store them with warehouseman. Depositor agrees to indemnify and hold harmless the warehouseman from all loss, cost and expense (including reasonable attorneys' fees) which warehouseman pays or incurs as a result of any dispute or litigation, whether instituted by warehouseman or others, respecting depositor's right, title or interest in the goods. Such amounts shall be charges in relation to the goods and subject to warehouseman's lien.

ACCURATE INFORMATION – Sec. 17

Depositor will provide warehouseman with information concerning the stored goods which is accurate, complete and sufficient to allow warehouseman to comply with all laws and regulations concerning the storage, handling and transporting of the stored goods. Depositor will indemnify and hold warehouseman harmless from all loss, cost, penalty and expense (including reasonable attorneys' fees) which warehouseman pays or incurs as a result of depositor failing to fully discharge this obligation.

SEVERABILITY and WAIVER – Sec. 18

(a) If any provision of this receipt, or any application thereof, should be construed or held to be void, invalid or unenforceable, by order, decree or judgment of a court of competent jurisdiction, the remaining provisions of this receipt shall not be affected thereby but shall remain in full force and effect.

(b) Warehouseman's failure to require strict compliance with any provision of the Warehouse Receipt shall not constitute a waiver or estoppel to later demand strict compliance with that or any other provision(s) of this Warehouse Receipt.

(c) The provisions of this Warehouse Receipt shall be binding upon the depositor's heirs, executors, successors and assigns; contain the sole agreement governing goods stored with the warehouseman; and, cannot be modified except by a writing signed by warehouseman.

At the time of this writing (May 1, 2008), this form is in the revision process by the IWLA and is being reproduced here for illustrative purposes only.

(2) To Whom Should the Warehouse Operator Deliver the Goods?

The warehouse operator is responsible to deliver the goods to the holder of a negotiable warehouse receipt or to the person to whom delivery is to be made according to the terms of a non-negotiable warehouse receipt.[52] A person is a "holder" of a negotiable warehouse receipt if the person is in possession of it and it indicates that goods are to be delivered to bearer or to the order of that person.[53] The initial holder of the warehouse receipt may "negotiate" it to somebody else so that the recipient becomes a holder. Negotiation is accomplished by the holder signing the receipt and handing it to the recipient, similar to how one would negotiate a check.[54] If the initial holder negotiates it simply by signing her or his name and not indicating to whom the document is being negotiated, the goods are then deliverable to the bearer of the document.[55] The document is said to be "duly negotiated" when it is negotiated in the manner stated previously to someone who purchases it in good faith with new value without notice of any defense against or claim to it on the part of another person and if it is done in the regular course of business or financing.[56]

A person who is the holder of a duly negotiated document receives title to the goods paramount to those of almost anyone else.[57] If, however, the goods were stolen from someone who then put the goods in a warehouse and obtained a warehouse receipt, due negotiation of that warehouse receipt will not defeat the rights of the person from whom the goods were stolen.[58]

One can see that negotiable documents are dangerous in that if they indicate that delivery of the goods is to be to bearer, there is a danger that the document will be lost or stolen and that the goods will wind up in the hands of someone who otherwise would not have good title to them. But negotiable documents may be useful in obtaining bank financing against the goods in that the bank may take possession of the document to secure its right to payment.[59] It is easier to transfer possession of the document than of the goods themselves.

(3) Warehouse Operator Liability for Misdescription of Goods on Warehouse Receipt

The warehouse operator is responsible to a good faith purchaser for value of a warehouse receipt for misdescription or non-receipt of goods listed in the receipt.[60] The warehouse operator may avoid liability by conspicuous disclaimers to the effect that it is unknown whether the goods described were ever received, for example, "contents, condition and quality unknown."[61]

Unlike a carrier, the liability of the warehouse operator for damage done to the goods while in the operator's possession is not absolute. The warehouse operator is

---

[52]UCC §7-403.
[53]UCC §1-201(b)(21).
[54]UCC §7-501.
[55]UCC §7-501(a)(1).
[56]UCC §7-501(a)(5).
[57]UCC §§7-502 & 7-503.
[58]UCC §7-503(a).
[59]UCC §§9-312(c) & 9-313(a).
[60]UCC §7-203.
[61]UCC §7-203.

responsible for any damage to the goods caused by negligence.[62] The warehouse operator may further limit liability by establishing a limit with respect to each article being stored.[63] Look at paragraph 11 of the Standard Terms and Conditions For Merchandise Warehousemen, reproduced on page 194, to see how liability is limited under the terms of the Warehouse Receipt.

One of the greatest financial scandals in American financial history, the "Great Salad Oil Scandal" of 1963, involved the issuance of warehouse receipts that were used as collateral to procure loans based on the salad oil that was represented by the receipts. Through various means, the unscrupulous vegetable oil dealer, Allied Crude Vegetable Oil Company, shipped and stored vegetable oil in ways that made it look like there was more oil than actually existed. For example, because oil floats, vegetable oil was stored on top of water. If a tank was inspected from the top, it would appear to be full of vegetable oil when in fact it contained mostly water. When the fraud was discovered in 1963, $175 million in salad oil was missing. The owners of the field warehouses issuing the receipts had a lot of explaining to do! American Express, which through subsidiaries issued warehouse receipts in the scandal, lost approximately $58 million.[64]

The rule that is applied in cases like the Great Salad Oil Scandal is that once there is evidence that goods have been presented to the bailee, namely, the warehouse operator, the bailee assumes a duty of care with respect to that property. The failure to return the bailed property creates a presumption of negligence. The burden of proof is then on the bailee to show how the loss occurred. If that burden is then met, the plaintiff must prove actual negligence on the part of the bailee.[65] Where the loss of goods is a mystery and cannot be explained by the bailee, the bailee will take the loss.

SUMMARY

■ A seller may insist on a letter of credit established by the buyer to make certain that the seller will be paid when goods are shipped.

■ A letter of credit will typically require that the seller produce documents showing the goods have been shipped, such as a bill of lading issued by a carrier showing receipt of the goods and an inspection certificate showing that proper goods were handed to the carrier.

■ The bank's obligation to pay under a letter of credit is independent of the underlying contract for sale. The bank is obligated to pay if the documents presented conform to the requirements of the letter of credit.

■ The bank is obligated to pay only if the documents strictly comply with the terms of the letter of credit.

■ If a bank properly honors a letter of credit, the bank has a statutory right to be reimbursed by the applicant for the letter of credit, namely, the buyer.

---

[62]UCC §7-204.
[63]UCC §7-204(b).
[64]For more information, read Miller, *The Great Salad Oil Scandal* (1965); see also *Proctor & Gamble Distributing Co. v. Lawrence Ware Corp.*, 16 N.Y.2d 344, 266 N.Y.S.2d 735, 213 N.E.2d 873 (1966).
[65]*Proctor & Gamble Distributing Co. v. Lawrence Ware Corp.*, 16 N.Y.2d 344, 266 N.Y.S.2d 785, 213 N.E.2d 873 (1966).

- In the event that the seller engages in material fraud, such as by shipping worthless goods or forging documents, the buyer may be able to get an injunction preventing the bank from paying under a letter of credit.

- In some cases, the contract for sale may not require a letter of credit but may require the buyer to pay against a presentation of documents before the goods arrive. The documents will show that the goods have been shipped. The buyer must pay if the documents conform for the buyer to obtain the goods.

- Carriers are required to deliver goods to the consignee named on a straight bill of lading and are required to deliver the goods to the holder of a negotiable bill of lading.

- The general common law rule regarding damage to goods during shipment is that the carrier is absolutely liable, subject to exceptions for acts of God, acts of public enemy, acts of shipper, acts of public authority, or loss due to the inherent vice or nature of the goods. Damages may be subject to limitation under international conventions.

- In terms of timeliness of delivery, a carrier is required to use due diligence in making delivery.

- A warehouse operator is responsible to deliver the goods to the holder of a negotiable warehouse receipt or to the person to whom delivery is to be made according to the terms of a non-negotiable warehouse receipt.

- The warehouse operator is responsible to a good faith purchaser for value of a warehouse receipt for misdescription or non-receipt of goods listed in the receipt. The warehouse operator may avoid liability by conspicuous disclaimers to the effect that it is unknown whether the goods described were ever received, for example, "contents, condition and quality unknown."

- The warehouse operator is responsible for any damage to the goods caused by negligence. The warehouse operator may further limit liability by establishing a limit with respect to each article being stored.

CONNECTIONS

Contract Formation and Terms of the Contract

Whether a contract calls for goods to be shipped by a carrier or whether payment will be by a letter of credit depends on the terms of the contract of sale, and thus it may be necessary to look at how the contract was formed. If the contract was formed via an exchange of forms, it may be necessary to analyze the contract under UCC §2-207 or under the CISG to see if the contract calls for shipment or payment via a letter of credit.

Performance of the Contract

Whether the seller shipped conforming goods is independent of a bank's obligation to pay under a letter of credit. With respect to goods shipped by carrier, if goods are damaged in transit, the issue of who has the risk of loss will determine who winds up suing the carrier.

Remedies

If non-conforming goods are shipped to the buyer and the seller makes a conforming presentation under a letter of credit, the bank is obligated to honor the presentation unless there is material fraud. The bank is entitled to be reimbursed by the buyer, and the buyer then can sue the seller for damages caused by the seller's breach. If the bank wrongfully honors a non-conforming presentation under a letter of credit, the bank is not necessarily entitled to reimbursement by the buyer. The bank is subrogated to the position of the buyer or the seller under the sales contract, and it will be necessary to determine which party is in breach under that contract and the amount of damages the breaching party owes to the injured party. The bank can step into the shoes of the injured party to recover. It is thus necessary to analyze which party to the sales contract was in breach and the remedy available to that party.

Leases of Goods

10

A party may prefer to **lease** goods rather than purchase them. "Lease" is defined in Uniform Commercial Code (UCC) §2A-103 as "a transfer

OVERVIEW

of the right of possession and use of goods for a term in return for consideration. . . ." A party may need the goods for only a short time, in which case leasing the goods is preferable to purchasing them. Many people prefer to lease automobiles rather than purchasing them, especially if they frequently wish to change to more updated models. Parties may also prefer to lease goods rather than purchase them for tax or accounting reasons. For example, a purchase of goods on credit may result in a liability on the balance sheet of the purchaser while a lease of the goods might not.[1]

This chapter considers the rights and obligations of lessors and lessees of goods. The chapter will focus on the similarities and differences of these rights and obligations to those governing sellers and buyers of goods.

A. GOVERNING LAW

B. IS THE TRANSACTION A LEASE OR A SALE?

1. The Conditional Sale
2. Factors in Determining Whether a Transaction Is a Lease or Conditional Sale
3. Consequences of Determining that Transaction Is Sale Rather than Lease

---

[1] See White & Summers, *Uniform Commercial Code* §21.3 (5th ed.).

C. IS THE LEASE A "FINANCE LEASE"?

D. RIGHTS OF THE LESSEE IN THE GOODS

E. PERFORMANCE, BREACH, AND REMEDIES UNDER A LEASE CONTRACT

1. Lessee's Right to Reject or Revoke Acceptance
2. Lessor's Right to Cancel, Withhold Delivery, and Repossess
3. Damage Recovery for Injured Lessors and Lessees
4. Actions for Rent and Specific Performance

A. Governing Law

Uniform Commercial Code Article 2A, added in 1987, deals with lease transactions. It was revised in 1990, and has been adopted in some form by every state except Louisiana. In 2003, proposed amendments to Article 2A were approved by the National Conference of Commissioners on Uniform State Laws (NCCUSL) and the American Law Institute (ALI). The 2003 proposed amendments are currently before state legislatures along with the 2003 proposed amendments to Article 2. References to the proposed amendments in this chapter are to "Amended UCC §2A-." Other references are to the unamended version of Article 2A.

For international transactions, the International Institute for the Unification of Private Law (UNIDROIT) approved the Convention on International Financial Leasing in 1988. At the time of this writing, it is in force in ten nations. The United States has signed the Convention, but it has not yet been ratified and is not in force. In this chapter, we will discuss only UCC Article 2A.

Table 10.1 discusses some of the areas in which Article 2 covering sales differs from Article 2A covering leases. Some of the topics in the chart are discussed in more detail in the pages that follow. Article 2A has many similarities to Article 2 on the

TABLE 10.1	Comparison of UCC Article 2 (Sales) to Article 2A (Leases) (Does Not Include 2003 Amendments to Articles 2 & 2A)	
Topic	Article 2 (Sales)	Article 2A (Leases)
"Sale" Compared to "Lease"	Passage of title to buyer for a price. §2-106(1).	Lessee obtains right to possess and use goods for a term. Lessor has right to goods on expiration of the term. §2A-103(1)(j).
Secured Party vs. Finance Lessor	A financial institution may finance a sale by lending money to the buyer and taking a security interest in the goods. The seller may also finance the sale on credit and retain title until the price is paid. The lender or seller in such a situation is called a "secured party" and the transaction is governed by UCC Article 9.	A financial institution or leasing company might purchase goods selected by the lessee for the purpose of leasing the goods to the lessee. Such a lease is called a "finance lease" and is governed by UCC Article 2A.

"Battle of the Forms"	UCC §2-207 provides complex rules dealing with contract formation when buyers and sellers exchange form purchase orders and order acknowledgments containing varying terms. See pp. 29-39, *supra*.	Article 2A contains no provisions dealing with the battle of the forms because parties in lease transactions do not typically contract through an exchange of forms.
Implied Warranties of Quality	Implied warranty of merchantability given by merchants who sell goods of the kind involved, unless properly disclaimed. §2-314. Implied warranty of fitness for particular purpose given when seller selects goods for buyer with reason to know of buyer's purpose. §2-315.	Same as Article 2, except not given by lessor in a finance lease. §2A-212.
Risk of Loss	Passes to buyer under circumstances set forth in §§2-509 & 2-510. See pp. 77-85, *supra*.	Stays with lessor during term of the lease, unless lease is a finance lease or unless otherwise agreed. §2A-219.
Revocation of Acceptance	Permitted under circumstances set forth in §2-608. See pp. 114-115, *supra*.	Same as Article 2, except no revocation of acceptance against lessor in finance lease unless lessor gives express warranty or assurances of repair that were breached. §2A-517.
Calculation of Contract/ Market & Contract/ Resale Remedies When Goods Not Accepted	Contract price — Market Price (buyer) & Market Price — Contract Price (seller) or Purchase Price — Contract Price (buyer) & Contract Price — Resale Price (seller). See pp. 139-145 and 161-164, *supra*.	Same as Article 2, except amounts due in the future must be discounted to present value based on agreed or reasonable interest rate. See pp. 211-212, *infra*.
Right to Reclaim Goods	Unless seller takes a security interest, right to reclaim goods from breaching buyer is limited. See pp. 168-169, *supra*.	Upon breach, lessor may repossess goods & use self-help as long as no breach of the peace. See pp. 210-211, *infra*.
Liquidated Damages	Reasonableness determined based on actual or anticipated loss.	Reasonableness determined based on anticipated loss.

questions of contract formation and enforcement. For example, §2A-204 on formation is very similar to §2-204 permitting informal contract formation without agreement on all terms. There is a statute of frauds under Article 2A, §2A-201, which is triggered for leases of $1,000 or more (as compared to $500 in §2-201). There is nothing in Article 2A comparable to UCC §2-207, reflecting the view that lease contracts are not typically formed through a "battle of the forms." There also are warranty provisions in Article 2A similar to the warranties given under Article 2 (although implied warranties are not given in finance leases, as discussed in more detail later). Unlike Article 2 where the risk of loss passes to the buyer on the buyer's receipt of the goods (if not earlier), the risk of loss in a lease remains with the lessor unless the lease is a finance lease or the lease allocates the risk of loss to the lessee.

B. Is the Transaction a Lease or a Sale?

The determination of whether a transaction is a "lease" or a "sale" is important in determining which law governs the transaction. It may also be important, as noted previously, because tax laws and accounting rules may give more favorable treatment to a lease as opposed to a sale. Parties may be tempted to label their contracts "leases" instead of "sales" to obtain favorable treatment. The law does not, however, permit the parties to define whether a transaction is a lease or a sale merely by labeling it as such in the contract.

The UCC defines "sale" as "the passing of title from the seller to the buyer for a price."[2] In a true sale, there is no reversionary interest for the seller, that is, the seller does not have any expectation or right to get the goods back.[3] Under a true lease, the lessor _does_ have a reversionary interest. Once the lease term expires, the lessor has a right to get the goods back.

(1) The Conditional Sale

There is a transaction, however, that combines elements of sales and leases and that can sometimes be disguised to look like a lease. That transaction is the **conditional sale**. Under a conditional sale, the seller sells the goods to the buyer on credit. The seller reserves title in the goods until the buyer pays the complete purchase price, at which point title is conveyed to the buyer. It is a conditional sale because completion of the transfer of title is conditional upon the buyer completing payment for the goods.

A conditional sale is governed by both Article 2 and Article 9 of the UCC. Article 9 of the UCC deals with secured transactions, that is, situations in which a creditor takes personal property of the debtor as collateral for a loan. The UCC provides that the retention of title by a seller to secure payment of the price is the reservation of a security interest under UCC Article 9.[4]

---

[2]UCC §2-106(1).
[3]As we discussed previously, there are limited circumstances in which a seller may reclaim goods that have not been paid for. See pp. 168-169, _supra_.
[4]UCC §2-401(1).

CHARACTERISTICS OF SALES, LEASES OF GOODS AND CONDITIONAL SALES

Sale — Buyer obtains title and Seller has no reversionary interest in the goods. UCC Article 2 governs the transaction.

Lease — Lessee has a contractual right to use the goods for the period indicated in the lease contract. The lessor has a right to recover the goods once the lease period expires. UCC Article 2A governs the transaction.

Conditional Sale — Seller retains title to the goods until Buyer pays the purchase price in full. If Buyer defaults, Seller has a right to obtain possession of the goods. Articles 2 and 9 govern the transaction. Seller's reservation of title generally needs to be protected by filing a public notice called a "financing statement."

UCC Article 9 generally requires creditors taking collateral, including sellers under conditional sales contracts, to take steps to notify others of their interest in collateral.[5] This requirement is similar to the requirement that somebody taking real estate as collateral record a mortgage or deed of trust to perfect their interest against third parties. Under Article 9, creditors will often file a document called a *financing statement* in the relevant state's secretary of state's office (normally in the state in which the debtor resides) to perfect their security interest in personal property.[6] By contrast, UCC Article 2A does not require a lessor to file any documents putting others on notice of its interest in goods.

A lease can look a lot like a conditional sale at times. For example, a "lease" may provide that the lessee is obligated to make payments on goods for five years and then at the end of the "lease" term may purchase the goods for $1. The parties are obviously contemplating that ultimately the "lessee" will own title to the goods and are only reserving title in the "lessor" for the purpose of securing the "lessee's" obligation to pay for them. They are calling the transaction a "lease" for tax or accounting reasons. As noted, the UCC does not permit the parties to determine the characterization of the transaction through a label. Instead, UCC §1-203 focuses on the economic realities of the transaction, requiring courts to look at all of the facts and circumstances of the transaction.

Sidebar

THE DIFFERENT TREATMENT OF LEASES AND SECURITY INTERESTS

It was previously noted that the law disfavors secret property interests and that is one reason why sellers are generally not allowed to reclaim goods when a buyer does not pay the price, unless the seller retains a security interest under UCC Article 9. See pages 168-169, *supra*. In the area of leases, however, the UCC permits the lessor to retain its reversionary interest in the goods without putting anyone on notice. For all the world knows, the lessee in possession of goods has title to those goods — there is no public record to check to see if the goods are leased. The drafters of Article 2A believed that it would be too burdensome to require lessors of goods to file public notices every time a good was leased. Lease transactions are similar to sales transactions in that they tend to be informal and conducted without counsel. See UCC §2A-101, official comments.

---

[5]Conditional sellers need not file a financing statement if the goods being sold on credit are consumer goods. Such a transaction is called a purchase money security interest in consumer goods. See UCC §9-309(1).
[6]UCC §§9-310, 9-501.

(2) Factors in Determining Whether a Transaction Is a Lease or Conditional Sale

Section 1-203 states that a transaction disguised as a lease is a conditional sale covered by Articles 2 and 9 if the "lessee" is legally bound to continue the lease for the entire duration of the lease and one of the following circumstances exists:

(1) the original term of the "lease" is equal to or greater than the remaining economic life of the goods as estimated at the time of the contract;

(2) the "lessee" is bound to renew the lease for the economic life of the goods or is bound to become the owner of the goods;

(3) the "lessee" has an "option" to renew the lease for the remaining economic life of the goods for no additional consideration or for nominal consideration at the expiration of the lease; or

(4) the lessee has an option to become the owner of the goods for no additional consideration or for nominal consideration at the end of the lease term.

   To give a couple of examples, assume that someone enters into a "lease" of a computer system for five years. The "lessee" is unable to legally terminate the lease during that time. The "lease" provides that at the end of the lease term, the "lessee" can become the owner of the computer system at the price of $1. This transaction would be labeled a conditional sale/secured transaction according to UCC §1-203.

   Assume the same facts except that the option price at the end of the "lease" term is $200, but the estimated economic life of the computer system at the time the contract is entered into is five years. The parties contemplate that the computer will not be worth very much at the end of the five-year period. Such a transaction would also be considered a conditional sale/secured transaction according to UCC §1-203.

   When you think about it, you can see that these transactions are really like sales in that the parties are contemplating that the "lessee" will ultimately realize the entire economic benefit of the good in question. There will be nothing of value that will go back to the lessor. In a true lease, it is contemplated that something of value will revert to the lessor at the end of the lease term.

   Except for the four situations discussed previously, §1-203 does not give a clear answer as to whether a transaction is a true lease or a disguised conditional sale/secured transaction. It does say that certain factors are consistent with both sales and true leases, and that the existence of one or more of those factors should not cause a court to overturn the parties' statement that the transaction is a "lease." Those factors are the following:

(1) the present value of lease payments that the lessee is obligated to make under the lease is greater than the fair market value of the goods at the time the lease is entered into;

(2) the lessee assumes the risk of loss;

(3) the lessee agrees to pay all taxes, insurance, filing, recording, or registration fees, or service or maintenance costs;

(4) the lessee has an option to renew the lease or become owner of the goods;

(5) the lessee has an option to renew the lease for a fixed rent that is equal to or greater than the reasonably predictable fair market rent for the use of the goods for the term of the renewal at the time the option is to be performed; or

(6) the lessee has an option to become the owner of the goods for a fixed price that is equal to or greater than the reasonably predictable fair market value of the goods at the time the option is to be performed.

To demonstrate how a court might examine various factors in determining whether a transaction is a conditional sale or a lease, we can consider *In re Hoskins*.[7] In that case, the lessees of a vehicle were required to pay $14,317.92 over a 24-month lease for a vehicle that was estimated to be worth about $24,000. The lessees had the option to purchase the vehicle at the end of the lease term for around $15,000, which was approximately the estimated residual value. The lessees were subjected to a penalty in the event that they tried to terminate the lease early. The lessees were also responsible for insuring the vehicle and for title, license, and registration fees.

The court ultimately determined that the transaction was a true lease. The option to purchase did not render the lease a disguised sale because the option price was roughly equivalent to what the parties agreed the car would be worth at the time that the option was to be exercised. That the lessees had to pay for registration and insurance was consistent with the transaction being a lease, according to UCC §1-203.

The key for the court was that the lease contemplated something of value for the lessor at the end of the term. A rational lessee might, or might not, decide to exercise the option to purchase when the lease expired. The consideration that the lessee was to pay to exercise the option to purchase was not nominal. In determining whether an amount is nominal, the court stated that the question was "whether the lessee has, in light of all of the facts and circumstances, no sensible alternative but to exercise the purchase option. . . . Under this test, if only a fool would fail to exercise the purchase option, the option price is generally considered nominal and the transaction characterized as a disguised security agreement."[8] The vehicle also had considerable value at the end of the lease term — $15,000.

(3) Consequences of Determining that Transaction Is Sale Rather than Lease

What are the consequences of a court finding that a transaction is a sale instead of a lease? If the "lessor"/conditional seller has not complied with Article 9's requirements for perfecting its interest, the seller will be considered to have an unperfected security interest in the goods.[9] This means that buyers of the goods and other secured creditors with claims to the goods may be able to take priority over the seller in the event that the buyer defaults.[10] If the buyer goes into bankruptcy, the bankruptcy trustee will take priority over the seller.[11] Even if the seller has complied with Article 9, lessors are generally given more favorable treatment under the Bankruptcy Code

---

[7]266 B.R. 154, 45 UCC Rep. Serv. 2d 1025 (Bankr. W.D. Mo. 2001).
[8]266 B.R. at 161.
[9]If a lessor is uncertain as to whether the transaction will be determined to be a disguised secured transaction, the lessor may file a financing statement anyway under UCC §9-505 without conceding that the transaction is subject to Article 9.
[10]See UCC §9-317.
[11]Bankruptcy Code §544 (11 U.S.C. §544).

than conditional sellers, meaning that the lessor has a better chance of being paid in full or getting back the leased goods.[12]

To summarize, if you are faced with a question where a transaction looks like it might be a sale disguised as a lease, you should think about what things you might expect to find in a "lease" transaction as compared to a "sale." You might expect that at the end of the lease term, something of value will go back to the lessor. If there is an option to purchase the goods at the end of the lease term, one might expect that it will reflect a price approximating the value of the goods at the end of the term and the rational lessee might either decide to exercise the option or not. If you see a contract in which it is contemplated that there will be nothing of value to return to the "lessor" at the end of the "lease" term or where no rational "lessee" would elect not to exercise the option to purchase at the end, then you should probably strongly consider the possibility that this contract represents a sale rather than a lease.

C. Is the Lease a "Finance Lease"?

In some cases, a third party will be involved in facilitating the lease transaction. The party interested in obtaining possession of the goods wishes to lease the goods rather than purchase them, and the supplier of the goods is not interested in a lease or a credit transaction. In such a case, a financial institution or leasing company may come into the picture, which will technically purchase the goods from the supplier and will then lease the goods to the party interested in obtaining possession. This type of lease may fall within the definition of a *finance lease* in UCC §2A-103(1)(g). Two fundamental characteristics of a "finance lease" under that section are (1) the lessor does not select the goods, and (2) the lessor acquires the goods in connection with the lease. In addition, one of the following additional events must occur:

(1) the lessee receives a copy of the contract by which the lessor acquired or will acquire the goods before signing the lease agreement;
(2) the lessee's approval of the terms by which the lessor will acquire the goods is a condition to the lease agreement;
(3) the lessee, before signing the lease agreement, receives a complete statement of warranties from the supplier or manufacturer of the goods, including disclaimers, limitations,

---

[12]A lease would be considered an executory contract and the bankruptcy trustee would be compelled to either assume or reject the lease. See *In re Architectural Millwork of Virginia, Inc.*, 226 B.R. 551, 39 U.C.C. Rep. Serv. 2d 36 (1998). An Article 9 secured party may be subjected to a "cramdown," meaning that the bankruptcy estate can retain the goods by paying fair market value rather than the amount owed under the contract. See White & Summers, *Uniform Commercial Code* §21-3 (5th ed.).

or liquidated damages, provided to the lessor by the person supplying the goods; or

(4) for leases other than consumer leases, the lessor informs the lessee in writing or in an electronic record before the lessee signs the lease agreement (a) of the identity of the person supplying the goods to the lessor if the lessor has selected that person, (b) that the lessee is entitled to the promises and warranties provided to the lessor by the supplier, and (c) that the lessee may communicate with the person supplying the goods and receive a complete statement of the promises and warranties or a statement of remedies.

Finance leases are given special treatment under Article 2A. The main advantage of the non-consumer finance lease from the lessor's perspective is that the lessee's promise to pay rent under the lease becomes irrevocable upon the lessee's acceptance of the goods, no matter whether the goods prove to be defective.[13] Article 2A thus codifies the "**hell or high water**" *clause* existing in leases that requires the lessee to pay the rent no matter what happens to the goods subject to the lease.[14] This rule make sense in situations in which the lessor does nothing more than finance the transaction. Remember that in a finance lease it is the lessee who selects the goods from the supplier; the finance lessor does not have any control over whether the goods will be suitable to the lessee's purposes or not. The lessee is given the benefit of any warranties given by the supplier of the goods under §2A-209, so the lessee can sue the supplier in the event that the goods do not conform to any express or implied warranties given in the sale of the goods to the lessor.

The issue of whether a lessee was required to pay the lessor even though the supplier of goods was allegedly in breach of contract was presented in *AT&T Credit Corp. v. Transglobal Telecom Alliance.*[15] In that case, Transglobal leased phone equipment from AT&T Credit Corp. The equipment was supplied by AT&T Corporation, an affiliate of AT&T Credit. Transglobal claimed that AT&T Corp., the supplier, was in breach of contract in not providing all of the equipment that it was supposed to provide, and thus refused to pay under the lease agreement with AT&T Credit Corp. AT&T Credit Corp. sued, claiming that Transglobal's obligation to pay under the lease was "come hell or high water" as the lease was a finance lease, and thus the breach of contract by the supplier of the goods was irrelevant. It was also irrelevant, according to AT&T Credit Corp., that it was an affiliate of AT&T Corp.

The court first held that the lease was a "finance lease," because Transglobal, the lessee, had selected the goods and AT&T Credit Corp. had acquired the goods from AT&T Corp. pursuant to the lease agreement. In addition, the lessor had notified the lessee of its rights to pursue AT&T Corp. in the event that the goods did not work. Because the lease was a finance lease, the lessee was obligated to pay the lessor even if AT&T Corp. was in breach of contract in not supplying proper equipment. It did not matter that AT&T Credit Corp. (the lessor) and AT&T Corp. (the supplier) were affiliated corporations.

---

[13]UCC §2A-407.
[14]See UCC §2A-407, official comment 1.
[15]966 F. Supp. 299, 33 UCC Rep. Serv. 2d 492 (D.N.J. 1997).

SOME SPECIAL FEATURES OF FINANCE LEASES

(1) Lessee can enforce warranties arising out of sale of goods from supplier to lessor. §2A-209.
(2) Lessor does not give warranty of title, warranty of fitness or warranty of merchantability. §§2A-211(2), 2A-212, 2A-213.
(3) Lessee has the risk of loss on goods. §2A-219.
(4) Once goods accepted, Lessee must pay rent in non-consumer lease "come hell or high water." Lessor not responsible for defective leased goods. §2A-407.
(5) In non-consumer leases, Lessee may not revoke acceptance unless Lessor made assurances that defects would be cured (and they weren't). §2A-517.

In the case of commercial entities such as those involved in the case just discussed, it probably is not a horrible hardship to require that the lessee continue to make payments under a lease and pursue the supplier for any problems with the goods. AT&T Corp. is a "deep pocket" and could be sued for breach of contract. The commercial lessee can hire a lawyer to pursue them. Consumer leases present another problem, however. A consumer lessee may not be in a good position to continue making payments under a lease for goods that don't work and then pursue the supplier of the goods for a remedy.

One of the most common consumer lease transactions involves the lease of a car. These transactions can involve finance leases if a leasing company winds up purchasing the car from the manufacturer pursuant to the lease contract. The lessee is the one who selects the car. The lease may contain a "hell or high water" clause obligating the lessee to make the lease payments even if the car does not work. One can see how this would be a hardship for a consumer lessee who needs the car to get to work and has to make payments even though the car isn't working. It would be difficult for the consumer to come up with money to obtain alternative transportation and also to hire a lawyer to sue the supplier of the car. The UCC does not take a position on the enforceability of "hell or high water" clauses in consumer leases, leaving the matter to consumer protection law. Official comment 2 to §2A-407 states "That a consumer be obligated to pay notwithstanding defective goods or the like is a principle that is not tenable under case law."[16]

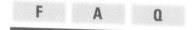

Q: Why ever uphold a "hell or high water" clause?

A: It seems unfair to say that a lessee must pay under a lease when goods don't work. It may seem unfair even in commercial cases. Upholding these clauses, however, encourages financial institutions to extend credit in the form of leases. If

---

[16]See cases cited in the comment and see also *Mercedes-Benz Credit Corp. v. Lotito*, 306 N.J. Super. 25, 703 A.2d 288, 34 UCC Rep. Serv. 2d 1 (App. Div. 1997).

the financial institution had to worry about whether the goods were defective, it would be less willing to engage in these transactions. Remember that it is the lessee who selects the goods that are the subject of the finance lease, not the lessor. So, the lessor should choose its supplier wisely. The finance lessor is really like a bank that extends credit to a buyer to enable the buyer to purchase goods. In such a situation, the buyer would look to the seller for recourse if the goods didn't work, not the bank. The buyer would generally be expected to continue to make payments on the loan, unless the lender was somehow affiliated with the seller.

D. Rights of the Lessee in the Goods

Just as the buyer of goods generally obtains no better title than the seller had, the lessee of goods generally obtains no greater rights in the goods than the lessor had.[17] There are a few exceptions to this rule.

One situation in which the lessee can obtain better title than the lessor is if the lessor had **voidable title** to the goods being leased. The concept of voidable title is discussed on pages 110-111, *supra*. One situation in which the lessor might have voidable title would be if the lessor purchased the goods with a bad check. A person with voidable title has the ability to convey good title to a good faith purchaser for value. The definition of "purchase" and "purchaser" includes people who take by lease.[18] So, assuming that a lessee from a lessor with voidable title acted in good faith and gave value, the lessee would take free of any right to reclaim the goods that the seller of the goods to the lessor might have.

Another situation in which the lessee obtains greater rights than the lessor is if the leased goods had been **entrusted** to the lessor by their rightful owner. For example, let us assume that Company A purchases a large piece of equipment from Company B. Company B agrees that it will hold the equipment for Company A until A has the opportunity to get rid of some old equipment that the new equipment will replace. During the time that it is holding the equipment, Company B unscrupulously leases it to Company C. Section 2A-307(2) indicates that a creditor of a lessor takes subject to the lease contract, unless the creditor holds a lien that attached to the goods before the lease contract became enforceable. Official comment 3 to §2A-304 indicates that in the factual situation described, Company A is a "creditor" of Company B because A could sue B for wrongfully leasing the equipment to C. Because A does not have a "lien" on the goods, A cannot take the goods away from C. A is entitled, however, to the lease payments made by C to B and is also entitled to the reversionary interest in the goods. C may continue to use the goods, pursuant to the lease.

A lessee can also obtain greater rights than the lessor if the lessor improperly leased the goods and the lessee qualifies as a **lessee in the ordinary course of business**. To be a lessee in the ordinary course of business, the lessee must lease from someone who is in the business of selling or leasing goods of the kind involved. The lessee must also act in good faith, give new value (i.e., the consideration is not forgiveness of an antecedent debt owed by the lessor to the lessee), and not have

---

[17]See UCC §2-403 & §2A-304, official comment 1.
[18]UCC §1-201(b)(29)(30).

knowledge that the lease violates the rights of a third person.[19] To give an example, let's assume that Company A leases office furniture to Company B. Company B is a furniture store, but the furniture being leased by Company A is not to be resold or leased to anyone else and is to be used in the offices of Company B. Company B unscrupulously leases the furniture it leased from Company A to Company C. Assuming that Company C acts in good faith and gives new value in paying the rent, Company C will take free of Company A's interest as Company C will qualify as a lessee in the ordinary course of business.[20]

E. Performance, Breach, and Remedies Under a Lease Contract

(1) Lessee's Right to Reject or Revoke Acceptance

The rules dealing with performance and breach of leases under Article 2A are very similar to the corresponding rules under UCC Article 2 for sales. The lessor is required to deliver goods that conform to the warranties given under the lease contract. Similar to Article 2, Article 2A distinguishes between cases in which leased goods are to be delivered in installments and cases in which the goods are delivered in a single tender. In a non-installment lease, the "perfect tender rule" applies, and the lessee may reject goods that do not conform to the lease contract, subject to the lessor's right to cure that is similar to UCC §2-508.[21] In an installment lease, the lessee is only allowed to reject if a nonconformity substantially impairs the value of the installment and cannot be cured. The contract may be canceled only if the nonconformity or default with respect to one or more installments substantially impairs the value of the contract as a whole.[22]

The lessee has a right to revoke acceptance under UCC §2A-517 similar to the right afforded buyers under UCC §2-608. Except in finance lease cases, the lessee may revoke acceptance if a nonconformity substantially impairs the value of the goods to the lessee and the goods were accepted on the reasonable assumption that the nonconformity would be cured and the lessor does not seasonable cure, or if it was difficult to discover the nonconformity before acceptance. Even in finance lease cases, the lessee may also revoke acceptance if a nonconformity substantially impairs the value of the goods to the lessee and the lessee's acceptance was reasonably induced by the lessor's assurances. Remember that in finance lease cases, the lessor is generally not responsible for the quality of the goods. It will be a rare case in which a finance lessor makes assurances to the lessee regarding the quality of the goods because the lessee selects the goods from a third party supplier.

(2) Lessor's Right to Cancel, Withhold Delivery, and Repossess

The lessor's rights on a lessee's default are similar to the rights of a seller under Article 2 if the buyer defaults. Article 2A distinguishes between installment leases and non-installment leases, permitting cancellation of an installment lease only if the buyer's

---

[19]UCC §2A-103(1)(o).
[20]See UCC §§2-403 & §2A-305.
[21]See UCC §§2A-509 & 2A-513.
[22]See UCC §2A-510.

default substantially impairs the value of the whole lease contract. Otherwise, if the lessee wrongfully rejects or revokes acceptance of goods, fails to make a payment when due, or repudiates, the lessor is given a number of options, including cancellation of the lease, withholding delivery in some cases, and disposing of the goods and recovering damages.[23]

There is an additional remedy given to a lessor that reflects the lessor's retention of title in the goods. If the lessee fails to make payments, the lessor may repossess the goods. In addition, if the lessee otherwise breaches the lease contract, the lessor may repossess if permitted under the lease contract or if the default substantially impairs the value of the lease contract.[24] Repossession can be by self-help as long as there is no breach of the peace.[25] If self-help repossession is attempted and the lessee is present and objects, it is probably prudent for the lessor to go to court and obtain an order rather than risking any breach of the peace.

(3) Damage Recovery for Injured Lessors and Lessees

In terms of damages, Article 2A like Article 2 allows the injured party to "cover" or to recover damages under a contract/market formula in cases in which the goods are not accepted by the lessee.[26] Lost volume lessors may try to argue for lost profits under §2A-528 just like a lost volume seller can obtain lost profits under UCC §2-708(2).[27] Because lease contracts are long term as compared to sales, it is necessary to make present value calculations when doing a contract-market analysis or when comparing the value of a breached lease contract with the value of a substitute lease contract. For example, assume that on the date that goods are repossessed by the lessor, the rent under the lease is $1,000 per month while the market rent at that time is $750 per month. If there are five years left on the lease, the court needs to do a present-value analysis, factoring in an appropriate interest rate, to determine the difference in the value of the leases at that time. "Present value" is defined in UCC §2A-103(1)(u) as "the amount as of a date certain of one or more sums payable in the future, discounted to the date certain." That section also permits the parties in the contract to set the interest rate that will be used, provided it is not manifestly unreasonable at the time of the contract. Otherwise, it is a commercially reasonable rate.[28]

Similar to Article 2's different treatment of buyers and sellers, Article 2A permits lessees to obtain consequential damages and incidental damages in appropriate cases but permits lessors to obtain only incidental damages.[29] As the 2003 approved amendments to Article 2 permit sellers to recover consequential damages in some cases, the proposed amendments to Article 2A permit lessors to recover consequential damages in some cases.[30]

To give an example of the analysis that a court might follow in a case in which the lessor wrongfully failed to deliver goods promised under a lease, assume that the present value of all payments under the lease is $50,000. The present value of market rent for comparable goods under a comparable lease is $60,000. If the lessee does not cover, that is, rent comparable goods, the contract/market differential would be

---

[23]See UCC §2A-523.
[24]See UCC §§2A-523(3) & 2A-525.
[25]UCC §2A-525(3).
[26]See UCC §§2A-518, 2A-519, 2A-527 & 2A-528.
[27]See pp. 165-167, *supra*.
[28]See official comment (u) to §2A-103 for a discussion of this definition.
[29]See UCC §§2A-520 & 2A-530.
[30]See Amended UCC §2A-530.

$10,000. What if the lessee were to hire additional employees at a cost of $30,000 to take the place of the equipment that was to be leased? A court might find that if comparable equipment was available, that the lessee could have reasonably mitigated its loss and the $30,000 would not be recoverable as consequential damages. If mitigation was not reasonably possible and if the hiring of additional employees was foreseeable to the lessor as a probable consequence of breach, then the cost of the additional employees would be recoverable.

Because of the difficulty of estimating present values and appropriate discount rates, parties to a lease contract may define how damages will be calculated in the event of a breach. UCC §2A-504(1) permits the parties to contractually provide for liquidated damages or a formula by which damages can be calculated as long as the amount or formula is reasonable in light of anticipated harm caused by the breach.

To give an example, assume that a lease contract provides that in the event of default by the lessee, the lessor is entitled to (1) any lease payments that are past due, plus (2) the present value of future lease payments at the time of default discounted at an interest rate of 3 percent, plus (3) the estimated residual value of the goods at the end of the lease, minus the value of the goods at the time of default. The agreement also provides that the residual value of the goods at the end of the lease will be $20,000. The contract provides that the value at the time of default is to be determined by subtracting from the initial value $5,000 per year in depreciation up to the time of default. The initial value of the good is $60,000. Assume that all of these estimates are reasonable at the time of contracting.

Assume that at the time of default, the value of the goods as calculated under the contract is $45,000. After taking possession of the goods, the lessor is able to sell the goods to somebody else for $50,000. If the formula for determining damages in the lease contract is enforced, that means that the lessor will arguably be placed in a better position than if the lease were performed. Nevertheless, Article 2A will enforce the damage calculation under the formula as long as it was reasonable at the time the contract was entered into. There is to be no use of hindsight to find that the formula has in fact turned out to be a penalty.

Sidebar

THE DIFFERENT TREATMENT OF LIQUIDATED DAMAGE FORMULAE UNDER ARTICLE 2A

Article 2A is different from Article 2 in analyzing liquidated damage provisions in that courts under Article 2 are required to take into account the difficulty of determining actual damages in determining if a liquidated damage provision in a sale of goods case has turned out to be an unlawful penalty. Under Article 2, a liquidated damage provision that was reasonable at the time the parties contracted may turn out to be unenforceable if it is clear that the liquidated damages exceed the amount of actual damages. Under Article 2A, the only question is whether the formula was reasonable at the time of contracting. The formula may turn out to be a penalty but still be enforceable. The drafters defend the more liberal treatment of liquidated damage formulae under Article 2A as being "critical" to modern leasing practice, where there is a need to provide for certain rates of return and also for compensation of any tax benefits that are lost as a result of breach. UCC §2A-504, official comment. Note that the formula for calculating damages may include "indemnity for loss or diminution of anticipated tax benefits." UCC §2A-504(1).

(4) Actions for Rent and Specific Performance

Lessors are given the right to sue for the rent under the lease contract in situations similar to those that give the seller the right to sue for the price under Article 2.[31] If

---

[31]See UCC §2A-529.

goods are accepted and not repossessed and the lessee has not tendered back possession, the lessor may sue for the rent. Also, if goods are lost or damaged within a commercially reasonable time after risk of loss passes to the lessee, the lessor may sue for the rent. The lessee's right to specific performance of the lease contract is similar to the right of a buyer to specific performance in a sale of goods case—basically, that the goods are sufficiently unique that the lessee cannot obtain reasonable substitute goods.[32]

SUMMARY

■ A lease of goods permits the lessee to use the goods for a period of time. After that time, the right to possess the goods reverts to the lessor.

■ True leases of goods, covered by Article 2A of the UCC, must be distinguished from conditional sales of goods, governed by Article 2 and Article 9. Parties will sometimes call a transaction a "lease" when it is really a conditional sale for tax or accounting reasons. The UCC disregards the label the parties place on the transaction and looks at the economic realities to determine if a lease or a sale has occurred.

■ If a transaction calling itself a "lease" gives the "lessee" the option of acquiring the goods for nominal consideration at the end of the lease term (e.g., $1) or the term of the lease equals the estimated economic life of the goods, it is likely that the transaction is really a conditional sale rather than a lease.

■ If a transaction is a lease, Article 2A applies. Article 2A is like Article 2 in some respects and unlike it in others. For example, Article 2A does not have a "battle of the forms" provision. For a summary of the similarities and differences between Article 2A and Article 2, see the table on pages 200-201, *supra*.

■ In a finance lease, the lessee selects the goods that are the subject of the lease transaction and the lessor purchases the goods for the purpose of leasing the goods to the lessee. Because the lessee selects the goods, the lessor does not take much responsibility in the event that the goods do not work properly. In such an event, the lessee is generally required to continue to pay the lessor and seek recourse against the supplier of the goods (i.e., the seller), at least if the goods are not consumer goods.

■ A lessee generally only gets rights in the goods that are as good as those that the lessor had. In situations in which the lessor had voidable title to goods, the lessee can take free of claims to the good if it gives value and acts in good faith. A lessee in the ordinary course of business can also take free of any security interest created by the lessor.

■ With regard to performance under a lease, lessees may generally reject and revoke acceptance of goods under the same circumstances as a buyer under Article 2. In finance leases, however, lessees may generally not revoke acceptance unless acceptance of the goods was induced by the lessors assurances (which is unusual).

---

[32]See UCC §2A-521.

■ The rights of a lessor under Article 2A are similar to the rights of a seller under Article 2. One thing that a lessor can do is repossess the goods in the event that the lessee does not perform under the lease contract. Repossession can be by self-help as long as there is no breach of the peace.

■ Damages for breach of a lease contract are calculated in a manner similar to the calculation of damages under Article 2 in sale of goods transactions. One difference is that damages under a lease need to be discounted to present day because payments under a lease are made over time. Parties may agree on the appropriate discount rate provided that it is not manifestly unreasonable.

■ Liquidated damage provisions in lease contracts are enforceable as long as they are reasonable at the time of contracting. Unlike the rule governing liquidated damages in Article 2, courts are not permitted to second guess the parties by looking at the amount of actual damages that resulted.

■ Parties' rights to specific performance in lease contracts are similar to their rights to specific performance in a sales contract. Basically, if substitute goods can be found or the goods can be leased or sold to somebody else, Article 2A prefers that the injured party obtain damages rather than specific performance.

CONNECTIONS

Choice of Law

If a transaction is a sale of goods transaction, the materials in the first nine chapters of the book apply. If the transaction is a lease, the materials in this chapter apply. As discussed in this chapter, a sale can sometimes be disguised to look like a lease. Courts look at the economic realities of the transaction rather than the label that parties place on it. If it appears that there is a meaningful reversionary interest for the lessor, courts are inclined to label the transaction a lease. If it appears that there is not a significant reversionary interest, such as in the cases where the "lessee" is given the option to purchase the goods for $1 at the end of the lease, then the transaction is likely to be labeled a sale, with the seller retaining a security interest in the goods to secure payment of the price. To protect its interest, the seller is generally required to file a document called a financing statement with the secretary of state's office.

Contract Formation and Terms

The rules of Article 2A governing leases are similar to the rules of Article 2 governing sales but also are different to some extent. For example, there is no "battle of the forms" under Article 2A because parties in lease transactions do not contract that way. Warranties are given by lessors in the same way that they are given by sellers of goods, except that if the lease is a "finance lease" the lessor does not give implied warranties of quality because the lessor is really just financing the transaction and is not making any representations regarding the quality of the goods. The risk of loss in a lease transaction, other than a finance lease, stay with the lessor unless the contract states otherwise. This rule is contrary to the rules governing sales in which the risk will generally pass to the buyer upon the buyer's taking possession of the goods if not before.

Performance and Breach

The rules regarding performance are similar to the rules governing sales, except that revocation of acceptance can generally not be made against the lessor in finance leases. In finance leases other than those for consumer goods, the lessee may be required to pay "come hell or high water," whereas in a sales transaction, the buyer may be excused from paying the price if the goods do not conform to the contract.

Remedies

As compared to sales transactions, damage calculation in lease cases takes into account the present value of future payments. Another difference between sales and lease transactions is that the lessor has a right to reclaim the goods after breach whereas sellers have limited rights to reclaim goods in a sales transaction unless the seller takes a security interest in the goods. With regard to liquidated damages, the focus is on whether the provision is reasonable in light of antici- pated damages as compared to the focus in Article 2 on reasonableness in light of both anticipated and actual damages.

Table of Statutes

---

[1]Uniform Commercial Code citations to Article 1 are to the 2001 revised version, unless the citation has an "F" in front of it, in which case it is to the former version. Citations to Articles 2 and 2A are to the versions without the 2003 amendments, unless the citation has an "A" in front of it, in which case it is to the amended version.

Uniform Consumer Credit Code (UCCC)

United States Constitution

United States Code

United States Code of Federal Regulations (CFR)

Index